Other books by Reid Matthias

The Amicable Circle Novels

Butcher

Baker

Candlestickmaker

Son of a Butcher

Blank Spaces: The Legend of Jerusalem Walker

The Sick House

A Miserable Antagonist

Website

reidmatthias.com

Email

apostle13_1997@outlook.com

Copyright © Reid Matthias 2025

All rights reserved. Other than for the purposes and subject to the conditions prescribed under the *Copyright Act*, no part of this publication may be reproduced, stored in a retrieval system, or transmitted in any form or by any means, electronic, mechanical, photocopying, recording or otherwise, without the prior permission of the publisher.

ISBN paperback: 978-0-6456882-4-5
        ebook: 978-0-6456882-5-2

This edition first published by A13 in November 2025

Typesetting by Ben Morton

Publication assistance from Immortalise

Front and back cover Reid Matthias using AI software.

WHAT YOU SEE MAY NOT BE

Reid Matthias

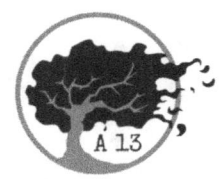

What do you do with your ideas? Once they get old, do you fold them up like laundry and place them in a dusty drawer in the attic of your mind? Or, do you wear them to see what other people think?

I'd like to think that all ideas have their own style. At some point, even the worst ideas are fashionable. If you wait around long enough, they'll become retro.

So it was with *What You See May Not Be*. Various iterations and titles were taken into the change room, spun in front of the mirror, and put back on the hanger until this one. When I first wrote it, the ending was very, very different; the first rewrite introduced a raft of new characters; the second was a culling of thoughts.

And finally, well…

You'll get there.

The characters of *What You See* are some of the nearest and dearest to my heart that I've ever conjured. To me, they are as real as some of my living, breathing friends. I hope that they become real to you, also.

Especially Dave.

This book could not have been written without the incredibly dark, disturbing, (and extraordinary) work of Thomas Harris in his books about a character named Hannibal. Throughout this work of fiction, I have included various quotes from both book and movie. You will see why shortly.

Enjoy what you can. Love what is most important. Laugh whenever possible.

Closer, please. Clo-ser...

Hannibal Lecter

For Christine.

1
Benson

When you look back at a time, and a place, with a person like Dave, it's fair to say that memories will be cast in many colors. Enviable green; contented blue; angry red. Dave could be golden in a moment, and then speak, destroying that moment with his strange radioactivity.

He was my best friend – a curious one, yes – and the way he left us still leaves a mark on my present – this, my wedding day. His departure is like a scar that never seems to heal. It itches and you can't quite reach it, and every day you wish it wasn't there for all to see, like malformed wings on your back. They were meant for flight, but they just don't seem to unfurl. That's the way my memories of Dave are.

My story with Dave, and so many others, will take a circuitous route. At times you will wonder who this person is. Do I really like him? Does he actually care? How do I put all the pieces of his personality together to find something akin to acceptance?

Bear with me, if you will, because as the story is told – with all of its truth, happiness and despair, you might find yourself changed.

Like I am.

Why am I telling you this? I don't know. I suppose it's cathartic. He was supposed to be my best man – he'd actually demanded it. Maybe now that the wedding has arrived, I've got cold feet. Maybe I need to talk about something other than the fact that my bride will be walking down the aisle in a few hours and I need distraction. Maybe I just want to talk about Dave. Maybe I just want to remember.

Where to begin?

How about his appearance?

Dave had long, bushy brown hair, a long nose with big nostrils, and a mole on his right cheek partially obscured by his facial hair. His wardrobe consisted of corduroy and long collars. Dave was tall, but stooped, if that makes any sense. He always seemed to straighten up or bend down to the height of whoever he was talking to.

When he arrived at the Palm Apartment complex a few years ago, Dave crawled out from behind the wheel of his 1987 Ford Escort – white with red and blue racing stripes – arched his back and cracked it. Then he reached to the sky and seemed to paint it with his hands.

I was standing on the balcony when this happened. To my right, three doors down, Vernon Russ, an octogenarian widower, raised his eyebrows. 'Looks like we've got a weirdo on our hands.'

'Yuh,' I said with my forearms resting on the balcony. I had an impending sense of doom. The only vacant room on the second floor of the western side of the U was right next to mine. Looking at this hippie filled me with trepidation, and visions of incense and seances filled my head.

Vernon pointed at the room next to me, shook his head and laughed. 'You're going to have a best friend.'

Hmmm.

Dave was unemployed. Or, at least, I never saw him *go* to work. He never seemed to be without money, though, sometimes surprising a local homeless man with loaf of bread and a fifty-dollar bill tucked on top. When we'd go out to eat, he always paid. We never went to nice restaurants, though. It was always the same place. Lefties Meatballs and Pickles. This was an establishment devoted to an entire cuisine of mixed hamburger and dill-flavored baby cucumbers. Lefties only hired left-handed people, although I suppose ambidextrous people could have applied. Dave loved Lefties, so ultimately, I did also.

One of the first times we went there, a young server wearing a brown vest and green shirt (obviously – meat and pickles) averted his eyes by pondering the cash register below waiting for our order.

'I'll have the special,' said Dave as he stared upwards over the server's shoulder. A full-length wall of meat and pickle choices were pictorially displayed above the serving counter.

'One special – Pickle pine trees and meat cones,' the server repeated robotically. 'And you?' He glanced at me quickly, his eyes watery above acne-pitted cheeks. The hat covering his curly hair sat askew on his head.

'I'll take a burger.'

The server frowned. 'A burger?'

It was as if I'd asked for steak at a vegetarian restaurant. 'Yeah, you know, a bun with a patty, some extras…' I motioned with my hands as if this would somehow free this young man's imagination.

'I know what a burger is, but we have so many other, better choices. What about fried pickleballs or a meat cannon?'

'Just a burger, thanks.'

The server stabbed angrily at the register in front of him and spoke to both of us. 'Anything else?'

'I'll have a Diet Dr. Pepper in a red cup, lots of ice, and a deep dish of catsup. My friend Benson here will have the same.'

'Soda machine is over there.' After wiping his nose with his finger, he pointed at the row of soft drinks on tap. 'Ice dispenser is in the middle. Catsup on the side.'

'Thank you, kind sir. We'll be dining in. Might I enquire of the usual table?'

'What?'

'We'd like to sit with an advantageous outlook over this fine restaurant.' Dave turned to wave at a table in the back directly in front of a window which blocked off the sound, but not sight, of a kids' playground. Three or four heavy children were being spewed from the mouth of an ogrish meatball in the shape of a head.

'If it's open, it's available,' the server said as he ripped off the receipt and handed it to Dave. 'Number 74.'

After retrieving our sodas, we took a seat at 'Dave's' table and were rewarded with sitting between two overweight families whose children appeared to be not only frequent fliers at Lefties, but most of the fast-food joints in Des Moines. One young boy slurped loudly from his cup then pulled his head back and emitted a ground-shaking belch. He laughed. So did his parents.

Dave sat with his back to the window.

Eventually, I would grow used to that which would ensue, but on that particular day, his weirdness hit me like a brick. He scanned the room and quickly postulated that 'the female server in the hallway was doing penance for showing up late for work'.

I turned to see a teenage girl wearing the Lefties uniform swabbing up the projectile vomit of a child who had one pick-kebab too many and a few too-many rides down the pickle tornado slide.

'How could you possibly know that?'

'Notice the way she mutters to herself, and the fact that she still has crusty sleep in the corner of her right eye. Her right hand drags slightly, as if it's still dreaming.'

'Dave, that's ridiculous.'

'At your 6:00 is another woman writing a note to her jilted lover. She's using a dulled #2 pencil, chewed on the eraser end. Her lover was a circus clown.'

I rolled my eyes and shook my head.

'Bensonimous,' he said as he leaned forward, 'you need to read life's clues. Learn like Starling.'

You wouldn't know what he was referring to at this point because I haven't told you yet about Dave's greatest strangeness – his affinity for *The Silence of the Lambs*.

If you'll allow me a short digression to show you the severity of this quirk, I'll be quick.

Dave loved to quote from both the movie and the book. It wouldn't have surprised me if he had it memorized – not just parts of it, but word for word. He could quote it chapter and verse as if it was his own personal Bible. And the quotes would come out at strange (and often inappropriate) times.

One time we went shopping at the local grocery store. Dave had a fascination and need for all things fiber. Some kind of finicky, gut-health thing. When we'd walk through the aisles, he would dump in beans, nuts,

1 – Benson

whole grains, Metamucil, anything that would keep his bowel movements normal.

At the end of this shop, though, as an afterthought, he dropped in a bottle of Jergens hand lotion.

'What are you doing, Dave?'

'What?'

I pointed at the lotion. 'Do you really need that?'

He lifted his hands to me. 'They're rough. Feel them.'

'I'm not going to feel your hands in the grocery store.'

'Where will you feel them?'

'Never.'

Dave shook his head and reached out for my cheeks. I pulled back, but not quick enough. He was right. They were rough.

'Do you understand my need?'

'Whatever.'

We carried our red baskets to the front and began to unload our articles onto the conveyor belt. The checkout lady began to scan the objects and place them at the end of the belt where we were to pack the groceries ourselves. I tried to move past Dave, but he blocked the way. As the articles began to pile up, the checkout lady said, 'Do you want me to bag these?'

'If you would be so kind,' Dave responded.

As the bread and tubers and Metamucil and shredded wheat went through, she peeked up at Dave but said nothing. The last thing to be scanned was the lotion.

'What would you like me to do with this?' She held the bottle near the end.

'It puts the lotion in the basket.'

'Yes, but do you want it on top of the...'

'It puts the lotion in the basket,' Dave said more stridently.

I knew what was coming. A quote. Sometimes, like an old cowboy, I can jump on that runaway coach and pull on the reins stopping the words, but not that day.

5

'What?' she asked.

'IT PUTS THE LOTION IN THE BASKET!'

The woman's mouth dropped open revealing an overly-chewed piece of Dentyne gum. Dave's shout had alerted half the grocery store, and no one knew what to do.

I shoved Dave out of the way and took the lotion from the woman's hand and placed it in the bag. 'I'm so sorry,' I apologized.

'Is there something wrong with him?' she whispered.

'Almost everything.'

I haven't watched *Silence of the Lambs* in years, and never will again, frankly, but I always knew when he was quoting it. His voice would mimic whichever character was speaking, whether Clarice or Lecter or Buffalo Bill, and a chill would settle in the air. Thankfully, he didn't do it all the time, but it was enough to keep us all on edge. Letitia hated it the most.

Poor Letitia.

If not for his incredible ability to connect people, we all might have dumped him in the garbage heap of previous-relationships. But he was so good with relationships, even with people he had never met before.

Thus, at Lefties, after he progressed from the vomit-mopping waitress to the love-letter-clown-writing woman, he twitched his nose in the air when our waiter brought our orders to us. 'I smell…'

'Don't say it!' I shouted and quickly grabbed the brown tray from the flummoxed waiter. I set the food out in front of us. 'Why do you do that?'

'Do what?'

'Quote from that movie.'

He slurped from his Diet Dr. Pepper, shrugged and moved on. He put a finger to the side of his nose and tapped it. 'You've got to learn to read the signs or you're going to be left behind. Stick with me and we'll go places.'

1 – Benson

I took a bite of my pickle burger which was surprisingly delicious. 'Don't you know that there are appropriate and inappropriate quotes, and definitely inappropriate moments in which to utter them?'

A drop of barbecue sauce appeared on his chin. I didn't tell him because knowing him, he would have been proud of it. I did rub my chin three or four times in rapid succession in a subconscious attempt to get him to wipe it away. He did, with the back of his hand, then licked it.

'Just like eating liver and fava beans washed down with a nice bottle of Chianti.' A greasy, meatball-encrusted smirk appeared, and he did that weird, tongue/lip-smacking sound that Hannibal Lecter used in the movie.

Slurpyslurpyslurpy.

'I don't think anyone even knew what fava beans were until that movie came out,' he said. 'I'd never heard of them,' he confidently stated between gulping bites and swallows of beef and pickle. 'I thought fava beans were like lima beans.'

'What are they?' I asked.

'They look like great big boogers.'

'Sounds delicious,' I paused mid-bite.

'They're not. I bought some one time, supposedly good roughage, and they tasted like…' he smacked his tongue against the roof of his mouth, 'like green beans except with a touch of blue cheese and a bouquet of athlete's foot that hits your palette like a freight train.'

My mouth was still open. Suddenly my pickle burger had taken on a very distinctive, brain-induced, foot-rotty taste.

Dave finished his meal and slurped his Diet Dr. Pepper. He wiped his hands first on a napkin then on his pants and stood up.

'Time to go, Benson.'

I couldn't eat anymore anyway, so I unceremoniously dropped the remains of my conglomeration into the little red basket, pinched the last few pickle shavings from the top, and we headed for the door. As we walked out, Dave tipped his non-existent cap to the waiter who stared at him. The waitress, still mopping up the bathroom corridor, paused, and watched Dave and I leave.

'Nice to see you again, Clarice.'
'What?'

2
Patricia

I'm an old nobody. A body with a heartbeat and history. My part in this story is so small that when you get to the end you'll go back to the beginning and say, 'What was that lady's name again? You know, the one in the apartment complex? The old snoop?'

I didn't set out to be that kind of person. I wasn't born with my rumor-feelers in the air, but I am Midwestern. Duh.

Every community needs a busybody – the watchful prairie dog who sticks her nose up at the faintest scent of danger. That's me. I'm a prairie dog. I sense danger and pass the threat along.

By the time my husband and I purchased the apartment on the opposite side of the complex, Dave had already moved into the Palms. He and Benson were two of the first people we met. They were like an old, odd couple: tall and short, thin and round, hairy and smooth. Some days before work (Benson's work, that is) they would sit on the balcony, just below the dinner bell Dave had installed on the beam outside their apartments sipping chai lattes and coffees. They would mumble and point; Dave suggesting various things and Benson shaking his head while laughing. To my knowledge Dave never had a job. I can't imagine what kind of work he would have excelled at.

Those first days of knowing them were lovely, and I look back on them with wonder. Sometimes when Gordon and I eat now, we glance across the way, the sun setting behind the western wing, and recollect those first moments.

Dave was so different. So very strange and lovely, like a moth, I suppose, all fluttery and dusty, hopping from topic to topic, pollinating and leaving trace behind him. There was one specific time when we came to realize what kind of delightful person Dave was.

Next door to Dave's apartment, on the other side, was a woman named Janice. She was generally a cranky kind of gal with a temperament bending towards Catholic-nun-having-her-monthly-in-a-school. I'm sorry about the crassness, but finding the right metaphor can be difficult for someone like Janice. When she came out of her apartment, it tended to be about yelling at kids on the swings, or someone playing their television too loudly. Hypocrisy, really, because Janice had a thing for Creedence Clearwater Revival which never seemed to be turned down until late.

One night, there was a bad moon risin', and the ambulance showed up around 11:00pm. I would know because the lights flashed across the courtyard, twinkling blue and red. The emergency personnel took their time and their gurney underneath the second floor and then carried the contraption loudly up the stairs. Surely, they could have used the elevator, but it was broken that week, if I remember correctly.

Anyway, when the paramedics entered Janice's room, Dave was already there. He met them at the door, shook their hands, and ushered them into the apartment. When they returned twenty minutes later, Dave led the way down the stairs. Janice seemed to be alert, but an oxygen mask had been placed over her nose and mouth. When they made it to ground level, Dave patted Janice's hand and leaned over to lightly kiss her head.

I thought it strange, but everything about him was strange. So, I guess it was normal for Dave.

Well, now you've met me and the way I make my way in the world. Please don't think badly of me because there will be moments when I insert myself into this story, but it will only be to snoop into what everyone else has said. They might want clarification on details. I'm good at those. Some might want to go into more depth regarding Janice and her final march towards doom, but if you need me, I'll be right here, on the eastern side of the U, stretched out on the balcony. Gordon will be sitting on the other side of our little table. He'll have a newspaper stretched out in front of him. Occasionally he will flick one side, a particularly irritating article, to give me the gossip.

The sun will set over the other side, and we will go to bed.

But we won't forget.

Most old people do, but we don't. Not yet anyway.

3
Benson

One day, Dave decided we would attempt to understand death. What I mean by that is, Dave's curiosity about all things taboo required we do things that most people wouldn't. That morning, a Wednesday, we went to Janice's funeral. I asked Dave how I was going to get out of work, and he responded that I simply apply for bereavement leave.

'How can I do that?'

'Just tell them a close friend has died and then ask for compassionate leave so you might grieve in totality.'

'Janice was not a close friend.'

'Sure she was,' Dave said as he adjusted his bowtie in front of his mirror. His long, wavy brown hair had been tied up into a bun near the back of his head. In the last months, Dave had been growing sideburns longer than normal, this time in the shape of an upside-down Mexico on each cheek. As we stood there, he pointed to the place where he believed the Yucatan Peninsula to be. 'Nice, isn't it?'

'Whatever.'

'Janice lives, or should I say 'lived,' two doors from you and one from me. That's pretty close.'

'That's not what 'close friend' means,' I said staring at the side of his face noticing that a mole punctuated the place where Cuba should have been. He had missed a few hairs near his nose, too.

'Your employers don't know that.' Dave straightened up, spreading his arms. 'How do I look?'

'Like something out of a comic book.'

'Thank you very much, Benson.' He reached into the pocket of his brown pants, found a quarter, and flipped it to me. 'Don't spend that tip all in one place.'

I stuffed the coin in his shirt pocket. 'Keep it to call someone who cares.'

'Ooh hoo hoo,' Dave hooted. 'Bingleberry standin' up for hisself.'

The irony of my statement is that Dave actually made phone calls from pay phones. I had seen him standing in a phone booth, handkerchief in hand, speaking loudly in a fake Russian accent as he pretended to be a KGB agent.

'Now,' Dave said as he smacked his hands together and rubbed them. 'Which cologne should I wear?'

'What difference does it make, Dave? It's a funeral, not a nightclub. It's *not* a first date.'

'Aah, you never know, my good man, who you might meet at an event.' He chose a cologne bottle from among the five that were sitting on his shelf. Each had significant chips in them. He found them in second-hand stores across Des Moines. Dave had an affinity for strange smells. No Drakkar Noir for him, no siree. The scent he chose on Janice's funeral day was from a dark green horse head figurine with a black spritzer on top. As he sprayed it, I smelled *eau de old man*. I wrinkled my nose.

'I've chosen wisely,' he said and brushed past me toward the door of his apartment.

Dave's apartment was almost identical to mine in size: two bedrooms, one bathroom, a moderately sized living area, small kitchen with an island, and a small laundry cupboard (except Dave never used the washing machine and dryer. He took his laundry to the corner laundromat four blocks away. There was great joy to be reaped by holding up his unmentionables in front of complete strangers and mumbling, *Hmm, those ARE sexy*).

Where our apartments diverged was that mine had some furniture from the current century in which we exist, whereas Dave's was from the last, upholstered in dusty paisley, aqua blues and greens, a brown swivel chair, and complemented by two coffee tables with mug-shaped coffee marks stained into their surfaces. There were a few shelves in his apartment, but none had pictures or even books. I'd never actually seen photos of Dave when he was younger, or any of his family. He never brought it up, so I never asked.

3 – Benson

Dave's kitchen was spotless. Not a single thing out of place. This was not because of being a neat freak. Dave didn't really cook. Whenever he wanted something home-cooked, he'd come to my apartment, or, if I wasn't home, he'd wander the corridors knocking on doors until someone took him in and fed him.

Before leaving for the funeral, I checked myself in Dave's mirror. I'm not even halfway near as handsome as Dave, and I'm six inches shorter, too. I have blue eyes and slightly chubby cheeks. I sucked them in hoping to look, I don't know, more Liam Hemsworthish, but it hurt to chew on my cheeks, so I let them pop out again. I have sandy-brown hair and an impressive cowlick. In the summer, freckles dot my nose; in the winter, I display a pasty-white complexion with a few straggler pimple scars from when I was in high school. The blue suit I wore to the funeral didn't fit very well, but it was the only one I had. In IT, we don't need suits.

Looking down, I reached for one of Dave's colognes. I smelled the sprayer on top. It didn't smell very good.

'Choose the blue one.'

I grabbed it and sprayed a little into the air to walk through the mist. It was not bad. I'd smelled it before, somewhere. It brought back memories.

Dave checked his watch. 'I ran out of cologne in that one last year, so I filled it with Windex just for looks.' He stood outside the door. 'Chop, chop, Gullible's Travels.'

We journeyed by bus to the church for the funeral. Dave had the Ford, and I have my car, but for the sake of appearances, we rode the bus. Janice didn't have a car, so we wouldn't either.

On the bus, people tried not to make eye contact with Dave. He liked to stare at people who were trying not to stare at him. For some reason it gave him pleasure to see people avert their eyes. An older lady with a white shirt and blue jeans sat uncomfortably behind us. Instead of letting her be, Dave adjusted himself in the seat to face her.

'Would you say you are wearing a blouse?' He pointed at her shirt.

'What?'

'A blouse.'

'Are you talking to me?'

'Yes, yes, I'm wondering about your shirt. It's blouse-like.' He pronounces the word 'blouse' like *blowze*.

She looked down and touched it. 'I suppose so.'

'It's very pretty,' he responded and turned back around. The woman smiled, touched her face, and pushed up her glasses. She blushed heavily, and I'm pretty sure that if we watched a little longer, she would have fanned her face.

I leaned towards him and whispered, 'Do you really think it's pretty, Dave.'

'No,' he responded. 'It is decidedly un-pretty. Utile, yes, a skin covering to be certain, but capturing the attention of wandering eyes, no.'

'Why did you tell her that then?'

'Because it's fun to be unpredictable. You should try it sometime.' He scanned the bus checking out passengers, looking for his next victim. One time he asked a woman if she was a size 14 as per *The Silence of the Lambs*. He was kindly asked to leave the bus pronto. I don't *think* Dave was a psychopath, but he was most certainly psychologically complex.

'I'm not predictable.'

'You're so predictable, I knew you'd say that.' He pointed to the front of the bus. 'See that man near the front, the one with the seed corn hat?'

A middle-aged man sat next to a middle-aged, frizzy haired woman. He wore flannel and she, a white turtleneck. The man held steadfastly to the metal bar while she clung to the back of the seat in front of them.

'He's missing the middle finger on his right hand.'

'Yeah, so? I suppose you're going to tell me he got it caught in a rabbit trap while hunting in Canada.'

Dave arched his eyebrows in surprise and smiled. 'You're getting better at this, Benson.'

3 – Benson

I knew he was pulling both of my legs at the same time, but I still felt pleased by his compliment as much as the bespectacled woman did two rows behind us, the one with the *blowze*.

The bus turned a tight corner and Dave's body crashed into me. Even as we straightened out, he didn't settle upright. He continued to lean against me. For a person so high on the weirdness scale, Dave had a surprisingly small aversion to physical touch. He seemed quite comfortable entering another person's personal space and erecting a tent there. As I pondered him, then pushed his body back vertical, I noticed his bow tie listing to one side like a sinking boat.

He could get away with things like that. In normal circumstances, with normal people, others would have quickly moved away, or worse, started to record him on their phone as if he was some sort of wild animal. He would have ended up in someone else's social media feed every day of the week, and yet there was something so… I don't know how to say it… but well, he broke down all your defenses. How was he so self-assured and ignorant of his power at the same time?

The person in front of us, an older woman with a head of hair the size of a regulation basketball, tried to ignore our conversation, but Dave took that as an affront to his conversational abilities, and tapped her on the shoulder. She flinched, glanced back and frowned, the expression revealing distrust and a vague sense of confusion. She did not have eyebrows but blue streaks where eyebrows had existed in ages past. Her wide, wire-rimmed multifocaled glasses, magnified her eyes and sat low on the bulb of her nose. She wore bright red lipstick emphasizing the whiteness of her pasty makeup.

'Hmmm,' Dave mumbled.

'Can I help you?' the old lady asked, her voice reedy thin, tremulous.

'Have you ever been to a funeral?'

'What?'

'A funeral. You know, where corpses are placed into wooden boxes, and then either burned or buried.'

'I know what a funeral is, young man.'

'And...?'

'Yes, I have been to a funeral before. Many of them, in fact. The last one,' her eyes shifted outwards beyond the grimy windows smeared with handprints of chocolate-eating children, 'was my husband's just a year ago.'

Normal people would have embarrassedly apologized saying, *I'm sorry for your loss,* but not Dave.

Before he prodded further, I wanted to reach out and request that he not dip his bucket into the reservoir of his strangeness. *Don't do it.*

'Tell me about that funeral, if you would, please.'

'I would prefer not to,' the old woman stated firmly and sadly as she turned around in her seat.

'It would mean so much to me,' Dave responded. 'We're going to our very first funeral today and we don't know what to expect.'

The woman turned again, and I spotted a dangly pearl earring that I hadn't noticed before. She sighed. 'You've never been to a funeral before? Was it someone close to you?'

Dave nodded. 'Very.'

I wanted to punch him. Very soon, a quote would pop out of nowhere, and this woman would have no idea, absolutely no clue, what he was talking about. 'I'm sorry for your loss,' she said as any normal person would (or should) have.

Dave's chin was perched on his forearms covering the back of her seat. She sidled sideways to face him. A faraway look came into her eyes, like she was netting a fluttering memory in the shape of a mental butterfly.

'Tony was a beautiful man, full of energy and life. He liked to go fishing and do puzzles. Every New Year's he'd set up one of those two-thousand-piece puzzles on the card table and that's what we'd do through the month of January.'

'What was your favorite?'

'My favorite what?'

'Puzzle.'

'There was this picture of Neu Schwanstein, that's in…'

'It's the Disney Castle,' Dave interjected.

'That's right,' she responded, surprised. She pushed up her glasses slightly, her middle finger on the bridge, not too much, only just past the bulbs of her nostrils. Dave mirrored her, even though he didn't have glasses, but she appeared not to notice.

'It took us until 11:00 on January 31. I remember placing the last piece myself – Tony always let me put the last piece in. He was like that. Always looking out for other people.'

Dave elbowed me, nodding at the thought of an old couple spending an entire month of their lives matching curves and straight edges making sure things fit together well.

Not that I've been around dead people a lot, but I've always heard that there are no flaws in the deceased. Once they've passed to the other side, their sainthood is assured. People talk about them as if they were the nicest, most beautiful, generous – whatever unselfish adjective you could think of – person who ever existed. For this reason, I took the woman's words with a grain of salt. The guy was probably a putz, and she wanted to cover up her guilt for marrying him.

'Now, about the funeral…?' It was a weird moment for me because Dave had a powerful, concentrated look on his face as if he was an arachnophobe confronting his greatest, eight-legged nemesis. Though these looks were rare, usually reserved when Dave met unstructured people like himself, it surprised me there on the bus talking about death.

'You're nervous about it?' The little old lady unconsciously fingered her old-fashioned purse, a green one with brass toggles.

'Very.'

I don't think Dave was nervous in the least. Perhaps the only time I'd seen him nervous was one Christmas when he had volunteered to be the little drummer boy for a live nativity play outside one of the neighborhood churches. Unfortunately for the organizers, Dave had been allowed to choose his own costume – red breeches, a tuxedo shirt with cravat, and green shoes (combo elf with penguin) – *and* which song he was going to play for the infant Jesus and his infinitely exhausted mother. As he waited for the Wise Men to arrive, he waved at me with one of his drumsticks and began counting his beats with his lips before launching into a very remedial version of *Smells Like Teen Spirit*.

'Funerals are sad affairs,' she began. 'I mean, that's obvious, I suppose; someone close to you has died. For me, grief has been constant since the...' she choked on the word, but it finally came out, '...death, and the pain has been transformed into numbness. But that doesn't necessarily make it hurt less. You sit through a ceremony, or ritual, and try to believe the best, but you feel the worst. All you know is that you'll never feel or hear them next to you again.'

'Your husband,' Dave motioned with his hand, 'was he incinerated?'

The old lady smiled. Dave knew fully well that the word was 'cremated,' but his feigned ignorance could sometimes put people at ease.

'Cremated,' she corrected.

'I always thought the word 'cremated' was strange, as if somehow they were being turned into cream.'

'Oh, dear,' she said as she put a hand to her mouth. 'I've never thought about it that way.' Her eyes filled with tears and her throat with giggles. It was the old lady giggles where they're afraid to show their teeth. Her glasses bounced up and down on her face and then we turned a corner. She untoggled her purse and retrieved an old-lady handkerchief, the very-used kind, crinkled and crusty, with faded flowers and tatted purple edging. She pushed up her glasses to dab her eyes.

'Tell me one more thing about your husband, something extraordinary,' Dave drew out the last word as he settled his chin back onto his forearms. 'Something you said at his funeral.'

She covered her cheeks with her hands, one holding the handkerchief. Not many people must have talked to her about her husband anymore. They probably assumed she was getting better or

3 – Benson

moving on with life; but the process of recollecting could be a reprieve from feeling like something was always missing.

'I remember his picture sitting on top of the casket, that picture of him in his boat, reclining back in his seat. He had a broad smile on his face, the one he revealed when everything in the world seemed all right. One time when we were in the boat, the sun was setting and we were just floating on the orangey water, he gave me that smile and said, 'You're a great catch, hon. I'd reel you in every lifetime'.'

Dave leaned back in his seat and sighed as if he'd been satisfied by a large meal. 'You need to find a woman like that, Benson.'

I felt my cheeks redden.

'I think,' he winked at the old lady and said to me, 'we'd better be on our best behavior.'

'Thank you for making me laugh, dear,' the old lady stretched her hand out to Dave who mimicked the motion, but they didn't touch.

'Gratitude has a short half-life, Clarice.'

I leaned my head back and rolled my eyes as the bus stopped at the station.

The church was a three-story building constructed of coppery-red bricks. The front entrance was overshadowed by a large steeple with a gigantic bell in its belfry, and running along both sides of the sanctuary were arched, stained-glass windows. Like most churches, the windows appeared dark from the outside. Dark, marbly eyes.

The last time I was in a church was when I was little and my parents took me to a Christmas service to, as my father said about me as his precocious son, 'get some religion in there'. While he could have used some religion in him more than me, I remember both the church, and the Christmas service, being quaint and sugary sweet.

We walked through a beautiful, well-kept garden along a delightful path. We were past the time of flowers, but the trees still had their leaves. As we neared the front steps, long granite tiers, worn by years of monotonous repetitive climbing, Dave suddenly grew jittery. He slowed, his arms got fidgety, and he started stroking his sideburns.

'What's wrong?' I asked.

He mumbled something under his breath that I couldn't catch and then started forward again as if caught in the undercurrent of something bigger than us.

Funerals do weird things to people, but the fearful uncertainty of what weird things a funeral could do to weird people like Dave made me shudder. We had never really talked about the ceremony itself – death, many times over, and usually with regards to Clarice Starling and Hannibal Lecter – so it was interesting to see that reaction on his face. Dread and curiosity. Loathing and adrenaline.

We paused outside the entrance. There was a gaudy sign with removable black letters with Janice Kipling's name and details on it. Something about seeing her name there made me feel sick, and for a brief moment, I imagined my own name there. Yuck.

Dave stopped at the sign, chin cupped in his hand. 'Did you know that when bodies are incinerated, there's not much left but ash, bits of bone, and a few teeth? The creamatoriums add ashes to help people not be so disgusted.'

'That's fascinating.' I ignored the fact that he had completely mispronounced 'crematorium'.

We approached the front steps and doors. Black-suited attendants guarded a brass stand where handouts were carefully arranged in a fan. Three photos of Janice were positioned behind these. It was as if Janice herself was making sure each attendee only took one. She had been frugal like that.

'May I have a funeral flier, please?'

The man seemed confused by the request, so Dave pointed at the bulletins with Janice's face on them. She looked younger and puffy, not at all like she did when she was sitting outside on the deck of her apartment smoking cigarettes and swatting flies with a swatter shaped like Texas.

3 – Benson

'Bulletin. Yes, you may have one.' The funeral attendant, a solemn looking man in his fifties, with an expensive looking tie, gold tie tack and cufflinks, looked up his nose at Dave and his appearance. The attendant's nose twitched as if he smelled something bad.

'Thank you,' Dave grinned. 'Being smart spoils a lot of things, doesn't it?'

'What?' The attendant frowned deeply and attempted to move on to the next grievers, but Dave tapped him on the arm.

'Do you prefer to be called 'undertaker?''

The man shook his head. 'We prefer funeral attendant.'

'What about mortician? It has a nice, shall we say, flare to it?'

The funeral attendant spoke to Dave through a fake smile. 'Thank you, sir. Please note that the front seats are reserved for close family and friends.'

Dave raised his eyebrows. 'I guess that means we're in the front row.'

'No, Dave, that's not what it means,' I responded.

Taking no notice of my disagreement, Dave proceeded to walk casually down the middle aisle to the front of the church. I followed, not because I wanted to, but because Dave would have made a scene – like waving to me as if we were at a baseball game and shouting, 'I got us some good seats over here!'

He found seats on the left side of the room near the front next to a young couple.

The seats were charcoal gray and springy. He bounced twice on them before speaking to the couple. 'Ooh, comfy!' The woman was particularly beautiful. Her boyfriend was handsome but not in a rugged kind of way, more like the cultured, mocha-coffee kind. He had a five o'clock shadow but it, too, had been carefully cultivated, unlike Dave's Mexico chops. The young couple reeled from Dave. She jabbed her femininish boyfriend and they quickly moved away from us.

Dave nodded. 'Mission accomplished.'

'What mission?'

'I needed two spare seats.'

'For who?'

'Letitia and Megsy.'

I tried to stifle the groan.

Letitia is like the anti-Dave. She is a petite, African American woman with a shaved head. And when I say petite, standing next to Dave, she looks like a Munchkin. I'm not even sure she is five feet tall. In theory, I am ambivalent about Letitia, but in practice, I could probably do without her. Nice enough, but she can be, how shall I say this diplomatically? Pushy and a little overbearing.

'What's wrong, Benson? You do not approve of my choice of dates?'

'Dave...'

He gave me the eye.

'This is a funeral, not a date!' I whispered loudly.

It was evident that Dave was unconcerned about the function of the function. His gaze was centered on me, but his voice seemed to be looking for someone else. 'Everything, my good man, is an opportunity. Letitia wondered what I was doing today and I told her about this event.'

My frustration boiled to the surface, and I bit my lip before responding. 'Dave, have a little bit of respect.' I made a pinch between my fingers.

Suddenly, Dave's eyes caught movement at the back. It took a few moments, but finally, she caught sight of him. Over the dirge-like music, Dave waved his hands above his head and shouted, 'Letitia! Over here! I got us some good seats!'

4
Letitia

No one understood Dave, just as no one understood *me* because Dave was my boyfriend – and almost fiancé. We hadn't been dating for that long, but when you get that feeling, your gut-instinct has to be correct, right?

We were a study in opposites. He was white, I was dark. Tall, short. Slow, fast. When we walked together, it looked like Dave was holding the hand of his adopted black child. He was obsessed with making sure everyone around him was happy, and I made it my priority to let everyone know it was *my* happiness that mattered. The physical appearances didn't matter. Not one little bit. It was just us and nobody else's opinion was worth a bucket of spit.

By the time of Janice's funeral, Dave and I had been dating for almost a year. In my past relationship experiences, a year-long 'romance' would not have been grounds for changing my social media status to 'not-single,' but it felt different. It sure as heaven *looked* different, that's for sure, especially after my ex – Meg's father. We'll get to him later.

Dave and I met at a fun little restaurant in downtown Des Moines where they served beer out of a cattle trough. (It is Iowa, for Pete's sake). As I was reaching into the trough, this strange white guy was staring at me. He had paused his drinking mid-sip, (it was a tropical blue cocktail with an orange umbrella), and he opened his eyes really wide as if he was trying not to blink.

I want you to know that I generally don't fish in the white end of the pool. Most white guys I know are nervous and connected to their phones. Black men, on the other hand, are loud and cocky. They have a degree of raw sexuality about them that white men lack, but for some reason, in my experience, they are *highly* allergic to commitment. Which, until I met Dave, gave me pause to dip a toe into the other end of the pool.

Antoine, my ex-husband, was a stereotype of what I have just described. He was confident, strong, and beautiful, but not at all concerned for his own offspring. Meg is our five-year-old daughter. She is the most beautiful creature in the world; dark, chocolatey skin, creamy brown eyes, and a smile that makes people gasp. She giggles at everything, like butterflies, ice cream cones, cold water on her toes, and especially Dave. Alternatively, Antoine is a self-righteous pig. Though not physically abusive, his abandonment struck us to the core, and we still haven't fully recovered. We got close with Dave, though.

About six years ago, Antoine and I met at a staff party. I'm a professor of African American Studies at Drake University. Antoine, one of the groundskeepers at the university, was charming and witty. He complimented me on all sorts of things, and his vocabulary was adequate, which was a nice surprise considering his line of work. After the staff party, we dated for about a year and a half, but as soon as he found out I was pregnant, things changed. It was as if he'd had a bucketful of fleas tipped on him. Itch. Itch. And suddenly his vocab turned churlish – infantile *What? You mean you want to get married? Make this permanent?* Scratch. Scratch. *I got plans, baby. Maybe we should just, you know…*

His idea of commitment was to erase what he called 'the little typo.'

I kicked his butt out the door. Last I heard, he was slumming in St. Louis. And no, in case you were wondering, he doesn't pay child support. That kind of commitment would be something he used to call 'financially adverse to his future prospects.'

Now, back to the restaurant where I first met Dave.

Instead of walking over to me from the cattle trough like a normal human, he got down on his knees and shuffled across the floor. He never took his eyes off me, not even when a waitress plowed into him and spilled a drink all over his head and down his back. With beer dripping over his eyelashes and through his peculiar sideburns, a waitress apologized without apologizing. Dave finished his knee-shuffle to me.

'Hello. My name is Dave.'

'What are you doing Dave?

4 – Letitia

'I've come to make your acquaintance.' He bowed to the ground. This was the first time his eyes broke contact with mine. He held his tropical drink off to the side where it began to spill out, but he didn't seem to care.

I laughed. I couldn't help it. His long brown hair drooped over his downturned face like a weeping willow tree.

'I'm Letitia.'

He finished bowing. 'I am full of joy that we have now met.' He reached out his hand, or should I say his fingers, as if offering them for me to kiss.

'Did you know that my name means 'joy?''

Eyes twinkling, he grinned again. 'All good things to those who wait?'

'What?'

Dave continued to hold out his hand to me. I glanced around and many people in the room were staring at us. I thought they were going to make fun of us, but what I came to realize was that the entire room (all knowing Dave, of course) was waiting to see what I'd do. They sat under bare wooden beams, road signs hanging above them, Christmas lights strung around their heads. Their eyes were wide – expectant – and drinks paused on the way to their mouths. A large woman, sitting on a black cushioned seat groaning under her weight, nodded and made a motion with her hands saying, 'Go ahead. Don't be afraid. He won't bite you.'

Now, staring into Dave's eyes and beer-dripping face, I shrugged and took his hand. The crowd waited with breathless anticipation. I kissed his fingers.

The patrons erupted with spontaneous laughter as Dave shuffled the last knee-step to me and wrapped his gangly white arms around my waist. Dave hugged very hard. He was so energetic about his hug that he spilled his tropical drink down my back. I gasped and pushed him away.

'What's wrong with you?' I shouted; my white shirt now streaked with blue.

'Only a few things,' he said quietly. 'But I'm well worth your time.'

The people in the restaurant returned to their drinks and continued their amicable conversations. They already knew Dave would get away with my Tropicana baptism.

Another person pulled up behind Dave, a shorter man, kind of chubby with a prematurely receding hair line and a splotchy complexion. 'Dave,' he said exasperatedly, 'maybe you should leave the nice lady alone.'

That was my first introduction to Benson, who, over the course of the next months, would play foil to various foundational moments in our burgeoning relationship. He frowned at me like a jealous lover.

Dave stood up and for the first time I saw how tall he was. And skinny. Not rail-thin, but sinewy, like a mongoose, and there was a raw, irresistible beauty about him. I would say it was his soul rather than his looks – even though he was a good-looking man. Dave held out the crook of his arm to me. I had to reach up to grab it, and we walked back to the bar where Dave promptly ordered another blue tropical drink with pineapple and an orange umbrella and stuck his hand into the ice-cold beer trough for me, producing a wine cooler with a gentlemanly flourish.

On the Wednesday afternoon of the funeral, Meg and I journeyed to attend the 'sailing away' ceremony (that's what Dave called the funeral) for his friend, Janice. I had never met Janice. I had no idea who Janice was, and Dave did not seem particularly shaken by her sailing journey, but he asked me to come anyway. He called it a 'date' which also made me nervous, but I went there to support him because I was curious to see what his grief looked like.

Dave was at the front of the church waving wildly to us at the back. Once he exclaimed over the crowd that he 'got good seats for us near the front,' I smiled. We passed many different kinds of folk on the way to our seats. There was a young, attractive woman sitting next to a metrosexual white man with a sculpted five o'clock shadow who whispered as I walked by. They had just vacated the seats by Dave and Benson.

4 – Letitia

Dave scootched Benson over a seat and tapped the soft gray chair next to him. Benson did not look particularly pleased. My guess is that he didn't even know I was coming.

Dave and Benson's relationship *appeared* simple, but it *was* incredibly complex. Benson lived next door to Dave. He was a computer programmer who, for all intents and purposes, was oddly non-reclusive for someone who worked predominantly online. They went everywhere together. Dave was Batman; Benson was Robin. To be fair, Benson attempted to flatten out the fluctuations in Dave's peculiarity, but it was hard to level a roller coaster that large.

Dave was still standing when I moved in next to him. He bent down and kissed me on the lips. It wasn't a peck on the cheek, either, but a lingering, meaningful kiss that caused the couple behind us to murmur disgustedly. I get it, it was a funeral, not a wedding, but it was just a kiss.

Finally, Dave broke away and sat down. His face beamed. 'You look absolutely ravishing.'

Dave's sense of beauty was radically different than anyone else I've ever met. Instead of focusing on thinness, age, skin color, curves, or anything that Hollywood sells us as most important, Dave looked through that as if it was a transparent mask. Okay, so yes, I am thin, I'm thirty-four, I'm black and curvy, but I've also heard him use the word 'ravishing' to describe a sixty-seven-year-old white man who had just come out of double-bypass surgery. Beauty is not about what you show, it's what you reflect. He not only saw beauty, he felt it.

'Hello, Megabyte.'

My daughter's face lit up like a flashlight in a treehouse. She shoved my leg to the side and clambered up onto Dave's lap. Meg squeezed his neck just like he squeezed her. Hugging her side to side, not once or twice but half a dozen times, Dave repeated over and over, 'I missed you! I missed you! I missed you!' This was the way they greeted each other every time they saw each other, as if Dave had returned home from war, even though they saw each other two nights before when we went to see a film together.

Dave turned Meg on his lap and leaned close to her ear. Immediately, she reached up for his sideburns and began to run her fingers through them. Arching her back into him, she tilted her head slightly and pointed at a place on his cheek where a shadowy mole was revealed under his right cheekbone. 'That's Chiapas, right?'

'That's right,' he responded as he patted the hand pointing at his cheek.

I leaned forward and greeted Benson who had sourly crossed his arms over his outdated shirt and tie. Benson was like a middle-school teenager in the way that he presented his jealousy. His true age is somewhere in the mid-20's (I think). He frowned, pulling his lips into a pout, and slumped a little lower in the chair, but he acknowledged my presence, even if he didn't want to.

'Hello, Letitia.'

For five minutes, Dave and Meg chatted beneath the muted organ music. Blessed Assurance, I think. I used to go to church almost every Sunday, but now not quite so often. Once a month, maybe, or every six weeks we attend a Baptist church on the south side. Quaint. Dull. Sedentary, sleepy people, nice but tolerable. Since I fell pregnant with Meg, we've stayed away. There are only so many sins that church people can accept. Greed and apathy were okay; outside-the-bonds-of-marriage-pregnancy, not so much.

Over the last six months, Dave asked me multiple times if we could go to church together. He said he was fascinated by rituals and sanctuaries. Dave said he had been to church before but refused to talk about where and when it was. Even on the day of the funeral, his eyes darted here and there, pausing, his frown appearing and dissolving as the funeral attendants prepared the sanctuary for the service. The spray of flowers. The easel and Janice's picture. The punctuating sound of a sob in the foyer. It was as if he was flinching while smiling.

The organ stopped like it was taking a breath to prepare for an impressive aria, then launched into Amazing Grace. I knew that song. It was sung at both of my parents' funerals. It's hard to believe that they both died so young. My dad died of a heart attack at forty-seven, and my mother breast cancer just two years ago. It's been a struggle, but Dave filled in nicely where my parents should have been.

The front stage of the church was bereft of religious artifacts. No crosses or bibles or anything. Just blue carpet and a podium for the lectern. Everything was pretty and neat, the very opposite of both death and the grief that had preceded the day. For some reason our culture has sterilized the end-of-life process to make it more palatable, as if that will make us heal better. From the flowers to the colored backdrop, the pretty people and their semi-formal outfits, the funeral display is one of reality-avoidance. We are preconditioned to avert our eyes from death, and yet we are drawn to it, center of focus, but not as the dark malevolent thing it is, but a saccharined enamel, like a gigantic Dinosaur Egg — remember those ancient choking hazards they'd peddle at the movie theater? Sugary sweet on the outside, but so tart on the inside it threatened to scrape away the inner lining of your cheeks. This is 21st century death, so very much like my parents' funerals, where the eulogists would extol the marvel and wonder of my parents' lives, when in reality, the sourness was overlooked. My father's spiritual indiscretions, not of the religious kind, but the one that came in liter-sized plastic bottles; and my mother's constant nitpicking and bemoaning of the fact that I would never reach her clavicle.

It was the same for Janice's funeral with its shields for grief. The music, carefully curated to give hope to the living and a syrupy journey on the River Styx for the dead, was low and numbing in the background. On the front wall of the chapel, the lyrics for Amazing Grace were projected in 44-point font on the screen. Obviously, Janice wanted us to sing along, or maybe the family did. Singing took the focus off the casket wheeled into the chapel by a long-faced mortician and his smartly dressed understudy. Two older people, most likely Janice's parents, trudged somberly behind the polished wood coffin containing Janice's body. Another spray of roses was thrown wreath-like on the lid.

After the undertakers positioned the casket in front of the stage, I returned my attention to the photo of Janice, a fleshy, salt and pepper haired woman who seemed annoyed that her image was about to be captured. While I wondered what Janice was so annoyed about, the funeral attendants resumed their positions at the back of the proceedings, and the service began when the organ finished. Dave rose and began to clap around Meg's body, but Benson stopped his hands. I heard Benson say, *Not appropriate, Dave*, though I'm sure the organist was quite pleased with her first standing ovation.

A dour pastor, berobed and becrossed, his thinning hair combed to the front hiding a large forehead, welcomed us, but judging by his expression, he seemed underwhelmed by it all, as if a yawn hunched at the back of his throat.

'What's that, Dave?' Meg pointed at the coffin.

'It's a sarcophagus, Megling.'

'I can't say that.'

'Try it,' Dave encouraged.

'Sarcoughingus.'

'Very good! Very good!'

'Why is it there?'

'Well,' David whispered, 'Janice's corpse is in there.'

Meg's face twisted into a frown. 'What's that?'

'A dead body.'

At this point, I felt a twinge of discomfort that some very difficult conversations were about to ensue, but if anyone was going to have them, Dave was probably the best person.

'What is dead?'

'Hmmm…' Even Dave wondered which valley of shadows to travel on that one. He tilted his head to the left and his eyes journeyed somewhere far, far away. He got that look sometimes, especially when he had to summon a different emotion other than happiness. It was hard for him – hard for all of us.

4 – Letitia

'Okay,' he began, his face even closer to her ear, 'as people get older, they start to lose the ability to live. In order to not be afraid of this inability, they do things that are not necessarily good for them. Janice smoked cigarettes and she drank a lot of Johnnie Walker Red.'

'Dave...' I warned with a lowered whisper.

'What is Johnnie Walker Red?'

'Entry level scotch.'

'Oh.' She thought hard about her next question as the obituary was wrapping up. 'Is Janice in the box?'

'Hmmm... Well, yes, but what made her who she is, is gone.'

'I don't understand.'

Dave patted her hair in a very touching and tender way. It was hard for me to comprehend the complexity of Dave. How he could be so incredibly gentle and caring with a small child and yet so abrasive with older, self-absorbed members of society.

'I'm not sure I do either, Megatron, but the best way I can explain it is, all the beautiful things that Janice was, are around us now. Like when you pop a balloon and the air just mixes in. Janice was a beautiful woman, very kind.'

This, in spite of all photographic evidence.

'What's going to happen to Janice's dead body?'

'They're going to incinerate it.'

At that point, a more-than-gentle reminder to Dave's arm was necessary and he rubbed it. 'What? What did I say?'

'Let's just stop at popped balloon.'

As he massaged his arm, I was suddenly struck by the fact that Dave had not looked at the casket. Even though he had answered all of Meg's questions, his eyes were distracted. They flitted between the altar and the pastor, to the organist with her blue hair and darker blue lipstick. He had studied Meg's hair and my hand, but not the coffin itself. Maybe he was more afraid of death than I imagined.

Meg leaned back and whispered again in Dave's ear who then mouthed the word, *Later*.

One of the family members stood up and Dave pointed at her. Meg nodded. It was the old woman who had been leading the procession. Grief was etched into her eyes as large chasms of pain and regret. Dried tears had left tracks in her mascara like fossilized footprints, but she was not crying at the podium. She ignored the gathered faces and reached into her pocket. Her hands trembled as she unfolded a sheet of paper and flattened it on the lectern. She was as uncomfortable as the sound of the paper's crinkling. The pastor lowered the microphone so that it was directly in front of her mouth. It made a loud creaking noise, and we all jumped.

She looked at Dave. He tapped his heart and smiled.

'My name is Helen, and Janice was my only daughter,' the woman started. 'She was not perfect. But, according to one of her friends, she was perfectly wonderful.' Her eyes darted back to Dave who nodded and urged her with prayer-tented hands.

'With Janice, we learned to look past what we thought were deficiencies in her character and found happiness with the way she was. Janice was a fifty-one-year-old woman caught between worlds. That was what she looked like, but when you talked to her, when you listened to her voice, there was a child-like wistfulness. A gentle spirit who only wanted to love and to receive it.'

Helen then launched into a poignant, heart-wrenching story from Janice's younger years.

In the meantime, I wondered if Dave was teaching me things like that – how to perceive a world, looking past people's peculiarities and struggles, to see similar souls wrestling with the same thoughts of meaningful life and meaningless death. I glanced at him. He had closed his eyes. A look of peacefulness settled over his face as if somehow he was absorbing Meg's (and Janice's) innocence into his own being. I was startled by the emergence of the word 'innocence.' Maybe it was the best way to describe Dave. An innocent traveler along a dangerous, meandering path.

'Today's loss reminds us of the power of the present,' Janice's mother continued. 'The more we worry about the future, the less joy we receive from today.' Dave reached out to put an arm around both Benson and me with Meg still on his lap leaning back against his chest. Dave stroked my shoulder with his thumb, and judging by Benson's reaction of jerking forward in his seat, he did the same on the other side.

'I'll close with the words of one of Janice's close friends: *Life is not what you make of it, but how you eat it.*'

I knew immediately that it was a Dave quote because I scanned the room to see multiple people frowning and mouthing the word, *What?*

'Thank you.'

Dave began to applaud wildly. At first, people were put off by the man in a brown and yellow outfit, bowtie, sideburns, shaggy hair, but then, something about Dave's spontaneous aura of love for life won them over. He lifted Meg who happily clapped with him to continue their march up Inappropriate Hill. Amazingly, others joined their clapping. A few scowling, older folks remained stoic, but some of the younger ones applauded, not quite as unabashedly as Dave, but politely golf-clapping nonetheless. The old woman blew Dave a kiss. I was surprised to see that Dave was crying. Tears streamed down his cheeks, and for some reason, I wondered if he was an angel. A peculiar angel that moved to a sub dimensional spiritual beat which no one else could hear.

The pastor closed his eyes and began to intone some pre-written prayers, and as he did, Meg tented Dave's hands in front of her showing him how to pray. I was startled that this small act of beauty had drawn out my own tears.

The pastor finished up the funeral rite, made the sign of the cross over the casket, and motioned for the undertakers to come forward. With deep solemnity, they approached, turned the coffin to exit the back doors headfirst, and started the long march toward the piercing sunshine outside the church.

As the people filed out behind the casket, I reached out for Meg who was reluctant to give up her Dave. She switched her head to the other side so she didn't have to look at me. With a shrug, I led us out into the aisle, carefully avoiding the stares of others.

Only Dave and Meg could see above the crowd. The stream of mourners, speaking quietly, stopped to hug Helen and Bill. Her mother thanked people individually and gracefully, very much like Dave would have, shaking their hands with both of hers. She was open and honest with her grief, and I wondered what she would say to us.

'Hello. You must be Letitia.'

Surprised, I nodded and looked up to see Dave winking at me. Helen reached out to Meg who hid her face in Dave's hair. 'You must be Megtropolis,' the woman spoke to Meg's back. Hearing one of Dave's nicknames for her, Meg turned back to Helen and smiled, a 10,000-gigawatt thing of beauty. Janice's mother fashioned a grin from her grief, and it paused briefly on her lips before fading back into the shadows of the day.

'Yeah, that's me.'

The woman squeezed into Dave who finally handed Meg to me. Helen wrapped her arms around him, enveloping him, using him as a life preserver for fear of drowning. It was Dave's nature to then invite all of us, including the father, into a collective hug. Meg giggled at the old man's hair in her face, and he seemed startled by this humorous turn of events. Dave smushed his face into Benson's shoulder. Benson, for his part, tried to wriggle out, but Dave's grip was strong. After a five second eternity, Dave released the ball of humanity, and like atoms seeking space, we separated quickly to find our own personal sacred distance.

'Well, that will keep us going for a little while,' he said.

Despite the release, Janice's mother continued to hold on to Dave. 'I can't thank you enough, Dave, for all that you've done for us, for Janice.'

'You're very welcome. She was extraordinary.'

'We'll pay you back when we can…' Her voice trailed off into emptiness.

4 – Letitia

Dave shrugged, and with no further ado, we moved outside into the sunshine and fresh air of the living world, where the shrubbery was neatly hedged, and the grass was emerald. To our right was a covered area where the non-casket-leading funeral attendants were setting up an array of sandwiches and coffee cups. A few of the mourners were already stuffing their gullets with what Dave muttered under his breath, *Death food*.

In the parking lot, we stood by my car. I grabbed hold of his elbow. 'What was that about back there?'

He grinned and scratched his nose. His bowtie was now almost vertical. Everyone who saw him probably wanted to straighten it. 'People are worth it.'

'What *exactly* did you do? Did you pay for the funeral?'

Dave raised his head and sniffed the air. 'Does anyone smell a barbecue? Mmmm, my stomach is rumbling.'

Nobody knew where Dave got his money. He didn't have a job. He didn't have any investments (as far as I knew). And he wasn't savvy enough to see things online. And yet he never seemed to be without means. It wouldn't have shocked me at all if Dave not only paid for the funeral, but he paid Janice's rent, also. Benson's eyes were wide, and his head was tilted to the side. His teeth ground together in frustration.

'Okay, Joy of My Life,' Dave said to me. 'I've got a plan for today. We don't need to head to the cemetery because Janice is being turned into cream, so…'

'Wait, what?'

'Cremated,' he pointed to Meg, 'you know, I can't say the 'incinerated' word.'

'How can Janice turn into cream?'

I gave him the *Nice-one, Bonehead* look.

'Have you ever heard of Little Black Sambo, Megs?'

I frowned at him. Dave had overstepped the line. 'Oh no you do not.'

'Okay, how about the same story but with the name changed? Megatroid, have you ever heard of Little Babaji?'

'No.'

'Well, there's this little Indian boy who fights with tigers and he tricks them into running around a tree so fast that they turn into black, white, and orange striped cream.'

Meg giggled. 'That's silly.'

'I know,' Dave tapped her nose. 'It's silly that people have decided that story is about racial stereotypes.'

Now, the hair on my bald head was standing up. 'You, Dave, don't get to choose what is appropriate for my race. I'm Black with a capital B and I'm proud of it. Don't you bring your white privilege into this, goin' all plantation master on me.'

Dave stood to his full height looking down at me. I should have been scared, but I was not because it was Dave. I was quite certain that Dave knew there were racial overtones to the story, but why did Dave share the story when Dave did not have a racist bone in his body?

'Letitia,' he spoke with great kindness, 'not everything in life is about what you look like on the outside.'

'I know that, *Dave*, but you've never had to live with my kind of persecution.' I placed my fists on my hips.

He smiled sadly – I wasn't sure what that was about – and then focused back on Meg. 'I'm very fond of your mother, Megalomaniac. Will you tell her when she can see me again?'

Meg giggled in my arms once again. 'You're silly.'

He turned to Benson. 'All right, Dipstick, how about we go rustle up some dead animals and chuck them on your barbecue.'

Benson seemed lost, as if he'd been watching a tennis match in the dark. 'I thought the tigers turned into butter?'

Dave seesawed his hand. 'Butter, buttah, patayta, patahta.'

'It's only 10:30, Dave. Barbecuing seems a little early.'

Dave leaned down to him. 'But in New York, it's 11:30 and on this Wednesday, let's pretend we're eating in New York.'

Turning his lovely face to me again, he tapped me on the nose. 'If you would be so kind as to grace us with your presence, my dear, we would love to have both of you keep us company for lunch.'

How did he do it? How did he deflect anger and never take things personally? I found my righteous indignation sliding butter on a hot stack of pancakes. Somehow, Dave made me feel as if I didn't have to be perpetually offended and angry. And I liked that. I *needed* that.

'Do you want a ride?' I asked.

'No, we'd rather take the bus.' His eyes sparkled. 'Can we take the Megadon shopping with us? You could have an hour to yourself and then make your way over to Benson's place and prepare the black, white and orange striped cream for us.'

I wanted to be angry. Kind of. 'Yes, that's fine, Dave.'

Meg jumped the short distance between us back to Dave and soon, they ran off toward the bus stop, Meg on Dave's shoulders bouncing with outrageous glee, and Benson dolefully following behind, hands in pockets staring at the ground.

As they faded into the distance, I gratefully pondered what I could do with an hour to myself.

5
Meg

My dad's name is Dave.

I know he's not really my dad. I'm little, not stupid. But he acts like a dad should, and I like that. And he's got a place where I can put my head, right between his fuzzy cheek and his shoulder. I can hear his heartbeat there. It's beautiful.

I see other kids at the park or at daycare, or in the swimming pool, and they have a male person with them. Usually that male person looks tired and distracted and is often staring at their phone while we kids play. But every once in a while, there is a dad that pays close attention and absorbs every moment with his kids.

That's Dave to me.

Ever since I met him, or my mom introduced me to him, I wondered how I got so lucky to have a dad like him. He likes to sing songs with me. He likes to go to movies with me. He likes to tell me stories. Basically, he likes me. Not like my gene donor AnTwerp (that's what my mom calls him) but I've never met him, and he can't be better than Dave. Nobody is better than Dave.

Dave doesn't treat me like a pest, and he's not annoyed even when I ask a lot of questions. Sometimes when we go out to eat, he will talk to me more than my mom. Or, he will talk to other people more than either of us, and pretty soon, Dave has invited someone else from another table to sit with us. I don't think my mom likes that very much at all, but I do. It's very interesting to be around strange people, but I feel safe around them with Dave nearby.

He's not afraid of answering hard questions, too. Today, when Dave was talking to me about the sarcoughingus and some other words I didn't know, I wondered why he does that when no one else will. Is being dead something I'm supposed to be afraid of? Why was that lady in the box? Could she breathe? I wondered if she was going to pop out like my Jack-In-The-Box and scare me. Why would a person go in there? I mean,

5 - Meg

I like to hide in places, sometimes under tables, in the closet, outside, underwater. When Dave plays Hide and Seek with me, I sometimes have him close his eyes and he is never able to find me until I shout, 'Here I am,' and then he laughs and laughs and bends over and sometimes farts — but why would a person get in that wooden box?

We left Mom behind us at the funeral place. I asked Dave what she was going to do.

'Your mother is going to have some personal space so that she is ready for adult interaction later on at the barbecue.'

'What is personal space?'

'Hmmm…. Think about it this way, Megsamillion. Have you ever just wanted to be alone? You're tired of dolls and toys and noise and videos and your brain is like AAAGH, LAAGAAHAL, BLAH.' His funny noises made me giggle. I was so high in the air while sitting on Dave's shoulders I felt like I could touch the tops of the buildings or pet a pigeon or something.

'Not very often.'

'Well, that's your mom sometimes. Old people like us need to breathe deeply, can you do that Megburger? Take a deep breath and hold it and then listen for the pounding in your ears.' I hold my breath and soon, it sounded like there were drums in my head.

'I can hear it.'

'What song is it playing?' Dave asked.

'Beat It.'

'A young lady after my own soul.'

'What's a soul, Dave?'

Dave bounced a few times and I made the Aaaaaah sound. It's my favorite. 'The soul, Megtastic, is what people see after you're gone.'

'She can't possibly understand that, Dave,' Benson said as he hurried up behind us.

'Why not?'

'Because she's five years old, that's why.'

'What does age have to do with it? You're what, thirty-six?'

'I'm twenty-three.'

'That's what I thought,' responded Dave as he twirled me in circles on top of his shoulders. The world spun. The clouds above us turned into a whirlpool in the sky. Turned to blue cream and butter.

'And?' Benson tried to step in front of us, but Dave dodged him. This was fun.

'You, Pumpkinhead, tell me what a soul is.'

Benson's stumpy legs were bouncing and that little bit of extra chin gobbler jiggled. I like Benson. He is nice. 'There is no data, factual or otherwise, that really suggests there is such a thing. It's just something religious people make up to not feel bad when they are dying.'

Dave stopped suddenly and wheeled on Benson. We leaned down together. It felt as if he was going to drop me, but I knew he wouldn't. 'Why are you with me, Benson?'

'Because you're my friend.'

'How did we get to be friends?'

'You live next door to me.'

'Yes, but so does Raji on the other side. Is he your friend?'

'No.'

'Why not?' Dave still hadn't straightened up. This was okay because I got to play with his hair and sideburns.

'Because... hell, I don't know. I suppose it's because I haven't taken the time to get to know him.'

'Why not?'

'This is ridiculous, Dave. What does this have to do with having a soul?'

Dave took one of his hands off my leg and touched Benson's shoulder. He spoke softly and it was hard for me to hear. 'When you look at every other person and know that they have a soul, something soft and excruciatingly beautiful, like a spiritual marshmallow waiting to escape, your life will change. Souls are songs.' Dave straightened up and we continued on our way.

5 – Meg

'Wait, Dave. But how do I... er... how do I find something, or listen for something I don't believe in?'

We looked up at the sky and then we turned to look at the flight of some birds. A fly buzzed past my face and I swatted at it. The sun was warm and wonderful on my dark brown skin and I hoped that it stayed in the sky for a long time. Maybe when we got to Benson's house, he'd have some toys I could play with on the grass.

Dave tapped on my legs but spoke to Benson. 'Start with her, Benson. She's singing loudly right now.'

'What should we sing, Dave?' I asked him. Because he was using my legs for drums, I used his head for a conga.

'How about ninety-nine bottles of beer on the wall?'

'I don't know that one.'

'You'll pick it up quickly.'

We sang all the way to the bus stop. I didn't know the numbers – Dave told me what they were beforehand, but I caught on to the song really fast. Kids are good at music. I always like to sing and dance. Sometimes I raise my hands up high in the air and spin and spin and spin. Sometimes I make up my own songs about nothing at all. It's fun. I don't know why big people don't do it. Dave does, but most adults are too grumpy.

We were at fifty-three bottles when the bus arrived. Dave tried to pull me off his shoulder, but I squeezed my knees shut real hard on his ears. He laughed, but I think it hurt him, so I let go.

As we rode the bus together, Benson stared at me and tilted to the side, his head almost touching Dave's shoulder. I crossed my arms and frowned at him like my mom does and he sat up straight. He's weird. Not like my dad.

'Dave,' I said, remembering the words my mom spoke, 'What's white privilege?'

Dave raised his eyebrows and glanced around the bus. 'We should ask some people. How does that sound?'

Benson did not seem real happy about that. 'Dave, inappropriate.'

'Why? What's inappropriate about talking to people. Why does everything have to be about the weather and the Cyclones?'

'Because that's casual conversation.'

'Well, phooey to that,' responded Dave and found two black teenage boys across the bus. 'Hey, my name is Dave. We,' he pointed to him and me. I was standing on my knees on the seat, 'want to know what white privilege is.'

The boys frowned at Dave as if he was crazy and then at me. 'What?'

'Recently, I was having a discussion with this young girl's mother, the joy of my life, a diminutive black woman, about racial tension in the United States. Can you explain white privilege to this young black girl for me?'

'You can't call her black. You white. That's racist.'

'Why can you call me white, then?'

'Because that's what you is,' the boy on the left mumbled, 'crazy white...' the rest was lost in a jumble of syllables about someone's mom and another word I did not know.

'What are you?' Dave asked.

The young black boy was now angry. 'Do you want to fight?'

'Why would I want that?'

'Because you talkin' to me with disrespect.'

'I just asked you a question and you got angry, but I'm not sure why?'

'All right, that's it.' The boy stood up and moved closer to Dave. I wanted to hug him. Benson told Dave to cool it.

'Do you believe in white privilege?' Dave asked. 'Do you think it's a thing?'

The boy looked around to see if he was being recorded. No one was paying much attention, although a few older ladies were holding their purses a little tighter. I saw the bus driver's eyes in the mirror, but they didn't look too worried. Not yet.

5 – Meg

'Hell, yeah.' He kept standing, but didn't look as angry with me sitting on Dave's lap.

'Where did you first hear about it? Was it in a book?'

The boy laughed and turned to his friend. 'Are you listenin' to this? A book.'

Dave smiled, it's the one I really like, the one that says, *You are the most important person in the world.* 'I first read about it a few years ago. Although I believe I understand the basic tenets, I can't fully know unless people of color help me. Will you help me?'

For a moment, the boy didn't know if Dave was pulling his leg. It was then that I noticed no one else on the bus had Dave and Benson's skin color. Everybody else was a healthy shade of chocolate or caramel.

'Okay, okay, it's like this. Look around this bus. How many white people do you see?'

Dave scanned. 'One.'

The boy frowned. 'There's two, dummy.'

'Where?'

Shaking his head, he pointed at Dave and Benson.

'You asked how many I see,' Dave responded, 'and I *see* one.' He pointed at Benson. 'It's all about perspective, isn't it?'

The boy shook his head. 'You crazy, man.'

'Only on Wednesdays.'

'White people don't take the bus. White people drive cars that they earned with money taken from us black people and they don't even know it. White people don't even know that they think they better than us black folk. White people,' he moved in closer to Dave who did not flinch even though Benson did, 'are always racist because they never change their perspective, only change their position.'

Dave's face lit up again. 'Then I'm not white!'

'What?'

'By definition of your perspective of what privilege is, I must be Black, or Asian, or Native American, because white people don't ride the bus. Benson,' he looked to the side, 'I never knew you were black.'

Benson face palmed. He was afraid Dave might have gone too far this time. I looked at the boy who shared my skin color. He was beautiful and I wondered if he was AnTwerp.

'Hey everybody,' Dave opened his arms to everyone on the bus. 'I'm woke!' A girl focused her phone on us. I wasn't sure why she thought it was important to record, but I must not be old enough to understand what teenage girls think is important.

The boy stared for a moment and then suddenly grinned. He tried to cover the grin with a hand, but then he burst out laughing. I liked his laugh. It was low and slow, like a swing that goes up and down and back again. He turned to his friend who had dipped his head and was laughing along with him.

'I like you,' the boy said. 'You different.'

This was where Dave's face slid a little bit. 'Yes,' he said quietly, 'different just like you.'

Benson put a hand on Dave's shoulder while I snuggled into him. The bus seemed smaller, I think. The windows squeezed me, and everything got real quiet. Then Dave stroked my head, and I felt better, and the bus got bigger again.

'What are you boys doing for lunch?' Dave asked them. 'We're about to head to Kroger to buy some meat for a barbecue. Do you guys wanna join us?'

'Ah, man, that's like stalkerness.' He smiled. 'What do you think, Dontay, should we travel to this man's house to eat his barbecue?'

The boy he called Dontay shrugged. That one had beautiful brown eyes and big black hair. Huge, like a midnight basketball. His clothes were very big for him, and I wondered if he was having trouble gaining weight.

'Man, you are crazy. But I am hungry. A nice T-bone would go down well with a few beers.'

'You're on,' Dave extended his hand.

The boy studied Dave's big, white paw. There was hair on his knuckles, and he had dirt under his fingernails, just like me. Well, I didn't have hair on my knuckles, but the dirt is a daily thing. My mom says I

5 – Meg

need to act like a lady and stay out of the mud, but that makes me unhappy. Like me, I think Dave likes to play in the dirt. Benson looked like he was curling up into a ball. I didn't know what was wrong with him.

'What's your name?' Dave asked.

'Rontrelle.'

'What a pretty name,' I said as I tapped Dave's cheeks. Chiapas was trying to hide from me.

'I'm Dave and this intrepid traveler next to me is Benson. Say 'hello' Benson.'

Benson had no intention of continuing his part in the conversation, but he didn't want to be rude. 'Hi.'

Dave spoke to the rest of the bus. 'If anyone else wants to come to my friend Benson's house for a barbecue, you're all welcome.' Benson was now slumping lower and lower into his seat. I think his back must have hurt, or something.

Rontrelle held onto the rung above him as we turned a corner. It felt like the bus was going to tip over. That was fun.

'Dave, what happened to you? Why you like that?' Rontrelle asked.

I crawled back on to Dave's lap and he rested his chin on my head. 'Nothing made me happen. I happened.'

A dark couple in their twenties, the man with black hair like mine, no bow of course, and the woman – she is a lot bigger than my mommy, a lot – they turned around in their seat. 'We'll come too.'

I clapped my hands. I love parties.

It looked like Benson was starting to cry.

6
Gladys

I am the superintendent of the Palm Apartments. There are 120 units built into a U. Inside the U is a central community space containing a small playground with a slide, a few rusty swings, and plastic animals that double as teeter-tottering toys. Unfortunately, the playground doesn't get used much.

The apartments were built in the 1980's and have very little to differentiate them from office buildings of the same time period, yet the residents seem to like them and their lack of individuality. All the distinctiveness comes from the residents themselves.

I remember the first time Dave rapped on the door of the super's office – my office. There was a certain Fred-Jones-of-Scooby-Doo look about him (without the blonde hair) in his sky-blue leisure suit and yellow socks. His sparkling white tennis shoes gleamed in the afternoon sun, and he had a yellow handkerchief poking from the chest pocket. His shirt was yellow, also. The tie he wore was something silky draped around his neck. Because the security cameras were facing the front entrance, I saw him coming in black and white, and I remember thinking to myself, 'Okay, here we go…'

He entered the office and studied my stuff as if analyzing a crime scene. There were piles of magazines, a ticking alarm clock, a scarred desk with an out-of-date computer at my fingertips. A few file drawers were open. I remember because I'd stubbed my fat thighs on them a few times. His gaze lingered on my pizza calendar, opened, as always, to May, 1984 (I never turn the page) where a seriously hunky (and hairy) man was on full display beside two equally yummy young ladies. Dave's eyebrow raised slightly, and he tilted his head, but whatever comment he was thinking remained tucked inside that shaggy head.

Dave bypassed the sagging coffee table in the middle of the room and approached the desk to touch the bell which had a little sign that read, *If unattended, ring the bell.* It irked me that, even though he had read the sign, he had decided to ring it anyway.

'Can I help you?'

'Hmmm...' He set down a gouged brown briefcase and flipped the latches to produce some documents. 'I'd like to rent an apartment.'

His appearance did not suggest what I'd call 'premium rental material.' People who looked like him tended to have parties on Tuesday nights, adopt cats from the parking lot, and list distinctly towards veganism, not that there's anything specifically *wrong* with veganism, but vegans tend to be a *little* bit pickier than your run of the mill omnivores.

'There's no parties allowed, and you can't have pets on the premises.'

'I'll limit my gatherings and drop the cats off at the pound.'

'What?'

'How much is a two-bedroom apartment?'

'Nine hundred.'

'I'll take it.'

'You haven't even seen it yet,' I said. 'It might be damaged or stinky or not quite right for, I don't know, you're...'

'Height?'

'Yes, that's right.'

'Are they?'

'Are they what?'

'Damaged, putrescent, or height limiting.'

Where is this guy from? Who uses the word putrescent? 'No, they are not.'

'Then let's not dither over specifics. When can I move in?'

It felt like I should be unsure about him. Someone dressed like that could only come from California, or Sweden.

He stared unblinkingly at me. This was disconcerting, so I averted my eyes to rummage through a filing cabinet for rental forms. As I rifled through them, I recognized that his vocabulary did not suggest he was mentally deficient. But there was something *different* about him. 'We'll need to get some background checks, one month deposit, and first month rent in advance.'

'Do you take bearer bonds?'

'Uh, no.'

'Good, then I'll use a check.' Suddenly, he smiled, and it was like my office lit up. He had these crinkles around his eyes and deep dimples obscured by the weird hair on his cheeks. He deposited his documents on my desk, wrote out a check for $1800, and snapped the briefcase shut. 'I'll have my people contact your people, and hopefully I can begin moving in later this week?'

'Which people are we talking about?'

'It's just something people who want to feel important say.'

After knowing Dave, I realized how strange that statement was because Dave didn't want to feel important.

When moving day eventually came around, the entire community watched from a hidden distance. A few remained in their apartments, but some, like Patricia and her husband, supervised from their balconies. Dave had this car, an old Ford, or something, and it was loaded to the gills with all sorts of odds and ends that looked like they came from Goodwill.

He whistled a lot. A few other neighbors, Benson and old Doc Grossman included, stood on their balconies and listened while he worked. He wore a pair of washed-out coveralls and a Pioneer Seed cap. The cap was sweat-stained, and the coveralls had grease spots on the elbows and chest. The name embroidered in white on the left breast read 'Zeke.' Inside the small rental trailer were a tattered double mattress and bed frame, a small cabinet, loads of crockery and dishware. His clothes had been balled up in the back seat of the car along with cleaning supplies and a tennis racket. Finally, with great delight (and a *Eureka! I've found it!*) he reached into the back of his car and held up a flyswatter in the shape of Canada. It was as if he had located the Holy Grail.

After he'd finished sorting everything in his house, he brought out an old card table, you know the ones with the fold out legs where you have to push the little slide things in and then it clicks into place, positioned three card chairs, and covered the table with a gingham tablecloth.

'Dinner is almost ready for any who would like to join me,' he announced loudly. A few residents laughed and returned to their apartments, but for those who remained, they got a show. Dave unzipped his overalls to reveal a three-piece suit – not the leisure suit, mind you – but a white dinner jacket with a red handkerchief and black pants. He did not change his tennis shoes, though.

It suddenly dawned on me that he had moved into his apartment wearing that suit.

No one took him up on his offer to dine with him, but a few did watch him eat with great relish. Whatever he had made smelled very good. Benson, for sure, looked like a stray cat that saw a bowl of milk set out on the stoop. Wary, yes, but tempted.

If I were to write all the stories of Davescapades at the Palm Apartments, this would be a very long saga, but a few will come to the forefront over the next while. The day I want to start with was the day of Janice's funeral.

When I saw Dave walking along Kenyon Avenue and turn into the apartment complex, followed by Benson, Meg, two African American teenagers, and a Latino couple, I thought to myself, *What kind of weirdness is about to happen?*

Dave carried Meg on his shoulders, and she giggled loudly while pointing at things in the sky. The Latino couple laughed and carried on animatedly in Spanish while the teenagers chatted with Dave. They toted two large shopping bags from Kroger's and two six packs of beer. Benson trailed behind kicking stones with his feet.

'Gladys!' Dave yelled out. 'We're having a barbecue. Come and eat!'

Sometimes he invited people off the street, sometimes just Palms residents. Dave and Benson were often seen dining together on the balcony, candles lit – this was a prerequisite of dining with Dave, eating al fresco, unless, of course, it was snowing. Then, he ate in other people's houses. The candles-thing was not entirely kosher due to fire codes and all, but as long as they did it outdoors, I put up with it.

Dave installed a dinner bell outside his apartment and affixed it to the beam. I begrudgingly allowed him to do it simply because it was easier than listening to his reasons why, according to the lease (and his careful reading of loopholes), the bell was allowable. Occasionally he would ring the bell, and minutes later, like Pavlov's dogs, people would start setting up for the meal outside their house. Then, Dave would walk around like a waiter asking after their drinks.

That morning, I watched the entourage ascend the stairs to the second floor. It did not surprise me that they went to Benson's place and not Dave's. One of the black teenagers asked, 'Where's the barbecue?' Dave replied, and the boy scrunched up his face and said, 'What?'

The barbecue is where it should be – in the center of the communal area. I had it regularly cleaned, but the only one who used it was Dave. He was always trying out new cuts of meats and different seasonings on them. Why, one time, Dave grilled up halibut with cayenne pepper and sprinkled it with chocolate. I'm not sure that worked very well, but when he was done eating, he licked his fingers and smacked his lips. On that Wednesday, instead of migrating to the communal barbecue, the group headed up to Benson's small grill on his front patio. I was not a big fan of barbecues near the apartments (for the same fire code reasons), but they were careful.

I checked my watch. It was just after 11:30 and I was due to take a lunch break. My work as the apartment complex manager (with the added perks of free rent and maintenance) is rarely hectic. The only moderately tough part was that I've had to knock on a few doors or send reminders to those whose rent is overdue. It didn't happen very often, and when it did, it was mysteriously paid within a few days. I've talked to other apartment managers, and it seemed like chasing down rent was the bane of their existence. Not for me. I've got good, money-managing residents. Thank God for small favors, I guess.

6 – *Gladys*

After logging off my computer, I grabbed my coat and closed the door behind me. My joints creaked as I walked across the courtyard toward the stairs. I know I've gained a few pounds over the last years because of all this sitting and staring at a screen, and it's not like I hadn't been eating more. Eventually, I suppose I'm going to have to have my hip exchanged. It'll cost a pretty penny, so I might ride out the tread on these tires as long as I can.

At the bottom of the stairs, I paused to catch my breath. Dave said something to the Latino man who nodded, and he came down the stairs to me.

'Can I help you up the stairs?'

'Thank you.' He grabbed me under my flabby arm and eased the weight from my hips.

His partner encouraged me from above like a lovely, condescending, stairway angel clapping lightly on the way to heaven. 'Come on, you can make it.'

Finally, like Edmond What's-his-name on top of Everest, I planted my foot on the top step and surveyed the roof of the world. Benson had fired up the grill and Dave wore a tattered apron with the large words *Classy, Sassy and a bit Smart Assy.*

'Gladys, this is Rontrelle and Dontay,' Dave pointed to the boys, 'and the one who helped you up the steps is Miguel, and that is his lovely wife, Carlita.'

'Hello,' I smiled at Carlita. 'How long have you known Dave?'

She laughed and replied in thickly accented English, 'Do you want that in minutes or seconds?'

'Ah. You were on the bus together.'

'How did you know?'

'Normal for Dave.'

Benson's grill wasn't quite as clean as the one downstairs, and whatever he charred on it the last time was now re-charring. Benson sourced a scourer and began to scrape off the burnt beef lacquer. Flakes of it floated to the floor and I mentioned to him that he'd have to clean that up later. He gave me a peeved look and rolled his eyes, but I knew he would do it. Dave had raised him well.

'Where are you guys from?' I asked Rontrelle and Dontay.

The one named Dontay (I think) sniffed. I could read him well: he had prejudged a fifty-seven-year-old white woman with weight and hip issues. I'm sure he was questioning my wardrobe fashion that day as I had chosen a particularly tragic outfit, pink, stretchy polyester pants and a white flowy shirt that Dave called his favorite *blouse* one time. I know, I know, it was something grandmothers wore, but it was comfortable, and *I* liked it. If there was any one thing I learned from Dave it was that your fashion sense should not be determined by the voice of another person.

'Over by the zoo.'

'I bet that's nice,' I responded, noticing his own slightly dated outfit of oversized jean-shorts with a stripe down the side, a Lakers jersey, and soccer shoes.

'Yeah, Me and Rontrelle like to go and spend fourteen dollars to look at animals.' His sarcasm was not lost on me.

I felt my face redden. 'I'm sorry.'

Rontrelle elbowed his partner and shook his head. 'No, ma'am, our fault. We're used to speaking with people who…'

'All right.' Dave raised his hands behind us. He had picked up a chef's hat from somewhere and was speaking into the grill. 'Who's ready for some meat?'

Of course I hadn't brought anything with me, so while the rest of the group chimed in with 'Me' or 'I am,' including little Meg who bounced up and down next to Benson while clapping her hands, I smiled and nodded.

'Gladys,' Dave said as he threw two large T-bone steaks, two thick pork chops, three pieces of chicken breast, and a hunk of tuna onto the sizzling grill, 'I got you a chicken breast, if that agrees with your peptic disposition.'

'Thank you, Dave. That would be nice.'

6 – Gladys

As the meat sizzled and scattered delightful aromas into the rafters of the balcony, I heard a car door slam out in the street. It was Letitia. She was wearing a black dress and looked entirely overdressed for a deck party.

Then it hit me.

Janice's funeral.

I had aimed to attend, as it was the proper thing to do for a resident of the complex, but I got busy, doing this and that and a bit of the other, and before you know it, the mourners were back and barbecuing.

Who am I kidding? I lost track of time watching soap operas. Television drama is so much more palatable than real life drama, and the people are better looking, too. Nothing like meaningful stares, desperate pauses, people dying and coming back to life, finding out your stepson is your first cousin – everything that is different to my own life. Sometimes I wish something drastic would happen, just so I could feel anything other than boredom. Then again, I'm not sure how useful I'd be in a crisis.

I didn't know Janice very well. She kept to herself and kept people away. Other than Dave, most people skirted her apartment not knowing exactly what to do with the perpetually drawn shades and the welcome mat that said, *NOT Welcome*. They went for walks sometimes, just her and him, not close – it was nothing like that – but Dave talked, and she listened. Or was it the other way around? I can't remember.

She was not attractive. Just a plain Jane, but when they were together, she smiled. When she walked up the stairs, she held Dave's forearm like a queen, and when he dropped her off on top by her room, he bowed. She would giggle into her hand while he retreated to his own apartment.

As I watched Letitia ascend the stairs, I was startled by the similarities of how Dave treated both Janice and Letitia. Where Janice was feeble, Letitia was strong, regal, really, and she held herself very well. I am jealous of Letitia – not just her youth, or size, but something less tangible, like poise or majesty, something like that. The two African

American boys behind me leaned towards each other, and I heard them *oooh, boy*, and slap their hands together. I guessed that Letitia was either complimented or offended, but I didn't know her well enough to know which way she leaned. Offended, most likely.

As she reached the top step, the boys continued to check her out. She rolled her eyes and approached Dave who was whistling over the smoky carnage.

'Hey, baby,' she said and briefly pulled him out of his chefery. From her lower altitude, she tugged him down to her and they kissed deeply. The boys' eyes were wide and disbelieving.

'There's something so wrong wit dat,' Rontrelle commented and covered his cringing mouth.

Letitia rounded on them. 'When you find someone like Dave, you hold on for the ride.'

I could see his face, his patient absentness, and Letitia was right, there was an inscrutable *indistinctness* about him. It's like trying to look at a star at night and only finding a blank space until you peer to the side of it.

'Yeah, he doesn't dress like most people and his sideburns are a little iffy, but he's solid. Solid gold, right, baby?'

'Hmmm…'

They were talking about him like he was not even there, not sniffing the air, not humming and whistling, not… present. Maybe he wasn't. Maybe he was in his own little world, even then, waiting to reenter ours at the right moment.

'Speaking of fascinating,' Dave licked each one of his fingers consecutively, 'I find it fascinating that you all are free on a Wednesday. What's that about?'

Rontrelle snickered. 'You know, me and Dontay, we was just goin' for a job interview, and, um, you sidetracked us.'

'How fortunate.'

Benson held out a tray for the meat which had finished cooking. 'And you, Miguel and Carlita?' He pointed at them with his barbecue spatula. It dripped sauce onto the floor. I frowned.

6 – Gladys

'We,' Carlita chuckled, 'were just at the... um... *Como se dice en Inglés – obstetra.*'

'Obstetrician,' exclaimed Dave. 'Congratulations! A day for a fiesta!'

'Yes, yes, we are very happy.' Carlita held her healthy middle.

'It's going to be a boy,' Miguel interjected with a beer raised to them all. 'And he's going to go to Lincoln – the University of Nebraska. He's going to be the smartest and nicest boy who ever lived. Why, I wouldn't be surprised if he won the Nobel Peace Prize.'

I love how pre-parents have such grandiose ideas for their children, as if somehow imagining the genes we have embedded within them are chock-full of superpowers. Even though I knew that Miguel and Carlita were not serious about the Nobel, I had the urge to tell them that my daughter was a lawyer. In North Carolina. I wanted to one-up them, to show them that even someone with my genetics could produce a highly respected member of society, even if...

'I don't get to go to school because I'm not old enough,' Meg shouted above the din.

'It has nothing to do with age, Megamix. You are just entirely too amazing for school yet. Give it another year and your shine will wear off.'

'What?'

'So, y'all met on the bus?' Letitia changed the subject. They all nodded.

'It's too bad Janice couldn't have been here,' Dave said. 'She would have loved meeting everyone.'

'Who is Janice and where is she?' Carlita asked.

Before anyone could respond, Meg piped up, 'She's dead and going to be incinerated.'

Conversation paused, mouths opened, frowns appearing. 'Okay,' Dontay said slowly.

'She died last week on Thursday,' Dave said as he flipped a piece of chicken onto a beautifully ornate plate. From Dave's apartment, Benson had retrieved the pearly, gilded china with river scenes from somewhere in Asia. 'It sucks to die in summer. You miss out on so much.'

'Uh, that's kind of morbid,' Rontrelle muttered under his breath.

'Why?' Dave responded innocently. Benson handed out a plate to each person and distributed the meat.

'Because we're about to eat.'

'Okay,' Dave responded with a poke of his barbecue tongs, 'we can talk about the sacrifice of all these animals for the sake of our nutrition instead.'

'Whatever, man.'

'Now,' Dave clapped his hands, 'let's dig in!'

Dave held Meg up to the dinner bell hanging from the beam. 'Do me the honor, would you?' With a large grin, Meg, in her little red dress and little red hair bow, rang it with glee.

Moments later, doors opened from all around the apartment complex. People brought out card tables and chairs, their own food, drinks, and set them outside their apartments. Greetings were lobbed across the courtyard like welcome-grenades. It seemed that they all had been waiting for the dinner bell, at least those who worked from home, and now were ready to tuck in to a good meal.

'Sit wherever you like,' Dave said. 'They'll all take you in. Good conversation, too.'

Meg picked up her plate of chicken and stepped deliberately down the stairs, tilting her plate dangerously which would have dumped meat and salads onto her dress, but she made it without mishap to an older gentleman's table setting. Doc was tucking a napkin inside the front of his shirt like a bib. He smiled and welcomed her, then scooped some of his green salad onto her plate.

'This is really different,' Rontrelle exclaimed.

'Messed up, if you ask me,' said Dontay.

Mr. and Mrs. Willis, a retired African American couple, waved to the boys. 'We've got some hot potatoes down here, boys, if you'd like some.'

'I'm gonna get me some of that,' Dontay mumbled as he shoved past some of the other diners.

6 – *Gladys*

It seemed like a miracle every time Dave did that. When people responded with generosity, you just got the feeling that the world was going to be all right.

7

Benson

Dave woke me up early. 4:00, to be exact.

For you, an early morning might be seven, or maybe six if pressed, but sometimes Dave decided that 4:00 was the perfect hour upon which to build the day.

If he would simply have called my phone, I could have ignored it, but somewhere during the day before, Dave had snuck into my apartment and set the alarm clock in my bedroom for that ungodly hour. What I really mean is: he snuck into my house and left *his* alarm clock under my bed.

It scared the crap out of me. There I was minding my own sleeping business – this was just a few weeks into August after Janice's funeral – when out of the darkness came this horrific clanging. After I'd located my bearings, I knew exactly what had happened. Dave had been mentioning something about going swimming. I told him, half-politely of course, that I would be declining the invitation on the grounds that I hate swimming, and wearing a swimsuit was too close to naked for this body. Add to that the fact that there would be dozens of screaming children there, some throwing things, some throwing themselves, a few teenagers trying to outdo each other in showing off, hot sun and sunburn (the smell of sunscreen makes me want to hurl, by the way), I couldn't think of one endearing thing about the local pool that would make me want to go there. Not even on the hottest day of summer.

But Dave, no, no, Dave was deaf to my protests. What he heard was, 'Blah blah blah swimming, showing off, blah blah blah make me...' So he did. That's the way it always was. I had no choice in the matter. Only Dave's will and timing.

I smashed his alarm clock with my fist and it felt really good to do that, as if I was telling Dave – *You're not the boss of me*. But as soon as that thought crossed my mind, four other alarm clocks, old fashioned ones with bells on top and a clapper between them – the kind you see in cartoons – had been scattered around my apartment and began ringing two minutes after I ruined the first one in the bedroom.

I roared with frustration, pulled myself from the bed, and hunted down the other alarm clocks. There was one behind the front curtain. One above the kitchen door. One behind the TV so far out of reach that I actually had to move the television. Because of my frustration, I was truly awake at that point. Unfortunately, there was one more still ringing. It was muffled. Somewhere in the kitchen.

It was in the refrigerator. Dave had stuck the alarm clock inside a defrosting chicken.

A shadow appeared at the front door, and I knew it was him. I just knew it.

When I opened it, he was leaning against the balcony, looking very normal in his jeans and t-shirt. 'Hello, Buttfinger.'

'Dave, it's four o'clock in the morning. I'm not happy about this. You have to know there are limitations to friendship.'

'Enumerate them, Benson.'

'Just come inside so we don't wake everyone else up.'

He did, but refused to sit down.

'Dave, come on, this is totally stupid. You can't do this to my house. You can't just... break in and leave alarm clocks everywhere. It's not right. And you can't always demand that I accompany you wherever you go.'

'Okay,' he responded simply and returned to the threshold. 'I thought you would enjoy a day outside away from your computer. Good night. Sleep well. I hope the bed bugs don't bite your grumpy gluteus.'

He didn't look dejected or even miserable. It was like I told him that water is wet. 'By the way, Dave, why did you wake me up at four o'clock if we're going swimming at the pool that doesn't open until ten?'

'I wanted to show you something.'

'At 4:00?'

'We have to take a drive.'

Dang it, my interest was piqued. 'Where is it? What is it?'

'Quid pro quo, Dr. Lecter.'

'Man, Dave, what does that even mean?'

'It means you have to give me something and then I'll give you something.'

'What do I have to give you?'

'Trust.'

I swallowed hard. Trusting normal people was relatively easy, but trusting Dave was like sticking your hand in a bear's mouth with a fist full of honey.

'So, I give you trust. What do you give me?'

Dave stared out over the balcony at the ground below. Everything was muted on the southeast side of Des Moines, Iowa. The only noises in the complex were crickets and cicadas. A far-off ambulance siren wailed mournfully in the distance, and the sound of buzzing lights above us was irritating. A few mosquitoes orbited Dave's head, but he didn't seem to notice.

'I give you meaning.'

'I have meaning in my life. I have my job and my apartment and friendships and weird adventures. I eat well. Other than the nights you wake me up, I sleep well. I...'

'Listen to you,' Dave interrupted. 'You don't have meaning – you have you. How can you find meaning only in yourself.'

'You weren't listening,' I said as I took up a position beside him on the balcony and lowered my voice. 'I have people in my life – friendships and the like.'

'Live life outside yourself.'

'Do you just make things up as you go, or do you have a bank of stupid things to respond?'

He ignored my jibe. 'Let other people have your song.'

'That's so convoluted, Dave.'

'You don't find meaning until people start singing with you. Geez, Benson, have you never noticed someone else so intensely that you wondered how in the world they came to be?'

7 – Benson

'No.'

'There you go,' he stated firmly as if everything was finally explained. 'Now trust me. Listen to Dave.'

I felt the same endless, emotional tug-of-war I always did. Every part of my physical being had no interest in swimming, hot sun, pool noise, and the like. Every part of my psychological being knew that I was being manipulated. My emotions were a mess – I was frustrated and upset, but I loved the guy, in a purely platonic way. He'd taught me how to enjoy life, and the shell I used to carry was left in the apartment.

I glanced to my left and saw him smiling over his domain waiting for the answer he already knew was coming.

'Okay.' My voice was full of resignation.

'Good,' his head bobbed, and his hair hid his face for a few seconds. 'Good. Get your swimming suit and meet me at my car in five minutes.'

'The pool doesn't open until ten, remember?'

'Who says we're going to the pool?'

Uh oh.

It was still dark when we drove out of the suburbs. We motored down Interstate 180 heading east. No one else was on the road because it was Sunday, and most Iowans were still in bed. We were almost to Iowa City before the morning sun made an appearance over the eastern cornfields. I had fallen asleep for a little bit because the hum of the tires droned the consciousness out of me. When I came to, I looked over to the driver's seat. Dave had tears falling from his eyes.

'Are you crying?'

'Yes.'

'What's wrong?'

'Why does anything have to be wrong? Why can't something be right? Or even neutral? Why can't the mere thought that the earth has been spinning for billions of years be glorious. Or that each day the sun appears on our eastern horizon, whether there are clouds or clear skies, the land wakes up, I am shaken from my apathy? Trees and living things appear out of nowhere, dude. Doesn't this just feel right and good?'

I'd never thought about it before. I just took it for granted that by the time the sun turned the clock to eight, I would wake up, pee, brush my teeth, and eat breakfast. I'd log onto the computer, check my phone for messages, and spend the day doing things that passed for work. I'd feed my stomach a few times, drink a pot of coffee, pee some more, shut my computer off, maybe stand outside and talk to the others, then go to sleep. Isn't that what life is all about?

'What does it feel like to you?'

Sometimes there were long and lonely roads between the strange things Dave did (and said) and the lucid depth of a highly intelligent and evolved, compassionate mind. What Dave did on most days was derivative of how he experienced life. He didn't just eat the meat of life. He sucked the marrow from it by crushing the bones in his teeth.

'It is a dream,' he responded with a stifled yawn. 'On the horizon of everything, there is an edge of eternity, something just beyond the veil and grasp of human understanding. When you look out over Iowa on a morning like this, the sky will be painfully blue, the green of the corn and soybeans will be startling in its intensity; the white-hot abandon of the sun and its need to bring life to all things – you can't help but wonder if this cosmic accident wasn't something more premeditated.'

'You're talking about God, aren't you?' I'm relatively agnostic about such things. Dave was too, in his own way, but he was also spiritual, if that makes sense.

'What do you mean by God? If you're talking about an altruistic version of a cosmic Santa Claus dropping blessing bombs on good people and delivering turd burgers to the sinners, well that would be a hearty 'no.' But if what you mean by God, that there seems to be a plan in everything, something that diverges human thinking away from its ego and pushes it to look outwards for the song in everything, then 'yes.' Can't you feel it?' he tapped on the steering wheel passionately, 'this, this, this subsonic trembling every day you wake up?'

7 – Benson

'No.'

'God, I feel sorry for you. I feel so alive at this time of day, and now that we're almost there, to the place I wanted to show you, my whole body is buzzing with electricity. So you can *feel* it like I can, Dude!'

'This isn't like the time we drove to Knoxville to go to the car races, is it?'

'No, Benson Bartholomew Dingleberry! Okay, well, kind of. You can get the same rhythm and pulse from people, but this time the melody is from nature itself. You need them both – people and creation.'

'Consider me skeptical.'

'I'm not going to talk now until we get there,' he stated with finality.

I wanted to ask him more questions, but it did no good to argue with Dave. It wasn't that you couldn't win an argument, you just never understood what the argument was about in the first place. He wanted me to feel something so I could experience anything to find meaning in it. How could you argue with that? I couldn't just say, 'Why can't we find a similar feeling/experience/meaning on Euclid Avenue over near the airport?' That kind of rational reasoning didn't work with Dave.

We passed Iowa City, West Branch, and a sign signaling for Tipton. We were almost to Davenport, and I hoped that we were stopping because I had to pee. And I needed some coffee. And I really was not looking forward to the rest of the drive for however long that might be. For goodness sake, it could have been Chicago…

'Stop thinking about you,' said Dave, breaking his vow of silence to interrupt my inner turmoil.

'What should I think about then?'

He didn't answer. He didn't need to because he had already told me many times: I should think about anybody else but me.

It's hard, you know. Gradually everybody becomes the center of their own universe, and every decision and thought orbits the perpetuation of their own, personal happiness planet. It's not limited to trips or food or even relationships, but how we stand in lines, how we wait, especially how we work through impatience. One time, Dave took me to Adventureland, the amusement park. I like roller coasters, and I like things that make my stomach rise into my throat. However, I do not like to wait. On that day, Dave engaged in twenty minutes of meaningless conversation with one of the park attendants who was using one of those portable dustpans, you know the ones that tip upwards when they lift them? The park attendant shared with great detail why she did what she did. She was under the impression that if she worked hard sweeping up the trash for the summer, she'd be on carnival row the next summer.

Like, who cares?

Anyway, I was tapping my foot, waiting, waiting, waiting (we didn't come to Adventureland to chat up the trash collector) while Dave watched me out of the corner of his eye. When he finished, he pointed to the biggest, baddest roller coaster at Adventureland: the Monster. It's green and huge. I Googled it and it said the top speed was 105 miles per hour. I walked quickly, like a speedwalker, you know, with my arms going sideways and my hips swaying. I was mongo excited. The lineup at the Monster read that it could take up to an hour, but for the Monster, I was willing to wait. So we inched along, inched along, leaned against the ropes, walked four steps, looked up at the lucky people who were already screaming their guts out above us as it whizzed by a billion miles an hour, got frustrated with the young couple ahead of us intent on staring at their phones the whole time and they'd left a four foot space between them and the next person and I just wanted them to move so I could move and be closer to the Monster. With about two more rides between us and glory, Dave turned to me and said, 'That's good. Very good. Let's go now.'

'What?'

'I learned something very important here, and that's enough.'

'But… but…' I stammered, 'It's *right there!*' I pointed to the freaking customers whose heads were being tossed from side to side. I could imagine their stomachs in their throats and their minds saying, *This is stupid but we love it!!!!*

7 – Benson

'I know where it is, Benson. We should let all these other people experience it now. That would be a kind thing to do.'

'I don't care about kind,' I pouted.

'That's why we have to leave, Benson,' he responded quietly.

'You leave. I'm going on it. Even if I have to ride by myself.'

Dave smiled sadly, sighed, and nodded. 'Okay.' He turned to duck out the Chicken Exit for the people who can't hack the thrill. There was nothing I would have liked less than to take that walk of shame. Dave was jeered by a few high school kids who were sucking on slushies and flicking through their phones.

Dang it, I muttered as I followed.

You might think I had no stones, or no gumption, or whatever, but Dave's relentless personality was irresistible. He didn't tell me what he learned from standing in line, only that his thoughts were more important than the Monster. And his thoughts should have been *my* important thoughts.

When he saw that I had followed him away from the rollercoaster, he didn't stop, and he didn't thank me. He just kept walking, and eventually, as we parked ourselves outside the flume ride (which, by the way, was very distracting for me. I love flumes), he said, 'When we learn how to be comfortable inside the time we've been given, waiting loses its pain.'

I glared at him resentfully.

We reached the south side of Davenport, and Dave took the exit to Credit Island. I looked at him questioningly, but he said nothing. Once we crossed the bridge, he drove around to a ponderous lagoon, still shadowed, with seagulls gently biding their time on the shore waiting to begin their workday. In the parking lot, he chose one of the back parking spots and cut the engine. As he opened his door, the car rolled backwards slightly. He groaned and stretched his arms high above his head, painting the sky like the time he moved into the Palms.

Dave grabbed his bag and his towel out of the back seat and strode toward the shore of the Mississippi. 'Don't you want to lock it?' I asked.

'If someone really needs a car, they can take it.'

'How will we get home then?'

'Providence.'

We stood along the northern shore of the Mississippi. Saying that is strange because the Mississippi runs north and south not east and west, or at least that's what my high school geography teacher told us when he pointed to a map on the wall (he was old school – it was made out of paper and everything) and banged it with a stick. 'Here is the longest river in North America,' he said.

'This is the longest river in North America,' I said.

'That's what your high school geography teacher said, I'm sure.' Dave was still striding away from me, so I hurried to catch up. It was difficult because I was wearing flip flops and a swimming suit which was about an inch too small for my waist, and two inches too short for the family jewels.

'But it's the truth, isn't it?' I asked.

He held up a finger as he walked. 'It's a fact, yes, but what is the truth *of* the Mississippi River?'

'That question refuses to make sense.'

'Listen,' he paused, and we listened. The Quad Cities were beginning to rouse from their weekend slumbers. Traffic, even on a Sunday, moved across the river from us like slow moving mud. Insects were awakening and fluttering and buzzing. Things smelled different, muddy and decaying. They reeked of heat and humidity, and I already felt the gooey air in my nostrils. My arms stuck to the sides of my chest.

'Ahead of us is, *in fact*, the largest river, but its *truth* is that it is the American aorta. They don't call this the heartland for nothing, Jackrabbit. Over the centuries, before white people, this body of water divided a continent and its beautiful inhabitants. People didn't cross this river, they survived it. The people who sighted its wide waters didn't look at it and think, 'Well isn't that nice? I wonder if we can waterski on it?'

He frowned and rubbed his chin as if pondering an entrance point in the lagoon. 'I learned how to spell the name of this river when I was four? You know the joke, 'What has four eyes and can't see?' The Ojibwe people named it the Misi-ziibi which meant 'Father of Waters.' The Dakota called it Wakpa Tanka – 'Great River,' obviously.' He drew out the 'obviously' to suggest that I take him seriously.

'This river has more eyes and ears and blood vessels than you can count.'

We continued walking towards the water. 'The Mississippi carries all the memories of all the rivers from the Rockies, via the Missouri River, to the Appalachians, the Ohio and its tributaries, and delivers them downwards, always downwards, through the rocky clefts, the mosquito infested estuaries, past the ugly cities, always downwards to New Orleans where they stack the stories like bricks and sing about them along the quays and in the streets, deep southern bass notes with high tremulous laughter from the storms of the plains and the winter whistles, melted snow into the swishing waves.' A faraway look settled in his eyes like he'd lived a thousand lives and was only remembering them then. 'The Mississippi is where the stories of the people and the stories of the land fuse to become truth.'

'Jeez, Dave, that's poetic.'

'That's the truth of the River, Benson.'

'How do you find the truth of stuff, Dave?'

As we paused on the northern side of the north and south river, the sun appeared above the trees on the far bank. I didn't want to think it, but it was a spiritual moment, an awakening, and even though I didn't want to tell Dave, I was glad we went – even for just that minute in time.

'Close your eyes,' he said. 'Your sight actually clogs truth.'

I closed my eyes and felt his hand on my arm. I opened them again to see what he was doing, but he shook his head. 'Trust me.' Once again, I shut them feeling the instinct to panic. Everything about my life was dominated by the visual. Screens, windshields, windows, and anything that caused my head to rotate. Once I didn't see, something amazing happened. I could listen. Without thinking about it, my sense of smell and touch barged to the front of the line. Each had waited patiently to get on the roller coaster. For so long I had ignored the sensual pleasure of smell which linked me to the past, and I had neglected my hearing, abused it, really, by how many hours per day I filled my ears with unnatural (and unnaturally) loud music.

Dave led me down an angled hill to the water's fingers. I stepped tentatively, hesitantly. There was some trustless hesitancy during the descent. What if there was a loose stone and I tripped? What if there was something sharp and I cut my foot? What if Dave pushed me into America's aorta? Suddenly, shockingly, I felt small pebbles near my toes, and I realized we were near the shore. The Mississippi was flowing past me, visceral and large, like when a tractor-trailer passes a bicycle pushing it aside by the force of its kinetic power. When I stepped into the first inches of the river, I recognized that the water was cold because my feet were hot. Dave urged me in up to my ankles and I was aware that no longer was I simply a universe of one but part of a complex system that wanted me but didn't *need* me. My presence or absence on the earth was irrelevant, and it was beautiful.

The pebbles changed into silty mud, and I wanted to open my eyes to see everything, but Dave encouraged me not to. He wanted me to trust him even more. I am not a strong swimmer, and even if I was, very few people could offer anything but a pitiful resistance against this ravenous waterway. If I were swept out, I'd have to float for a long time, perhaps to the nearest lock and dam, where they would fish me out, Benson Bartholomew Olson, late of Des Moines, Iowa, with the flowery-overly-tight swimming trunks, drowned like a rat.

The deeper we went, the more the cold water bit my skin. I never realized water had teeth before, and when it nipped at my knees, I felt the incisors. I tippytoed onto my now desensitized feet and held my elbows up as if suddenly a wave was going to take me out.

'Relax,' Dave calmed.

I couldn't relax because the experience had all but eroded my sense of self. No longer did I feel capable or partially strong. I was just a pebble being rolled along the cosmic river of life and there was nothing to stop me on the way to the delta. A leaf, or something like it, snagged my thigh and my imagination transformed it into a fish of some sort.

Without warning, the river's teeth took a piranha nip at both testicles, and no longer did I want anything to do with wading in the Mississippi off Credit Island.

I sucked in a deep breath. 'Enough, Dave. Enough. My balls. I need them.'

'Just two more minutes. Try to go a little deeper. Up to your belly button.' Dave released my arm, but I was not sure I could keep my eyes closed any longer. I inhaled deeply as the water crept over my groin until it made contact with my navel. With shocking, metaphorical reality, I understood that I was umbilically connected to all the stories flowing past me. I could feel them.

The Native Americans who lived off this land and waited patiently for the seasons to change.

The Spanish explorers seeking the Fountain of Youth, Cibola, anything that might change their lives.

The white explorers, the trappers, the brave and the stupid, who traipsed across the vastness of the Great Plains, unprepared for the deathtrap winters to plant them in the ground as fertilizer for the next crop of humanity trudging west.

The farmers and bakers and millers and quarrymen who toiled and struggled against, and with, this mighty river. All their songs seem to be plugged in to my stomach. Even just faintly, I heard the song of the past.

'Holy crap, Dave.'

'I knew you could do it,' he whispered. 'Now, open your eyes.'

When I did, I was slain by the slicing rays of the sun as it rose up and over the river trees. Undone, I gasped, not just by the river, but by that... unfortunately there was no other word... miracle. Dave's eyes glittered in the reflected light of the Mississippi as it sparkled and glinted on his face. I felt like shading my eyes, but I didn't want to spoil the effect.

Without warning, Dave dove headfirst into the river and came up ten feet from me spluttering and screaming. 'Hot damn! That's cold!' His voice echoed in the lagoon and across the river. Its resonance was all around us and I thought that I, too, could take the plunge.

Except I made the mistake of dipping slightly first, and it felt as if my nipples were stripped from my chest.

'Aaaaah, aaaah, aaah,' I gasped as I stumbled backwards. The cold water stabbed me in the back, thus making a human Weeble Wobble out of me until finally I tripped and fell sideways into the water, gracelessly and painfully. Thankfully, I was not in the current, but I sensed that Dave was swimming against it which meant he was swimming in place.

Now inoculated against the cold, I dunked my head again, and in the silence under the water and the darkness of the beneath, I felt fully alive and yet dying. I needed breath, but I wanted to stay.

I was resurrected from the water with an arcing spray over my back and hair. The water clung to me, to my face and cheeks, my eyebrows, the hollow at my throat. It was a baptism of truth and mercy. I felt reborn. The river's amniotic fluid sluiced from my skin, and I wiped my eyes with the palms of my hands. I wanted to shout and laugh and pluck Dave from his water-treading. When I could finally focus again, I saw him swimming towards me. He was smiling, but his attention was fixed over my shoulder. He was waving at someone else.

I turned to look, and by God, when my eyes caught on the focus of Dave's sight, I'll be danged if it wasn't the sexiest State Park Ranger I'd ever seen. Not that I'd been to many Ranger get-togethers before, but still...

Unfortunately, the sexy State Park Ranger did not look happy.

8
Wendy

Occasionally, when I return home at night after hours in the sun, I shed my uniform, put my gun and belt in the safe and think to myself, 'Now, I've officially seen it all.' Whether it's people doing stupid things on jet skis, fishing in restricted zones, hiking on islands with unexploded munitions, waterskiing during floods, I sometimes wonder if the world is not going to choke to death on its stupidity. It wouldn't surprise me, you know. We get dumber by the day. And more arrogant. And riskier. And I get front row tickets to see all of P.T. Barnum's Circus clowns' actions out here in the Quad Cities – each sideshow armed with mobile phones and less than the recommended allowance of brain cells. Believe you me, you want to see some morons? Spend a weekend in Burlington.

Five days per week my job as a Mississippi River Park Ranger is to drive a heavy-duty, forest green boat (with a 250 hp motor) up and down the River to make sure people are doing the right things (read, safe things) so that everyone can enjoy the great outdoors. Most of my stops are relatively enjoyable: a quick chat, a check of safety equipment and fishing licenses, spot checks of coolers, and on the rare occasion, a breathalyzer test. Very rarely is someone in trouble, but when it happens, because the Mississippi River is so unforgiving of stupidity, invariably an ambulance is called.

The Mississippi and I have had a six-year relationship. She looks different every single day. Sometimes she is grumpy. Other times she is singing. In the winter, she is lazy, frozen over in hibernation. Like good, long-lasting partnerships, I know beforehand what she will be like when I motor down to Credit Island in the mornings.

When I drove down to the Mississippi that day, I expected a beautiful, sparkling sunrise and an hour of contemplative peace before the loonies blistered the water with their noise. Instead of peace, a couple of yahoos from Des Moines were having an early morning dip. At first, I thought they were hippies. You know how they are, retro wannabes needing to 'express' themselves by connecting with nature (usually in the nude). Hypocritically they drive gas guzzlers to the parks and use mobile phones which are probably worse for the environment than the cars. I see some of the young ones, the dyed hair, dreadlocks, tattoos, nose-rings, all-talk-and-no-action-next-gen hippies who record themselves sitting cross-legged on yoga mats, humming and pretending they give a flying fig about sustainability, but really, it's only for the purposes of ingratiating themselves with their 'followers.'

God, I hate social media and beautiful people. I can't stand them.

No one has ever described me as thin and beautiful, and less than no one has mentioned to their friends, 'Wendy'll grace the cover of Vogue one day, mark my words.' Maybe it's because I wear a uniform. Maybe it's because I'm stronger than many of them. I don't know.

I think my face looks blocky, like a cement slab with eyes. My cheekbones seem to hover somewhere behind the curtain of my skin, and because I don't take the opportunity to smile much, my cheek muscles are a little flabby. I have mottled brown eyes and bleach-blonde hair from all the time in the sun. My mother calls it sandy blond, but I'm not sure that's a compliment or criticism. For a medium-sized woman of twenty-seven years, I have large hands, and my fingers are tipped with recreationally chewed fingernails.

My uniform hugs my figure, but I would not begin to call that flattering in any way, shape, or form. I have big hips, big thighs, big calves, and big feet. Birthing attributes, my farming mother would say. Charming. Just how I always wanted to be remembered.

But I'm happy, because I really do love what I do. And the unpredictability of every day gives me joy when I wake up in the morning, roll over to see my cat, Tiptoe.

Back to the unpredictability of that day, though. The two presumed Hippie-wannabes, one shorter and one taller, were frolicking in the water. The taller introduced himself as 'Dave,' and waved when he saw me.

'Hello. My name is Officer Johnson. What are you two doing here on this fine morning?'

8 – Wendy

The shorter, cuter one, a man in his mid-twenties, with a round face and receding hairline, seemed to be struggling in the sluggish water along the shore.

'We've come from Des Moines to connect with the Mississippi.'

Aaah, I called it. Hippies.

'And, how is it?'

'Enlightening,' the one with the weird sideburns acknowledged as he pulled himself from the current back towards the shore. The shorter one continued to stare at me, which I found slightly disconcerting.

'Did you know that swimming here is prohibited unless you have a life jacket on?'

'No,' Dave responded. 'Do you have some for us?'

'Those are user supplied, sir.'

'Too bad for us, I guess.'

'Yes, too bad for you.'

I looked at the shorter one who was holding his arms across his chest, the international sign for cold and/or breast-concealment. 'And what's your name?'

He pursed his blue lips together and looked to his friend for help.

'Go ahead, you can tell her, Benson Olson.'

'My name is B...B...Benson Olson.' His teeth chattered in the cool morning air.

'I never would have guessed.'

'Are... are... do you need to write us a ticket?'

'I think we'll let it go with a warning this time.'

'Th... th... thanks,' said the shivering Benson.

Dave pulled himself into the shallows and began to shake himself like a dog. When he was finished, he grinned at me. 'Have the lambs stopped screaming, Clarice?'

'What?'

The smaller one held up his hands in front of him. 'Please don't change your mind about the ticket. His favorite movie is the Silence of the Lambs, and he quotes it all... the... time... even when the quotes don't have any connection with the context.'

'Fascinating,' I responded. 'I enjoy movies, too, but probably not on the Lecter end of the movie store.'

'How about Benson and I buy you a nice cup of coffee this morning, Officer Johnson?'

'I don't know if that's such a good idea.'

'Sunday mornings are a great time to have a java, and most people won't arrive here for a while, right?'

I was tempted. No one had ever offered to buy me a cup of coffee before. I don't even mean while on the job. Not ever.

'Shall I plead with you on my knees? Maybe Benson should.' He motioned to his friend who had his head down and was shaking it.

'That would not be necessary, sir.'

'What do you think, Officer?' Dave asked again.

I hesitated, but after checking the river and seeing no one else, I made a snap decision. 'Okay. I accept. Back on the Iowa side there is a nice little cafe.'

'What's the name of it?'

'Human Beans. It's a little franchise shop from some small town in western Iowa. Amicable, I think. It's good coffee. Good people.'

'I'll bet it is. Come on, Benson, let's get out of here.' He strode from the water, his hair still dripping, his arms goosebumped and red from the Mississippi's teeth.

Benson waited in the shallows.

'What's wrong? I thought you were cold.'

Benson shook his head, embarrassed.

'Do you want me to leave before you get out of the water?' I asked.

Benson made a little sound like *heeah* and nodded.

'All right, I'll meet you at Human Beans in fifteen. If you're not there in twenty, I'll have to head upriver.'

As I strolled back to the car, I had this strange little glow in my stomach. And it wasn't even indigestion – or at least not yet.

8.5

Benson

'What the flippin' heck, Dave?'

Dave was standing on the shore, arms crossed, bouncing back and forth from foot to foot. 'I know you like her, Buttmoon.'

'What?'

'It's obvious.' Dave sniffed and wiped his nose with a finger then went back to putting his hands in his armpits.

'That is completely beside the point.'

'What is the point then?'

'The point, *Dave*, is that even if there was something there, you know, that she returned the liking-thing, there's no possible way we can meet her for coffee.'

'And why is that?'

'Because when I fell over the last time, I split the back of my shorts.'

Dave began to laugh. It's not rare for him to do so, and his laugh is so different from anyone else I know. It's kind of hiccuppy, with a brief staccato, and then back to hiccups.

'It's not funny.'

'Of course it *is*, Benson. It's hilarious. It's the perfect jumping off point for your wedding speech delivered by me, the best man.'

'DAVE! You're not listening to me. Read my lips,' I pointed to them and overexaggerated every word. 'My buttcrack is exposed and my testicles will not be far behind once they thaw out.'

'You're funny.'

'And you're not,' I pouted. Unfortunately, Dave had already planted a seed in my mind that I would be marrying the gorgeous, sexy park ranger named 'Officer Johnson'.

Dave turned away from me and made his way back to the car. He opened the back door and grabbed one of the towels. He dried himself starting with his lambchop hair, then taking particular care to make sure his underarms were dry. Dave then tossed the towel back into the car. 'I'm leaving in two minutes. You can either get out now and dry yourself, wrap a towel around your middle and ride with me to Human Beans, or you can wait until I'm gone and expose your buttcrack and thawing testicles to the early morning Davenport traffic as you walk across the bridge.'

'Dammit, Dave, this isn't funny!'

'But why *can't* it be funny? Why can't this moment be so utterly ridiculous that you'll talk about it for years? Why does everything have to be normal and forgettable.'

'Because this is me.'

For a moment, Dave paused and then, without warning, reached behind his own swimming suit and ripped the hem running from north to south. He turned around to me to reveal the horrific nightmare: his buttcrack and one family jewel.

'What are you doing?

'You said, 'This is me,' and then you got this pouty look on your face. So, I'll join you.'

'We can't go into the cafe like this! They'll throw us out! Arrest us, probably. And the park ranger will be mortified. Do you hear that, Dave? Mortified!' I threw my arms in the air because it was the only thing that I could do. 'And turn around! I don't want to look at your junk.'

'Hurry up, Benson, we only have minutes before Officer Johnson is going to desert us.'

I grumbled as I dragged myself out of the water. For some reason, I believed it was important to try to cover my backside with one hand as I walked to the car, even though there was no one else in the parking lot. I grabbed a towel and dried myself before wrapping it around my waist. In the driver's seat, Dave was softly singing a song by some nameless 80's band.

Don't let go while I'm hangin' on. 'Cause I've been hanging on so long. It's so hard to be all alone. I know you're not that strong. Our love's in Jeopardy, baby. Ooooooooooh.

I slammed the door behind me, and I mean I slammed it. The entire car shook. 'You and your big mouth.'

He smiled at me. 'I got you a date.'

'This is not a date, dipstick.'

'Listen to you gettin' all uppity.'

'Dave, this is my life we're talking about.'

'Which,' he lifted a finger as we began to drive towards the exit, 'I happen to be a large part of. But let's get back to the big picture of what we're experiencing here. Didn't you just mention what a profound moment you'd felt, a real connection with the stories of the River? Guess what? Now you added your story to the river.'

'That's not how it works, Dave.'

'Tell me, oh Master of Spirituality, how does one join one's story with those of the past?'

I harrumphed. The appeal of embarrassing myself was so small that I almost wanted Dave to keep driving back to Des Moines, back to normal life, back to me being me. If the park ranger had been less attractive, I would have begged him to.

As it was, we left the Credit Island parking area and merged back onto the interstate. Dave had me Google Map where Human Beans café was, and within five minutes, Dave had parked his Ford across the street from the coffee shop. In my side mirror, I saw the mascots for Human Beans – coffee beans with legs and arms. The park ranger sat on a tall black barstool checking her watch with irritation. Dave jumped out and waved his arms. 'Hello! We're here!'

I tightened the towel around my waist and walked with squishy flip-flop footsteps across the street. Finally, I got a really good look at her.

Stunning.

Without sounding perverted, a lovely body was enveloped by her green and khaki uniform. There was a little gold badge on her left breast and her name on the other.

She lifted a hand shyly, not to Dave, but to me. Suddenly, it felt quite like I was floating on the Mississippi. Out of control. Far from safety. Feet dangling from innertubes, fingers linked…

Dave snorted.

'What?' I asked.

'Of each particular thing ask: 'What is it in itself? What is its nature? What does she do, this woman you seek?"

'Oh, shut up.'

8.75
Wendy

When Benson crossed the street, I thought, *There's not an individual thing about him that screams – Meewow, but the entire package is... what? Hot? Is it his hair, his little eyes, his fleshy arms? Or is it something less tangible – the kindness in his expression, a hitch in his step as if walking in a towel is uncomfortable for him. By the way, why are they wearing towels into the café?*

'You can't wear those towels into the cafe, you know. Did you not bring other clothes?' They were halfway across the street.

Benson's face turned red. 'We didn't think we'd be caféing this morning, so, this is what we got.'

'Fair enough.'

'Now,' Dave said as he pulled a twenty-dollar bill from his wallet, 'Can you do us the favor of getting the order.'

'Yes, I can do that. What would you like?'

Dave was much, much taller than Benson, but Benson was not *too* short, thankfully. *Why did I add 'thankfully' at the end of that? Am I honestly considering...*

'I'll have a black coffee,' Benson responded quickly, and then added, *'Please.'*

'That's what I like, too.' *Good Lord, how long had it been since I flirted. So weird.*

Dave's eyes shifted back and forth between the two of us knowingly. 'Hmmmm... I'll have a chai latte with a lemon twist and sprinkle of cinnamon.'

That was my first closeup of Dave. Everything about him seemed kind of blurry and indistinct. Even as I watched him, it felt as if I'd seen him somewhere before, like in a painting or movie or something. His tallness did not seem intimidating but comforting, like standing next to a giraffe.

Benson stammered a whispered apology as if Dave was not standing next to him rubbing his chin between thumb and forefinger.

Dave acted as if he had completely forgotten we were there. His gaze was drawn to the awakening city around him. The Quad Cities do not have a huge skyline and wouldn't be considered a top exotic destination for world travelers, but there are some perks for Midwestern living. The people are good, river life is nice, and crime is low. Better than Des Moines, but a long toss from Chicago.

I entered Human Beans to get the orders. I turned around once to catch Benson staring at my butt. He looked embarrassed that I had caught him. I felt a warm glow in my stomach because he was ogling me. *Heavens, I feel like a twenty-seven-year-old teenager.*

After purchasing the coffee (and whatever it was that Dave asked for), I took them outside and we sat on wrought iron stools.

After placing their drinks in front of them, I situated myself across from Benson. 'So,' I started, 'you guys are from Des Moines? When did you get here?'

Benson waited for Dave to speak, but Dave refrained and smiled contentedly over his chai. 'Uh, this morning about 7:00.'

'What time did you leave? 4:00?'

'Yes,' said Benson.

'What else are you going to do while you're here?'

Benson's eyes shifted to Dave who was suddenly very interested in what was happening across the street. Squirrels, maybe. 'We're, uh, I don't know. We hadn't thought past the river thing. What would you suggest?'

'Well, if I was new in the Quad Cities and kind of...' I didn't know how to say 'strange' without it sounding as if I was insulting them.

'On vacation,' Dave inserted.

'Yes, on vacation,' I agreed, 'depending on how much time you had and what your resources were...'

'Honestly,' Benson leaned forward, and I heard a little ripping sound. He sat up quickly. 'we'll have to go home after this.' He glanced down at his towel. 'These are the only coverings we have.'

8.75 – *Wendy*

'That's too bad.' *What in the world are you doing, Wendy? Just move 'em down river.*

Benson swallowed hard. His Adam's apple bobbed. 'Yes, I suppose if we had more time.' He cleared his throat, and his eyes dropped to his hands. 'Say we were to return someday, what should we do? I mean, it's a hypothetical, of course.' The scarlet embarrassment had turned almost purple.

'Well, okay then, I would for sure check out the downtown area – some good shopping. If you're into American Pickers, their antique store is there. You can go on a riverboat cruise, that's always nice. Romantic, if you're into that kind of thing.' *Wendy! What the frickity frick!*

'I… uh… romance…' Benson's mouth was moving far slower than his mind was racing.

Clearing my throat, I moved on quickly. 'Since you boys are interested in islands, there is a tour of the Rock Island Arsenal.'

'That sounds fascinating.'

'And for you, Dave, William Cody's farmstead is outside of town. I'm sure you'd like that.'

'Why would he like that?' Benson asked.

'Because, Captain Ignorant, William Cody's alias was Buffalo Bill.'

Benson's mouth sagged and he appeared flummoxed.

'Do you always call him names like that?' I asked Dave.

'Yes. It's how he knows I like him. I have pet names for everyone I like.'

'How is Captain Ignorant a pet name?' For some reason, Dave calling Benson a name rubbed me the wrong way.

'My apologies to you, Wendy.' Dave did not seem offended or put out by what I said, but he also didn't apologize to Benson, only me.

'You didn't hurt my feelings,' I pointed at Benson.

With a wry smile, Dave turned his attention on Benson. 'For any offense you have been given, please take the skin from my back.' His reference to Buffalo Bill in Silence of the Lambs was not lost on me.

Benson sniffed and blew the air out through his lips. 'Thank you, Dave. You are forgiven.'

'I feel better already.'

Unsure whether his statement was sarcasm or genuine, I hedged on genuine.

'We were going to talk about your movie preferences, Officer Johnson.'

'So we were,' I said. 'I'm partial to romcoms.'

'That's what I like, too,' Benson interjected.

'Really?'

Benson nodded, but his eyes shifted to Dave. 'Maybe if...'

My heart started beating a little bit harder. Dave's eyes were moving back and forth between the two of us and suddenly, he stood up. Both Benson and I were startled and jumped. 'I feel the need to urinate,' he stated with great precision and force. He left the table and did not turn to look at us. Within seconds, he was holding up his hands like a crossing guard to stop what little traffic was coming up the street. I had no idea at all why he recrossed the street to go to the bathroom instead of using the café's facilities.

In embarrassed silence, I waited for Benson to continue.

'You were saying?' I can't remember the last time I had accepted an invitation for a date. *Was he really going to ask me out?*

'Uh... well, maybe if I can... uh... get back to Davenport, or if you're in Des Moines, we could uh...'

'Yes?'

'Ah, man, when I come back, I'd love for you to take me on the cruise.' He cringed. 'Am I being too forward? I mean, you don't know anything about me. Like, what I do for a living, what things are most important to me, etc...'

'How about you give me your number,' I was the one now being forward, but it seemed like the only way to make him feel more comfortable, 'and I'll call you so we can get to know each other.'

8.75 – Wendy

A jet of air escaped his mouth. 'Oh, that would be great. Really great. Do you have a pen?'

I tapped my chest pocket for a pen. His eyes were drawn to the pocket, and he blushed again. 'No, but how about you just tell me what your number is, and I'll punch it into my phone.'

'Great, great.'

Taking out my phone, I turned it on and glanced up. 'What's your last name, Benson?'

'Olson.'

Benson Olson, I mouthed and entered it in my known contacts. 'That's right. You told me at the River. Number?'

He gave it to me and our eyes met. There's something exciting and somewhat erotic about trading phone numbers now, like you've given them the password to your underwear drawer.

'Okay, I've got to get back to the River, but I'll call you.'

'Yeah, yeah, yeah,' he responded quickly and stood up. Unsure of what to do next, he awkwardly stuck out his hand which I shook – firmly, but not too firmly. I'm still a woman, you know.

Benson, beaming, turned away from the table and started to walk away from me. Unfortunately, his towel must have been touching the ground because he stepped on it ripping it away from his waist.

'Oh my God!' He shouted at the top of his voice and reached down to grab the towel, which in hindsight, (ahem) was probably the worst thing he could have done.

'Whoa, Benson,' I murmured quietly to myself as his lunar landscape with orbiting twin satellites was enough cosmic view for a lifetime.

'So sorry!' He shouted behind him as he ran to the car holding the towel to his backside. 'Dave, you buttmunch!' he yelled, 'I told you this would happen.'

Dave met him at the car, and they opened the doors simultaneously. Dave took off his towel also and I saw that Dave and Benson had matching shorts.

What you See May Not Be

I began laughing very hard.
Just when I thought I'd seen it all.

9

The Honorable Ignatius Stackworth

I do not speak of Dave much anymore, though he is often on my mind. It's his youthful face, freckled and inquisitive, open, like a window to his soul. He never really changed, except for the last years. He was always like that curious teenager who sat erectly in the front row of my courtroom nineteen years ago.

His was the third case on the docket that day. Dave's lawyers were attempting to shed him of his guardians, the Mannings, Dave's aunt and uncle. They sat on the left side of the courtroom. His uncle was a strong-jawed, under-unemployed construction worker in his mid-30's, and his aunt was a wiry-thin woman wearing a floral dress with white pumps, whose chin displayed a prominent chocolate chip-like mole. Two long hairs sprouted from it like miniature bamboo. Jane was every bit the nearing-middle-aged trailer dweller (even though they didn't live in a trailer) I'd come to detest in my courtroom. Their kind were continually bringing outrageous litigation to my courtroom which, for all intents and purposes, could have been settled outside of court.

Gold digging. I hated that.

Their lawyer, a calm and secure young graduate from the University of Iowa, had prepped their case well, but I felt sorry for her. The Mannings were not enjoyable people, and as much as I tried to be impartial, it was difficult with people like them. Over the course of the morning, they interrupted multiple times only to be cautioned by their lawyer before I needed to do it.

Dave had hired his lawyers for the purposes of *divorcing the Mannings* as he put it. While they were blood relatives, he had a feeling his aunt and uncle were only trying to get their hands on his inheritance to spend it on their four 'natural born' children.

Dave sat beside his three lawyers from Walker, Kelso and Monroe, hands folded on the table in front of him. As a thirteen-year-old, he wore an Oscar the Grouch t-shirt and corduroy pants. Scuffed Puma shoes stuck out under the table. The bemused expression on his face never quit, even when his aunt and uncle pled their distress that Dave was a burden on their financial resources. If only they could have access to Dave's trust, then they could help him achieve all his life's ambitions. *Riiiight.*

As the morning wore on, the case was going nowhere, Dave finally reached out to Richard Kelso and said, 'I'd like to speak for myself.'

Dave stood up, straightened Oscar the Grouch's face and said, 'Your holiness, I think it's best if we just figure out how to let me live my life outside the constraints of people who are only interested in money.'

Who is this kid?

The uncle, Ted, pounded the bench in front of him and yelled, 'Objection!' I patiently overruled the objection and asked Dave to continue, but the aunt, Jane, decided to try the same ploy only with more volume. 'Objection, Your Honor!'

I pulled down the glasses on my nose. Their lawyer placed a hand on Jane's arm and tried to get her to sit down, but she refused.

'What exactly are you objecting to?'

'We... we are not after his money! We love Dave. He's been with us for five years, since his parents died.'

Dave had crossed his arms, but strangely, he was smiling. And rolling his eyes, too.

'What's his favorite color?' I asked.

Jane looked towards Ted who shrugged. She answered, 'Blue.'

Dave shook his head. 'Magenta.'

'Oh, come on,' Ted responded testily, 'that's the same thing.'

'Your holiness,' Dave said, 'this man needs to go back to kindergarten to learn his colors.'

'What is Dave's favorite hobby?'

The woman leaned forward and mumbled, 'Being a smartass.'

'I'm sorry,' I said. 'I didn't quite catch that.'

'He likes to play with his Matchbox cars.'

'Guilty as charged on that one. I've got a whole track set up through the house.'

9 – The Honorable Ignatius Stackworth

'What does Dave want to be someday?'

Stumped, they looked at each other and shrugged. 'He's only thirteen,' the man stated forcefully. 'How could he possibly know what he wants to be when he grows up?'

'At thirteen years old, I wanted to be a baseball player, and then an astronaut, and then a fireman – this was all in one week. But you still have dreams. What do you think Dave's dreams are?'

'We have worked tirelessly to provide for Dave,' Ted responded as he ignored my point, 'but we need help – financial help, even just a little bit would allow us to assist him in fulfilling those dreams and…'

'I want to be a kind and generous person,' Dave exclaimed loudly. 'I want to be a good friend. Those are my dreams.'

It's been said that it takes time for wisdom to accumulate, as if somehow age would attract it like dirt on duct tape. Some people, like the Mannings were made of Teflon, while Dave had already collected enough wisdom for the entire family. He was a smart, odd child, a mere teenager, but kids like him were rare. Diamonds in a bowl full of ice. His answer made me want to take care of him myself.

'And how much… financial help… would you need to help Dave along the way?'

The man lifted his hands and then looked to his lawyer before sitting. The lawyer shook her head imperceptibly and then sighed before speaking on behalf of the Mannings. 'My clients are asking for full access to funds given that they are the full-time carers of the child.'

'So, you want my parents' money,' Dave said.

It's important for you to know that by the time of the trial, Dave had already been separated from the Mannings for roughly six months. Having been placed in foster care with Edward and Mai Soto, he had flourished, or so his lawyers had told the court. Dave was satisfied with his life and where it was going. But when the Mannings had responded with a suit against Dave's estate, Dave had *regressed* somewhat. In no way did Dave want to live with his aunt and uncle again.

Dave's lawyers contested that the Mannings had been neglectful of Dave's needs. His physical requirements were met minimally (and involuntarily, mind you), but his social and emotional needs were not being provided for. According to WKM, Dave was not allowed out of the house to visit anyone. The Mannings responded that 'In order to protect Dave from the bullying he was experiencing, we picked him up right after school.'

WKM had interviewed the school, and they said Dave did not seem to be experiencing any specific bullying. In fact, according to the principal, Dave always seemed even-tempered and somewhat 'Pippi Longstocking-ish' in his outlook on life. Nothing phased him, whether significant achievements (he was a decent student) or perceived taunting by other students. His response in almost all situations was to smile and move on.

When I read the part about Pippi Longstocking, I thought to myself, *What a wonderful way to live.*

'Are the foster parents here?' I asked to the courtroom.

Four rows behind Dave, two hands raised slowly – a middle-aged Asian couple in dress clothes. They appeared out of place, afloat in the confusion of the proceedings. The father held his hat in his hand and stood.

'You are the Sotos?'

'Yes, Your Honor,' Mr. Soto responded. His hands shook slightly.

'Can you characterize Dave for me? What has it been like since he's lived with you the last…' I sifted through my papers, '…six months.'

Mr. Soto nodded in the Mannings' direction. 'We agree with those people over there to a point. He does have a little bit of impishness about him, that's for sure, but he is a nice young man. No problems with us. He keeps his room tidy, his schoolwork is done, and he helps around the house. He watches a lot of movies, but what kid doesn't?'

'Are you finding yourselves financially strapped while Dave lives with you? Does he require extra support, special needs, or anything else.'

'Objection, Your Honor!' shouted Mr. Manning.

9 – The Honorable Ignatius Stackworth

'I wish you'd stop doing that,' I said, 'I'm trying to understand what is best for the boy.'

'*Dave*,' said Dave.

I lost my train of thought momentarily before moving back to the Soto's. 'Please, if you would, answer the question.'

'Well,' said Edward slowly, 'like most teenagers, he does eat a lot, but he's no trouble, really. We are given a stipend to look after him, so we haven't really experienced any financial difficulties.'

'Our situations are different,' Mrs. Parker finally spoke. 'We have four other children who need to be cared for. And, and, and I have to work as a full-time mother which doesn't pay at all.'

The foster mother cleared her throat and spoke quietly. She seemed peaceful, as if the proceedings were a luncheon that she was patiently enduring. Her black hair framed her face in such a way as to make her seem strikingly close to angelic as humanly possible. When she spoke, her mouth barely moved. 'So do I.'

'How much money does the stipend pay you per month to take care of Dave?' I asked her.

'It's about five hundred dollars per month.'

Mr. Manning grumbled out loud. 'Dave's parents left him seven million dollars. Surely, we, as relatives who love him and care for him… well, he can afford to help us out a little bit for all the stress we're under.'

I sighed. 'Mr. Manning, how much of Dave's inheritance would help your family give *Dave*,' and I stressed his name, 'the best care available.'

He looked at his wife. 'Six thousand.'

'That's certainly reasonable,' I was surprised.

'Per month, Your Honor.'

'Six thousand per month. Seventy-two thousand per year?' I was incredulous. 'You do realize that is higher than the average annual wage of an Iowan adult?'

He held up his hands and nodded. 'Living expenses are high and as you said, we want to give the best possible care to young Dave.'

I turned to Dave. 'What do you think about this?'

Dave, who had taken a seat, leaned forward onto the table in front of him. His hair fell over his eyes. He propped up his chin with the palm of his hand and thought for a moment. Oscar the Grouch's large white eyes were barely visible over the desk. 'I guess if that's what makes them happy, Your Honor. It's just money.'

Mr. and Mrs. Manning's eyes widened with disbelief and excitement.

'But,' Dave held up a forefinger, 'if it's all right with the court, I'd rather stay with the Soto's. They're really great people.'

Mai Soto clasped her hands in front of her chest, head tilted to the side, and smiled at Dave. Edward nodded, pleased with Dave's response.

'It's obvious that you are a special young man. How very noble of you to be willing to hand over your money to make others happy.' I turned towards the Mannings. 'Mr. and Mrs. Manning, thank you for your care for Dave over the last years. I recommend a lump sum of $30,000 be given to you from Dave's estate, but that Dave would remain under the custodianship of Mr. and Mrs. Soto.' I banged the gavel.

The Mannings were overwhelmed with happiness. They didn't really want to take care of Dave, so he was off their hands, and they got a piece of the pie – $6000 per year for the last five years of taking care of him.

Dave reached over to solemnly shake his lawyers' hands before they began to tidy up the table in front of them and place attaché folders in their briefcases. On the other side of the room, Jane and Ted were hugging each other intensely and thanking their young lawyer who appeared pleased to be done with them.

'Dave,' I called out, 'can I talk to you for a moment?'

His eyes, intense and yet amazingly gentle, blinked a few times. He nodded and approached. I took my time stepping out from behind the bench. I laid my robe over the railing, and we met in front. We were roughly the same height. There was no fear in his eyes, only curiosity.

9 – The Honorable Ignatius Stackworth

'If you don't mind, I'm going to keep track of you. If you ever need anything, you give me a call, okay?'

'Yes, your holiness,' Dave responded.

I wrote out my number for him on the desk pad and handed it to him. He looked at it, nodded once, then carefully folded it and tucked it in his pocket.

'Goodbye, Dave, and good luck.'

'See ya.'

The Mannings left with their arms thrown around each other's waists. They didn't even say goodbye to their 'beloved' nephew. The Soto's, on the other hand, waited for Dave at the gate. Mr. Soto put a hand on Dave's arm while Mrs. Soto hugged him. Her head barely reached his chest. They spoke quietly for a minute and then left the courtroom.

When Dave turned eighteen, he graduated from high school finishing near the middle of his class academically. I went to the ceremony, and after five years of watching him from afar (sometimes nearby), I felt somewhat like a proud father. Stella and I never had any kids of our own, so Dave's accomplishments were a decent substitute for us. I was glad that Stella could see him graduate, too. She used to say how much she enjoyed the chats with him. Stella's death was, and still is, a horrible nightmare that even Dave can't wake me from. When she died, he took it very hard. The time between his visits grew and I wondered if he felt guilty about not coming over. At least I still know where he lives.

On his graduation day, as he accepted his diploma, I noticed that Dave was wearing bright white dress shoes with gold buckles on them. He was taller than the principal – much taller – and when he bowed to her to receive his diploma, his mortarboard cap fell from his head and onto the principal's before landing on the floor. She jumped and laughed, unsure of what to do next. Dave smiled, picked up his hat, and touched her arm before peeling off the stage to study the document in front of him.

Dave never went to college. In fact, he simply faded into (or should I say floated on top of) the system. Every few months or so, Dave would push open the doors to my courtroom (not large at all by Hollywood standards) and sit out of the way, but where I could still see him. After the docket cleared, we would usually go out for lunch, and he would tell me of his adventures in being a kind and helpful friend. Some of his friends were strange and straight off the bus. Others were normal people but a little bit down on their luck. Dave had no interest in hanging out with the populars nor with the snobs. Perhaps this had to do with the Mannings. Who knows? We enjoyed our time together.

In early September last year, he asked if he could see me after the day was finished. It had been three or four months since I'd last seen him. I'd grown worried that maybe something had happened to him – one of his newfound 'friends' might not have been as kind as he. He had been pondering Alcoholics Anonymous which I thought was silly because Dave didn't drink, or if he did, it was not very much.

I agreed to see him. He showed up on a 'date' (his words) with a tiny black woman who shaved her head, accompanied by a little girl, cute as a button, who was attached to Dave like moss on a rock.

'Hello,' I greeted the little girl, 'My name is Ignatius Stackworth.'

The little girl turned her face away from me, but the woman extended her hand. It was so small, like shaking the hand of that child.

'I'm Letitia.'

'You're a friend of Dave's?'

'Isn't everyone?'

'This is Meg,' Dave said as he brushed the hair out of the girl's face. 'Meg, this is Iggy Popsicle.'

Meg giggled and turned around.

'Why are you wearing a dress?' she asked.

'It does look like it, doesn't it? It's my uniform.'

'It's funny.'

I straightened up from Meg and began to take off my robe. 'What can I do for you all? Would you like a cup of coffee? Some lunch maybe?'

'We'd like to get married.'

That was not what I was expecting. I knew Dave had friends, and he had told me once of a passing infatuation with a lounge singer, but marriage? Not so much.

'How wonderful,' I said hesitantly.

'Life is short, your holiness. We thought we'd give matrimony a shot.'

'That's not exactly a ringing endorsement, Dave.' I glanced at Letitia whose jaw jutted out indignantly.

'That's a good pun,' Dave said.

'What?'

'A *ringing* endorsement.'

'Aah.'

'We are in love, Ignatius,' Letitia said.

'How long have you been seeing each other,' I asked.

'It's been quite a while,' Dave responded. 'About a year.'

'A year?'

'It sounds quick,' Letitia added hastily, 'but when you meet Mr. Right, you don't turn left.'

I studied the young woman. Her diminutive size appeared not to matter to Dave, nor did the fact that she had a child, which I assumed was *not* Dave's. In fact, those two things worked for him. He liked opposites.

She came off as confident, intelligent, and honest, but knowing Dave's net worth and how… naïvely he could respond to things, I wasn't quite sure of her true intentions. In my line of work, I see a whole lot of relationships with nice, intelligent people who enter into quick romances, assumptions of love, a need to pool resources, marriages. Then, frustration and a splitting of resources. Worst of all – children.

'Well…'

'Dave was insistent that we tell you. In fact, we would love it if you would officiate the wedding.'

'That sounds… interesting, but tell me the logistics.'

'We've got you and we'd like to get married at the zoo.'

'At the zoo?'

'Yes.'

'It's not just about the place, time, and officiant, have you done any pre-marriage counseling? Any financial planning? Where are you going to live? How will you... uh... afford it.' My words sounded callous, but I felt it was my job to help Dave make good choices.

Letitia's jaw twitched. 'Dave and I have life experience. I am an associate professor at Drake and... as far as I know, Dave is independently wealthy. We'll buy a small house together in the suburbs – hopefully somewhere not too far out of town because Dave likes to ride the bus.'

'Wait,' I said. 'You don't know anything about Dave's finances?'

She studied Dave with adoring eyes. 'What difference does that make? He treats Meg and me like royalty?'

'What are your thoughts?' I asked Dave.

'If it will make Letitia happy, I'm all for it.'

Suddenly, almost viciously, the small woman turned on him, frowned, and tilted her head to the side. 'What did you say? Tell me now, because I thought I heard you say that you're all for it if it makes *me* happy, but what about you? Don't tell me you're doing this just because of your... Daveness.'

He shrugged.

'That is *not* the correct answer,' she snapped as she held a finger up towards his face.

Dave was about to grab hold of her finger and pretend to bite it, but she stopped him, 'Don't even think about trying to make me laugh. Right now, you are an inch away from becoming *the* ex-Dave.'

Her words were slow to register with him. 'I'm sorry,' but it came out as a question, as if he was asking whether an apology was the right response.

'Oh, I see. You're getting cold feet already.' She took Meg from him. 'When you have a timeline for when your feet are going to stay warm, you get back to me, okay?'

Meg complained about being taken away from Dave. Twin tears formed in Letitia's eyes as if she'd been hurt. Strangely, Dave didn't seem to understand what the issue was. He touched her on the shoulder and said, 'I'll call you later.'

'A lot later.' She wheeled from him and hurried through the back doors of the courtroom. Meg was still reaching for Dave as the doors closed behind her.

'Hmmm…' Dave said to me. 'I suppose that could have gone a little bit better, don't you think?'

'Dave, do you really understand what marriage is?'

'What a silly question, Popsy. Of course I do. It's about living with someone and giving everything you have to keep them happy.'

I shook my head. 'That's a small part of it, but you know what? No matter what happens, *you* can never make anyone else happy. They have to do that for themselves.'

'But I want to.'

'Think about it. Letitia just told you that for her to be happy, what has to happen?'

'I have to marry her?'

'No,' I replied sternly, 'she needs *you* to be happy. It's no good for just one person in love to be happy. Do you think she could ever be happy without you?'

'I hope so.'

I sighed. 'Until you reconcile this, Dave, she's not going to marry you.'

Dave didn't frown very often, but at that moment, one furrowed its way across his forehead, gouging out understanding. My guess was that it had been a long time, very long indeed, since he had thought about his own wants and needs. To be selfless was a truly noble thing in the short term, but it could be frustrating for people who also wanted to help.

'Think of it this way,' I said. 'Let's say you made cookies for Letitia, and she was really thankful for them. How would you feel?'

'Wonderful!'

'Now, suppose she made cookies for you, and you decided that you didn't want them because you were the only one who was supposed to make cookies, how would she feel?'

'I would never turn down her cookies.'

Exasperatedly, I put both my hands on his shoulders. 'If you don't allow her to make you happy, you'll just end up making her angry. Got it?'

Dave raised a forefinger. 'Maybe I'll go ask her for some cookies.'

I groaned. 'Just go talk to her. That will be a good start.'

'Okay.' Dave patted both of my cheeks, something he'd done since he was young. I didn't normally let him do it publicly. The bailiff snickered as it happened. I allowed it, just this once.

He turned quickly and rushed after Letitia. His hair fluttered as the doors shut behind him, and I wondered if he'd figure it out. I hoped so. He deserved it.

10
Letitia

It took me a long time to finish being angry with him after that moment in the courtroom. Most times, he would do something silly or distracting and I couldn't hold on to my anger, but when he didn't understand what marriage was (or even love, for Pete's sake), I felt it burning inside of me. I didn't need another AnTwerp.

There were times when his... oh, how do I put this... his emotionless nature was so overwhelming that it set me off to no end. I'm sure you, of course, would love to be in a relationship with someone who is never angry, never petulant, never overexcited, but alwaysalwaysalways even-keeled and good humored. Yes, it sounds nice until they inadvertently piss you off with their niceness. What do you do with that? Yelling at them makes no difference because it only makes *you* feel guilty, and swallowing it only increases the degree of being pissed off. It's no fun to be angry with someone if they don't allow you to release it – do you know what I mean?

After we left the courtroom, I was really fuming. Meg had seen me furious with her father, or at least heard me raise my voice on the phone, but she had never really had a relationship with him. During those conversations, Meg could hear the little buzzing bee voice on the other end, a tirade about how selfish I was always needing money – *I was a college professor and I made three times as much money as he did*. As his voice droned, Meg must have noticed my clenched eyebrows, and she mirrored my facial expression. She always does that. My little Megling is a true reflection of me.

Oh, listen to me, I'm starting to sound like Dave, dammit! I've never called her Megling in her life and now I've gone and done it.

That's what he did. Dave found a way to change you imperceptibly, one phrase, one gesture, one clothing choice at a time. It's like the temperature of a pond lowering in winter and it's only after a while that you notice the surface is covered by ice. See, Dave had these quirks, small things, really, words and ideas, and expressions and idioms. I don't think he did it purposefully, but what I do know is that over the time we were together, I noticed myself changing. Not for the worse, mind you. I was more patient with Meg and others. I was less critical of my appearance. I didn't feel quite as impassioned about my race or gender. I felt like I was part of a community rather than a voice screaming from outside of it.

But that doesn't mean I had to become him. I didn't have to be a diminutive African American Dave dressing like it was the 1970's and calling people nicknames. I didn't have to be his sidekick, and I certainly didn't have to put up with his inability to disinter emotions.

Because he didn't curse or scream or go off into a rage about a dent in his car or lost video game, (you can probably guess what was most important to Meg's father) or… or… or… he didn't berate me for things I *didn't know*, I couldn't stay angry with him. Unfortunately, I needed him to *feel what I felt*.

During the two weeks after the courtroom experience, Dave called me twice. I almost didn't answer either time, but I'd come to know the pay phone number quite well.

'Hello.'

'Letitia, my joyful pincushion. How are you?'

'Why are you calling from the payphone, Dave?' I could imagine him standing in the corner of it curled up, hand over free ear, staring out over the early morning, misty street.

'If something is really worthwhile, one should not worry about the cost.'

'Dave,' I responded, 'you pay a monthly fee for your cell phone.'

'Hmmm… Yes, well, I suppose that's true.'

'And?'

'And?'

'Why are you calling?' I checked the clock on the wall of my apartment. 'It's 6:30 in the morning. A Thursday, in case you forgot.'

'No, no, no, I didn't forget. I just wanted to…'

Could it be true? Could the man be calling to apologize?

'I wanted to thank you.'

'For what?'

'For being perfectly lovely in all that you do.'

I ground my teeth. 'Don't sweet-talk me, mister.'

'I wanted to give you a quote that I thought was appropriate.'

'Are you serious? A quote? Like from that movie...?'

He cleared his throat. 'Yes. But from the book. Here it is. *She had come to learn that inattention can be a stratagem to avoid pain and could be sometimes misread as shallowness or indifference.* Do you see?'

I shook my head. 'I understand what the quote means, Dave, but what does it mean to you?'

'I believe,' his voice sounded crooked as if he was too far bent into the corner of the phonebooth, 'that you might misunderstand my idiosyncrasies (*your* words) as shallowness, indifference, or a strategy to avoid any sort of negativity in life, but they are not.'

'Then what are they for, Dave?'

'I... well... I don't really know. To me, they aren't idiosyncrasies, even though that's what people like you and Benson and Ignatius say. Frankly, it seems like everyone else is idiosyncratic – not me. But that's neither here nor there.'

The mere fact that Dave was speaking like this reinforced his idiosyncrasy, in my honest opinion.

'What I mean to say, Letitia,' I was pleased that he refrained from adding, subtracting or transposing my name, 'is that I have... deep feelings for you and that I'm... very... um, apologetic? Is that the right word? For any misgivings or misunderstandings I might have inadvertently deposited onto you the other day.'

'Dave.'

'Yes?'

'Repeat after me.'

'Okay.'

'Letitia...'

'Letitia...'

'I'm sorry for hurting your feelings.'

'I'm sorry for hurting your feelings.'

'And I will try to express my emotions...'

'And I will try to express my emotions...'

'In the future.'

'In the future.' There was a pause. 'Can I ask you a question now?'

'Just a second. Dave, do you understand exactly what we've just modeled right now?'

More silence. 'Yes?'

'And that is?'

I could hear his deep breath whistling through his nose. God love him, he was trying so hard to get it right without angering me. 'You are teaching me how to ask for forgiveness?'

'Yes, Dave, and I'm also asking for you to learn how emotions are *good* things.'

'Yes, Letitia.'

I could tell he hadn't learned a thing from our role play, but baby steps were still steps.

'Now can I ask you the question?'

My turn to sigh. 'Yes.'

'Can you take me to your church this weekend?'

I told my friend Raquel about that conversation. A day later, we met in a café on the west side of Des Moines. It was morning and the café was half-filled with young urban professionals needing a jolt before heading into their offices to pretend to work for the day. I didn't have classes until the afternoon, and Raquel, who also worked at Drake as a secretary, had the day off.

Raquel and I are about the same age, although she is married (on most days, happily) and has a son roughly Meg's age. On that morning, Meg and Dylan were coloring across from us as they chatted merrily about toys and parks and birds.

10 – Letitia

'Look, Letitia,' she responded softly with an eye on the kids who might have been listening, 'you really need to be careful with Dave. I'm no love expert, but it sounds like he's got a few loose screws.'

I put my head in my hands over the coffee. 'I know. I know. I keep cautioning myself, too.'

'After your first failed attempt, you should be very wary.'

'Yes, Raquel, I get it.'

'Do you think Dave really wants to get married?'

I pondered the question carefully before responding. I could only come up with one answer: Dave didn't really know what marriage was. I think in his mind, he just assumed it was more time he could spend with Meg and me. We'd go on day trips together, and we would continue to meet strange and thoroughly interesting people. The thought that we'd be living together, sharing finances, arguing, conciliating, using the same bathroom, having sex! None of these things had probably crossed his mind.

'He… I don't know. I assume he likes the idea of it, but the practicalities might be a little beyond him.'

Raquel nodded. 'He sounds very immature.'

'I suppose. Immature isn't the right adjective, though. Naïve?'

'What does his family think?'

I felt a strange pressure around my temples. Over the last months of getting to know Dave, there had been an itch I couldn't quite scratch. Something he hadn't told me and a question I'd been ignoring. When Raquel posed it, the fog suddenly lifted.

'You know, he's never really talked about family before. You know how families can be. Until they're in your business, it's none of your business.'

'It sounds like a recipe for a psychopath.'

'You don't know Dave. There is no way someone like him could be a cold-blooded killer. I've seen him save mosquitoes from a spiderweb.'

She raised her eyebrows. 'Maybe not psychopathic, but that's definitely psycho. Why do you think he's like that? You know, weird-ish?'

'I have no idea. The only thing I know is that he loves new experiences – adventures. He grabs onto them with all his senses and sucks them dry. It's a real high for him.'

'He's not a junkie, is he?'

'No. He doesn't even drink that much.'

'He's not into kink…?'

I rolled my eyes. 'Just yesterday, he asked me if I would take him to church.'

Raquel snorted into her coffee. 'Are you serious?'

'I suddenly felt an urge to protect him. 'What's wrong with that?'

'Why would he want to go to church?'

'Like I said, he loves new experiences. I was hoping that by attending my church, he would want to check it out for a wedding venue.'

'Girl, you better be careful.' With that warning, Raquel collected Dylan, and after brushing the crumbs from his shirt and accepting his five-year-old art, she said goodbye to us and was quickly on her way out the door.

Sooner or later, I knew this church-thing was going to happen. He'd been skirting the edges of spirituality, gazing fixedly through boutique, New Age windows, pointing out the gems and crystals, lots of *ooooohs*, and *that looks yummys*. One day I caught him meditating in the park. His legs and fingers were crossed. When I mentioned to him that Buddhists don't cross their fingers, one eye popped open and he said, 'Not yet, they don't.'

I think he knew there was something empty inside of him, and his newly-found cognizance of it was startling and somewhat frightening for him. This realization created a lust for control over it. Instead of filling it with one idea of spirituality he wanted to cram them all into the soulful, empty space, gorging himself on the entirety, rather than tasting them individually.

10 – Letitia

As I briefly mentioned before, I attend a Baptist church. It is by no means impressive in size nor in worship style. The smattering of attendees on Sunday mornings tend to be well upwards of sixty years of age. What few children show up are carefully corralled into 'Sunday School' for a weekly dose of coloring pictures of Jesus and water, or they are taken to the parenting room to crash around without disrupting the other folks who are looking for whatever panacea of soul they need for the sicknesses within.

If I really wanted to impress him with churchy stuff, I'd have taken him to the affluent west side with their Gen Z bands and smoke machines. Lots of ten-minute anthems and a carefully crafted forty-five minute sermon detailing three different ways to live my best life. No, that's not really for me (and especially not for Meg). I'm comfortable with my Baptists and their rinse-and-repeat worship. Ninety percent old white folks and the other ten of us darker. But we get along for the most part, albeit from different sides of the aisle. No commotion, just contented Christianity. We Des Moines Baptists limit ourselves to a few perfectly placed 'amens' and a smattering of 'mmm hmmms' around the end of the sermon to hurry things up a bit. When Dave badgered me into taking him, it gave me pause to unleash him in a worship service where unbridled expression of thought (and sound) was somewhat encouraged.

'Why would you want to do that, Dave?' I asked him.

'I haven't really been to church much since I was younger. And I thought you could introduce me to a few of the professionals.'

'Professional what?'

'Christians.'

'Dave, there's no such thing.'

'Hmmm… Then what do they need all that money for. I went over to Gilda's apartment last Sunday and she was watching an interesting man in Texas. Gilda was pointing out the preacher's wife on the stage and her expensive jewelry. Gilda said, 'I'd like to get me a piece of that pie, – you know, preying on all those poor people so they can fly their fancy jets and buy some big ol' houses.' And I asked her, 'Now why would you want all that stuff. You don't even like to clean the house you live in, and you certainly don't like to fly.' Gilda asked me to leave right after that.'

'So, what you're saying, Dave, is that a professional Christian is someone who gets paid to be a Christian – like a pastor, or minister?'

'I expect that's so.'

'And you want me to take you to my church so that you can, what? understand them better?'

'Why not?'

'Why don't you just go by yourself. There's a nice Catholic church not too far from you. I'm sure they'd welcome you in.' I'm actually not sure what the Catholics would have done with Dave – probably an exorcism.

'Because I want to go with you.'

'How about we go to a Lutheran church. The college has a tidy Lutheran service. You might like that. They might be a little more… capable of helping me, uh, introduce you to the faith.'

'Lutherans?'

'Yeah, Lutherans.'

'Aren't they the boring ones?'

'Dave. We're talking about churches. They're all boring.'

'Well, nothing is boring when I'm around you.'

Finally, he made me smile.

'So, shall we attend then? What time? What is appropriate attire do you think?'

A door opened in the hallway of my house and Meg stumbled from her room to the living room with her blanket attached firmly to her arm. Her hair was mussed and sticking up high over her head like a frizzy brown halo. She plopped down beside me and leaned her head against my arm while I spoke to Dave on the phone.

'Even if I told you what *normal* people wear, my guess is that you don't have those kind of clothes anyway.'

'Just give me a 'for example'.'

10 – Letitia

'Well, someone your age is probably going to wear blue jeans and a t-shirt, some tennis shoes, and then probably comb their hair.'

'I don't have any blue jeans. I have black jeans and green jeans, maybe a white pair…'

'I guess we're not going to church then.'

'Okay. Okay. I'll go get some blue jeans. There's a good second-hand store not far from here. I think I've still got a decent t-shirt somewhere in my closet.'

'Don't forget tennis shoes,' I said.

'Check. Tennis shoes. And the time of church?'

'It starts at 10:00.'

'That's on Sunday, right?'

'Duh, Dave.'

'Why is it always on Sunday? Why can't it be on Tuesday morning or Thursday at lunch? I'm sure there are people who would appreciate not having the interruption on a weekend.'

'Focus, Dave.'

'10:00. Right.'

'Anything else?'

'Thank you for being amazing.'

I felt the familiar glow rise to my cheeks.

'I'm looking forward to our date on Sunday morning,' he said.

'It's not a date.'

'See you then!' He hung up the phonebooth handset.

On the Sunday morning I would take Dave to church, I checked my watch. It was 9:16. Dave had called me at 5:47 a.m. (I did not answer the phone because I knew he would simply expound on his excitement for the morning), but I could not get back to sleep. Fortunately, Meg did not wake up to the sound of my phone. Normally, she is up between 6:30 or 7:00 anyway, but I was happy to have a little time to myself.

At 9:24, I heard the slamming of a car door.

I checked my appearance in the mirror and noted that there was a rosy glow in my cheeks. My makeup was subtle and my head freshly shaved – not to the skin, mind you. I've got a few dents and scars from mishaps over the years – a woman has to have some vanity, mind you – and my red dress accented my dark brown skin nicely. Generally, I am not a person who wears dresses, but for some reason with regards to church, old habits don't die as easily as the recent ones. To complete the wardrobe, I dressed Meg in the same kind of outfit – red dress and shoes, but I tied up her hair with a bow.

Footsteps, light, and some humming, a few dance steps near the front door. I intuitively knew that Dave didn't want me to open the door until he had rapped on it. Seven times. *Tap tappity tap tap*. I waited for the last two taps, but he refused to finish it.

I opened the door to find my pseudo-fiancé standing, or should I say, bouncing on the threshold.

'Good morning, Lady Letitia,' he bowed, then crossed over to kiss the top of my bald head.

'Good morning.' His cologne was new. Not *bad*, but *different*. Orange blossoms and turpentine, he would have described it. His eyes were glowing, completely alive. That made me nervous.

'Is the Megalomaniac ready to accompany us?' He poked his head behind me where Meg sat at our kitchen table, feet swinging above the floor, moving to an inner beat. Black hair had been tamed to float above the red bow.

'Dave!' she shouted through a mouthful of cereal. Flecks of oats and milk spurted from her mouth and onto the table in front of her.

'What's happenin,' Wonderball?'

Meg leapt to the floor where she almost tumbled. She caught herself and precariously navigated between the discarded toys and furniture, rugs and other obstacles in her path to get to him. She jumped into his arms where he hugged her hard, back and forth, back and forth, legs flopping out to the side. She squealed with glee, and for a moment, I was stunned not just by his unconditional joy for the little girl, but the mosquito of jealousy I felt. Why didn't Meg make those sounds for me?

10 – Letitia

'Are you ready to go to church, Davey Wavy?' Meg said as she laid her head on his shoulder.

'Sure as shootin'.'

I picked up my bag and jacket from the sofa and then it hit me: Dave was wearing exactly what I told him to, and he looked so odd – so… normal. I frowned. This was not Dave. This was me wanting to make Dave into something the world wanted – I wanted.

'You look different.'

'You look torturously beautiful,' he responded through Meg's hair. 'My heart is pinched to bruising.'

'You say the nicest things.'

'What do you think of my get up?' He set Meg down to reveal blue jeans hovering just above his ankles. The jeans sported a belt with a buckle in the shape of a John Deere tractor. Below the rolled cuffs of his pants, he wore sparkling white Adidas tennis shoes with red stripes like velociraptor claw marks. The t-shirt was new, though. It was a 90's Nirvana album cover of a smiling (though dead) happy face with a bullet hole in its forehead. Ironic, considering how Kurt Cobain died.

'Different, Dave. Do you even know who Nirvana is?'

'Ahem,' he said as he turned back to the doorway, 'Nirvana is a *place*, not a person, and methinks we will be informed about that place in church this morning.'

I rolled my eyes and followed him out the door. By the time he reached the stairs, I noticed his blue jean pockets carried the distinctive 'W' stitching of Wrangler. The 'W' had a loop in the middle. Dave was wearing women's jeans, which was why they were so short.

It was a beautiful September Sunday. Most of my neighbors were already up and about. Two young, African American men sat on the front porch across the street. I had met them before, just once, but their stares were uncomfortable, and I was sure they were wondering why a tall, gangly white man was carrying my daughter to…

Oh, Lord.

Dave had driven a purple Lamborghini to my house.

A few other neighbors had noticed and were pointing at it. The car shimmered in grapey, sparkling sunlight.

'Dave,' I stopped. 'What is that?'

'It's my ride. My wheels. My locomotion to the house of the Lord.'

'Why do you have it?'

'That's what professional Christians drive, right?'

'I think you've got the wrong idea.'

'If the guy on TV and his megawatt wife,' he giggled into Meg's curls, 'have all that money, I want to fit in, you know – be able to talk to them.'

'You bought a Lamborghini to go to church?'

Dave flipped up the gull-wing door and inserted Meg into the back seat. Amazingly, there was a child seat in the back. 'No, silly, I rented it on Friday.'

'You rented it so that we could go to church in style?'

'Good, isn't it?'

I finished walking to the car where he stopped me. 'Wait, wait!' He held out a hand to assist me into the passenger seat. Dave shut the door gently and then grinned through the windshield as he crossed in front of the car. When he reached his door, it lifted smoothly but Dave was speaking to the young men on the porch across the street.

'Yeah, we're going to church! You wanna come?'

Muffled voices. 'Dave, just leave them alone. We're going to be late.'

He ignored me. 'I'm serious. You can come with us. It will be a great time! I'll even let you drive!'

'Dave!' I shouted. 'That's not cool. Don't tease them.'

Suddenly, two humans and their slapping footsteps appeared at the opened driver's door. They were big boys with bruising feet, legs covered by wide fraying blue jean pant legs hanging indecently low. I couldn't see their faces, but their backsides and thick-banded underwear were unmissable.

10 – Letitia

Dave leaned down and put his head in the car. 'This is Jeravious and Duwayne. It seems they are looking for Jesus too.'

'Color me less than comfortable, Dave.'

'Hop in the back seat, beloved,' he said as he pushed the driver's seat forward.

'No.' I crossed my arms and fixed my gaze forward. 'No offense, Jarvarious and Dwayne…'

'It's Jeravious, Ma'am,' he stuck his hand across the driver's seat. It was big and calloused, hardworking. Dirt and grime were stubbornly stuck beneath the half-moon cuticles.

'I'm sorry,' I apologized and meekly accepted his hand. 'But put yourself in my place. Would you trust your five-year-old daughter in the hands of strangers?'

Jeravious's face fell, and I felt a stab of guilt.

'Yes, you're right. I'm very sorry.' He took a step back before Dave bent down and put his face back into the car.

'Live a little, Pumpkin Pieces. You never know where new friends might come from.'

'I want to go for a ride!' Meg shouted from the back.

'Me too!' Dave grinned back at her. 'Pleasepleasepleaseplease,' Dave whined.

Against my better judgment, I nodded. 'Okay, but you drive.'

'All right, boys, hop in the back seat! You can drive on the way home!'

Jeravious and Duwayne shoved their bulks into the back seat bookending Meg. I turned to see her small, car-seated body squished between the two young men who had attempted to fold themselves in half to accommodate the seat. 'Her name is Meg.'

One of the two young men reached out and Meg shook his hand. 'Jeravious.'

Dave pulled his seat forward which released Jeravious's legs slightly but made Dave look sufficiently sardined into the driver's seat. His long legs were planted on both sides of the steering wheel, and his head was dangerously close to the ceiling.

'Dave, you can't drive like that.'

'Jeravious needs a little more room.'

'Put it back,' I demanded. 'Safety, please.'

Dave forgot how to start the car until Duwayne squeezed into the space between seats and explained that he had to push the automatic start button. Dave cracked his head on the ceiling, pushed the button, and put the car in first gear before pulling out slowly into the street. 'All right, navigator. Directions.'

We settled in for the ride. Dave glanced back at the boys who had engaged in conversation with Meg. He smiled into the rearview mirror. 'It's a good thing you boys were wearing your church clothes already.'

'Yeah, good thing,' Duwayne responded. 'Where did you get this car?'

'I rented it.'

'You must have lots of cash to rent a Lamborghini.'

'Is that what this is?'

'You serious?'

Dave grinned into the mirror and turned right when I pointed at the intersection. 'I liked the color.'

'Why you get a fine ride like this?'

'Because we're going to church, and I want to take my princess to church in style – you know, like Cinderella in a fancy carriage.'

'You ever been to church before?' Jeravious asked.

'I was at a church not that long ago for a funeral.' We turned left and Dave accidentally squealed the tires which caused Meg to giggle.

'Um, okay, but like for Sunday.'

'No, sir, not for a very long time. But I have heard a lot about it.'

'Whatchoo hear?'

'It's a place where they talk about Jesus and rules about Jesus. Like, how you're not supposed to drink or kill people.'

10 – Letitia

Jeravious and Duwayne exchanged expressions. 'Okay,' said Jeravious slowly, 'but there's a little more to it than that. My grandma used to take me when I was younger. She made me sit in the front row all quiet and sh…'

I held up a finger.

'Uh, sorry, Ma'am.'

'My name is Letitia, and profanity will not be appreciated.'

'Yeah, sorry,' he repeated. 'So we sat all quiet and the preacher kinda talked for a while and then people sang a couple of boring songs and then they opened up their wallets when the old guys walked around and they paid people for the service.'

We watched the endless scenery of two-story houses pass by, endless houses with their old porches and fake-shuttered windows. Generational maples, elms, and oaks lined the streets, their ancient roots distorting the sidewalks, rippling them. A few early birds were raking up September leaves. Soon, everything would turn a rusty orange, then people would be longing for their summer vacations and trips to the lake.

Duwayne agreed with Jeravious's assessment. 'It depends, you know, like what kinda church you wanna go to. Like, sometimes people talk during the service, but not in white people church. They be like all tight, rigid, as if it's a crime to feel the rhythm. No offense,' Duwayne patted Dave on the shoulder. 'But it coulda changed. I haven't been for a long time.'

'Well, I'm sure the people will be very welcoming and affirming, right Letitia?' Dave smiled at me sideways.

'Hmmmm….' I copied one of Dave's most meaningful sounds.

We pulled into the parking lot of Grace Baptist Church. A few of the faithful flock stopped and stared as Dave braked in front of the church. Lifting the door, he hopped out, scratched his sideburns, and adjusted his John Deere belt buckle while Jeravious extricated himself from the small back seat with difficulty. Then, Dave ran to my side and repeated the process. After I was out, Duwayne stretched by twisting his back. Meg had already undone her belt. I've cautioned her about that many times, and she normally was very good about not undoing it. Released, Meg jumped out of the car, past my arms, and straight to Dave. I frowned. Dave handed her to me, then reversed the process of getting back in the car, and proceeded to park the Lamborghini. There were plenty of spaces in the parking lot, but Dave chose one far away from the entrance.

Most people stared at us – four black people who had arrived at Grace Baptist Church in a purple sports car, chauffeured by a tall white man with bushy sideburns, wearing a bullet-holed, smiling happy face.

11
Jon-Nathan

When Dave and company rolled into Grace Baptist Church on that nondescript Sunday in September, I can recall almost every detail about that day. For one thing, they were early. Not many people show up more than five minutes before church, and the only people who do that are the elderly, or the extroverts who need their first conversations to get going.

Guiltily, I must confess, that I sometimes stay in my office a little bit longer than I should so I don't have to hear, for the umpteenth time, the minutia of Ed and Doris Erickson's medical conditions and accompanying pharmaceutical details. Nor do I have to listen to Ali Humphries ramble on about her interior renovations. Ali, as opposed to Ed and Doris, has a loud, shrill voice which is a deterrent for any other member chatting with her. Honestly, I *want* to talk with her, but I don't really want to *listen* to her. The struggle is real.

At Grace Baptist, we have a cross-section of people from the community. They come from all walks of life – retired farmers relocated to the city, dentists, hairdressers, homeless people. They sit uncomfortably in the pews continuing their church attendance habit formed from years of Sunday discipline. Honestly, they could probably preach better than I do. Many of them feel guilty if they don't come, and feel guilty when they do, that's why I try to make our services upbeat with some newer music. It ain't perfect, but nothing ever is.

I knew Letitia in passing. I knew that Meg was born out of wedlock (what a word, I know – 'wedlock' – it sounds like a prison sentence), and Letitia was a single mother who worked as a professor at Drake. They were not frequent attenders, and when they did show up, the two of them usually left quickly after a doughnut for Meg.

It's not that I didn't want to talk to Letitia, but on Sunday mornings, I am usually cornered by the traditional church goers who want to complain about things, or tell me that I need to give more 'life application' sermons. In my humble opinion, if they haven't learned to apply the Bible to their lives already, it wasn't going to happen by listening to my sermons.

That day, I saw Dave strolling across the parking lot, hands in pockets, bobbing as if he was listening to music. Dave was like a Slinky, if you know what I mean. His legs moved forward, and his head eventually pulled up behind it.

He was wearing a Nirvana t-shirt and Wrangler blue jeans, neither of which seemed entirely appropriate at Grace Baptist. Most people still dressed up for church, but I was open-minded enough to understand that attendance on Sunday mornings shouldn't be about clothes. I knew a few of the older chins would wag when they caught sight of the bullet hole in the forehead, though.

As Dave finished his walk across the church's parking lot, he stepped up over the curb and ambled over to Letitia, Meg, and the boys. I know this because I was watching both Ali's stupefied reaction next to me and also the senior choir who were dressed in their robes and making their way into the sanctuary. I stood near the front door in my suit waiting for them to approach while the whispers echoed behind me.

Letitia led, the boys followed, with Dave holding Meg at the rear. We stood in a semi-circle while Letitia introduced them to me.

'Reverend Jonathan, these are my neighbors, Jeravious and Duwayne.'

'How are you? Please call me Jonathan.'

The young men nodded and uncomfortably shook my hand. We didn't have many African American young men at Grace. I guiltily remember thinking at that moment, *Maybe we could get them on a brochure or something.*

'And this is Dave, my boyfriend. You've met Meg before.'

I didn't want my eyebrows to raise, but I couldn't help it. I thought maybe one of the African American young men would perhaps have made a better match than the lanky, side-burned white man towering over us.

'Hello, I'm Dave.'

11 – Jon-Nathan

'What do you do, Dave?'

'I collect church collapses, recreationally.'

I was sure that Dave was a whacko, but the church has to be open to all kinds, doesn't it? 'Is that a quote from a movie? It feels like I've heard it before.'

'Silence of the Lambs,' Dave responded. 'Lecter speaks of evil in the world and why it happens.'

'Ah,' I nodded and crossed my arms, 'why does God allow bad things to happen to good people.'

Dave scrunched up the side of his mouth and frowned. 'No. Why does God allow bad things to happen to anyone.'

An uncomfortable silence ensued as someone – anyone – attempted to find some words to follow Dave's deep thought. Jeravious and Duwayne crossed their arms and scuffed their feet while Meg played with Dave's hair. Then, Dave smiled. 'But that's not really applicable this morning, is it, Jonathan? Good things only!'

'By the way,' he continued enthusiastically, 'did you know you have two first names? Jon and Nathan. I like that.' He said the names 'Jon Nathan' three times in rapid succession as if tasting my name with his mouth.

Letitia pushed Dave and Meg forward through the front doors and then impatiently motioned with her hand for Jeravious and Duwayne to follow. As she entered the sanctuary, I noticed the discomfort of the strange quintet, as if they were entering hostile territory. Was this how most people encountered my church? Were citizens welcoming of immigrants or did they build walls to keep them out?

I cringed watching them walk through the church down the middle aisle. The wooden pews, with their equally wooden inhabitants, posed as sentries guarding the entrances with stoic indifference to the visitors. These were 'their' seats. If anyone else attempted to sit there, even guests, they would be moved out as soon as the members pointed to the seats and said with a fake smile, *I'm sorry, but that's where we belong.*

As they walked, Dave gave a running commentary of the dimmed lighting, the muted colors on the altar, the arched ceiling with shaded lights. Letitia attempted to quiet him, but he was bound and determined not to be silenced.

My congregation members watched them and looked away even quicker when the boys' eyes connected with theirs. Not one person shifted to allow them a seat. Not one person stood to shake their hands or have a brief conversation. Not one person made them feel welcome.

Tim and Denise Nelson entered next, and after pleasantries with me, I watched them run the same gauntlet as Letitia and her friends. They walked down the middle aisle greeted by no less than half a dozen people with smiling white faces and flashing white teeth. I felt sick.

Dave and Co. sat off on the left side near the front. Meg bounced up and down happily on Dave's lap, her curls jiggling gaily around her head. Jeravious and Duwayne glanced around cautiously as if expecting a tap on the shoulder asking them to leave.

When the service began, I welcomed the congregation, nodded and smiled to members and visitors alike (the five being most obvious), and after a few self-deprecating jokes, we launched into the service. The songs were sung with lukewarm fervor, while the Bible verses were read monotonously. I mouthed the words of the verses as Ardys Olson read them, frowning as she mangled 'Gennesaret.' Yes, I know they're hard, but practice, for Pete's sake.

I'd rehearsed my sermon three times that week, each with pregnant pauses and ponderous moments of self-reflection. I knew that the flock came to hear me preach, to give them tips on how to live, what to stay away from, and where green pastures were located, where they could munch healthy grass to their hearts' content. During the sermon, I noticed the auditorium was half-empty, and that was being generous. The hundred-or-so graying-haired sheep were a minute from sleep. I encouraged the flock to open their hearts to the Spirit's calling and be guided by Jesus.

11 – Jon-Nathan

A hand shot up to my right. It was Dave. Letitia was trying to pull his arm down, but he refused.

'Yes?'

'How do I open my heart?'

'What?'

The congregations' heads swiveled in unison like the radar array in Arizona, or New Mexico, or wherever that is.

'You just mumbled something that we should all have open hearts. The open-mind thing I get, but what does it mean for me to open my heart?'

I cleared my throat searching the flock for help, but they were all silent. *You made the mess. You clean it up.* It was a Baptist Church, sure, and we were (in very small ways) used to throwing out an 'amen' or 'preach it, brother,' but to ask a question *during* the sermon? God forbid.

'In spiritual terms, that's allowing the Holy Spirit to speak to our souls and invite the Word of God into the core of our being.'

Dave screwed up his face as if he'd just sucked on a lemon. 'What the heck does that mean?'

'Well… I guess… um, the easiest way to put it would be that you would hear what God has to say to you today.'

Dave squinted at me. 'Are you God?'

Uncomfortable laughter.

'No,' I held up my hands. I could feel my painful smile stretching across my face. 'We'll save that for the Savior.'

'Then how can I hear what God has to say if you're the only one talking?'

I shook my head and put my hands on my hips. 'The sermon is about a Bible passage which I've studied through the week and then, as this community,' I included them with a sweep of my hands, 'has given me the authority to preach about it. I relate what I think God has to say to them.'

I was hoping that would be enough, but unfortunately it wasn't. 'So, you're the only one God speaks to?'

'Dave!' Letitia whispered furiously. 'Shut up!'

'No, no, but let's have a chat after the service, shall we?' My voice echoed plaintively as if I was begging him for a favor.

'That would be fine, thank you. Continue,' Dave waved his hands forward.

What ensued would be in my estimation the worst sermon I've ever preached. Every time I came to a point of theology or biblical wisdom, whether the use of a Greek word (which Dave politely raised his hand and said, 'What does that have to do with the price of eggs in Ethiopia?') or a highfalutin religious phrase I had practiced over and over, stressing the right syllables to ensure that the congregation thought me the most intelligent pastor on the planet, Dave would question me. By the end of the sermon, I was checking on Dave before I continued. The congregation was frustrated. They just wanted to get the sermon over with.

Finally, and mercifully, I wrapped up the sermon about the demon-possessed man walking in the tombs. For some reason, after this particular message, I felt I could relate. Chained to the graves, breaking free momentarily and then put back there by the crowds, what was it about Dave's questions that had me troubled of soul. There I go again — what does that even mean?

I can remember lowering my head at the end of the sermon and slinking back to my throne in the corner. From there, I noticed two things regarding two distinctive groups of people: the congregation seemed to be puzzled that I'd been whipped by an outsider; and Dave and Letitia with the young black men smirking into their hands. Dave appeared untroubled as if he just walked through the mall and was asking the price of a few items that had caught his eye. Meg had fallen asleep on his shoulder. As the band restarted the sputtering engine of our last hymn (the offering was being collected so we needed a longer tune), Dave closed his eyes and buried his face in Meg's hair.

11 – Jon-Nathan

What was it about him that was so frustratingly refreshing? Was I jealous of the simple way he phrased things, or the childlike questions he asked?

It had been a long time since my faith had been questioned (or threatened, if I was being honest), and I was unsure of the complex emotions that stirred and spun, a spiritual vortex pulling me downwards (or maybe even upwards).

As the last guitar riff disappeared into the wooden beams above us, the crowd began to disperse. A few approached me at the back as I perched myself by the exit of the sanctuary. Tim Nelson patted me on the shoulder, a condescending symbolic 'better luck next time,' and left the long way around. Almost everyone avoided Dave and Co. like the plague.

Finally, as the last of the parishioners walked through the back door, I wandered over to them who were waiting quietly.

Dave held up his hand greeting me and his face radiated a happiness I certainly did not feel. 'Hello, Jon Nathan!'

'Hello.'

'You did a great job today. Your performance was spectacular!'

It was not a performance, and certainly not an act. Or was it? I'd practiced my sermon three times, the band had rehearsed Thursday night and this morning, and the worship coordinator made sure that the music style matched the emotion of the song. Even the techs coordinated with headsets. Was he right?

'Thank you, I think. But I'm not sure that 'spectacular' would be the right adjective.'

'Which one would you choose?'

'Mediocre, at best.' I suggested ruefully.

'You're being too hard on yourself.'

'Thank you, Dave. Do you want to have a cup of coffee?' Our eyes strayed back to the area where a few people were whispering over their steaming cups of liquid.

'If you think that would help.'

'Help what?'

He shrugged.

Letitia moved in. 'Dave doesn't drink coffee.'

Dave nodded over Meg's shoulder. 'It dilutes my zest for life.'

Looking up into his eyes, I noticed the good humor in them. For some reason, at that very moment, Dave seemed much like the Jesus I always wanted to meet.

'Do you want to sit down again?' I asked.

Jeravious and Duwayne did not appear pleased by the suggestion and Dave noticed. 'No, that's all right.' He passed off the sleeping Meg to her mother who accepted the sleeping child gracefully.

Dave rolled his neck. 'Now, tell me about this demon guy who got the exorcism. Is that real?'

'Yes, it happened.'

The boys looked at each other.

'I take it you have doubts?' I said to them.

'Oh, you know...' Jeravious's voice faded out.

'Please, tell me.'

'Well, um, no disrespect, but... um, we were like raised with this, um... these stories and they always seemed like, um, fairy tales, you know,' he looked at Duwayne as if to say, *Take over, will ya?*

'Yeah, um, the idea of Jesus and all, yo, that's cool, but some of the stories seem a little, like, you know, silly. No offense.'

'It's not the first time I've heard that,' I said.

'I mean,' Duwayne continued, 'it's good that people put their trust in an afterlife in like, um, someone else, but, like, how does it really help us now?' His eyes flicked back towards the assembled coffee drinkers. 'I bet they all drink their coffees every Sunday morning, and they be like pattin' themselves on the back and shit,' he paused, embarrassed, 'excuse my English.' I waved it away. 'So they sit there in their expensive rich people clothes, drivin' their rich people cars, and they cruise home to their rich people houses, all the while I walk, um, like, into this church, and you can tell out there,' he pointed at the coffee drinkers, 'they're like – just be born again and then you can be like us. Rich.'

11 – Jon-Nathan

Jeravious then whispered, 'But not white.'

Their truthful responses were a spear to my side, and I was crucified by the honest reflection regarding my congregation.

'See?' Duwayne said as he spread his hands. 'I know you thinkin' this black boy doesn't know the first thing about religion, but, I know the last thing about religion.'

'What's that?' I asked with trepidation.

'The world don't need no more born-again Christians. The world needs born-again Christianity.'

I felt myself blinking rapidly trying to process his prophecy. Maybe I'd misplaced my thoughts about the Jesus-ness of a person. Maybe Duwayne was more like the Savior than even Dave. I couldn't get the right words out, and as I pondered the conglomeration of beautiful people standing in front of me, I felt the chains to my own personal tomb break. 'Tell me what you mean. I really want to hear.'

'Okay, so like, um, lots of religious people have told me to be born-again, whatever that really means, but it sounds like a way to control people. When the religious people tell you to get born-again, it's all about you. Just you and God. What you can get God to give you so you can be comfortable, and then when this life is over, you get to be even more comfortable in a bright, shiny, sparkling white heaven surrounded by bright, shiny, sparkly white people.' He swallowed and it seemed like tears were forming in his eyes. 'But I ain't comfortable. Me and Jeravious, we scrapin' by – we tryin' to keep jobs so we can help out the family. You know, our mamas they have health problems, and the house needs fixin', and we got to ride the bus wherever we go so like when it snows, the buses don't run on time and we're late for work,' he looked embarrassed. 'I ain't got time to be reborn, and no amount of bein' born again is going to pay the bills, get my mother healthy, and make the bus run on time.'

I waited. I couldn't help it. There was nothing I could say that was righter than Duwayne's righteousness. For many years I'd been trying to put my finger on exactly what was *off* or at least *tilted* in my heart – there I go again – but here was a visitor from the neighborhood filling in one of the last pieces of the puzzle. Sure, I'd thought a lot about service projects in and around the church, and sometimes I'd convince a section of the guilt-ridden congregation (or the youth group) to pick up some trash or rake the lawns, but never had I thought about helping people solve real-life, long-term problems. Serving the community not as a project but as the life of the church. We were very good at speaking big but walking little.

'You're a prophet,' I said.

'Don't be like that,' he blushed with an embarrassed laugh.

Jeravious clapped him on the back. 'Yeah, boy, you're like a modern-day Moses.'

'I didn't mean to offend you,' I said.

'You didn't offend me,' Duwayne responded and crossed his arms. 'You know, I'm just talkin' sh… crap.' His eyes flashed to Letitia who had jabbed him in the arm. 'I don't even know what I'm sayin'.'

'Yes, yes, you do,' I insisted. 'It's very refreshing. Something I needed to hear.'

Duwayne sniffed and scanned my expression to see if I was being serious. 'You got a nice building here and plenty of money, probly got some extra stashed for those rainy days that don't affect white people.'

I was embarrassed. Even though the church finances were down over the last years, we were not at risk of foreclosure or storm damage.

'The way I see it is, why don't y'all invest some of that easy-earned money into some programs that help the neighborhood. Maybe then you start fillin' this place with people instead of words.'

Shocked by his audacity and his honesty, I reeled. The truth was a spleen-shredding gut punch.

'Are you okay?' Letitia asked as she stretched out an arm just short of connecting with me.

'Yes. Yes, most certainly.' My gaze returned to the people in the back – beautiful people, well-meaning people, who had been led not through the valley of the shadow of death where there were pleasant streams and pastures galore, but to the wastelands of prosperity. This was

11 – Jon-Nathan

not their fault, but mine. As my eyes settled on Dave, he shrugged again. Later, he would tell me that he had brought the Lamborghini to church because he thought all church people were rich, which reinforced and reminded me that the church indeed needed to be born again.

Meg began to stir in her mother's arms. 'I'm hungry, Mommy.'

Relieved, we nodded and felt released from the tension of walking along this narrow edge of indecisiveness. Jeravious mentioned that he and Duwayne were going outside. Dave stopped them and handed them the key to the Lamborghini. If I would have known then, what I do now, that Dave had only met them that morning, I would have marveled anew. After Jeravious and Duwayne left, Letitia and Dave walked together down the middle aisle like a bride and groom carrying their illegitimate child between them.

Once again, Dave took Meg who had grown too heavy in her mother's arms. They seemed an odd couple, the oddest, really, and yet the three of them were like the 21st century version of the holy family. For a moment I simply watched. Meg slowly lifted a hand towards me in blessing. Her small fingers were smooth and dark. Her expression one of contented love. I returned the gesture snatching at the air as if grabbing her blessing and holding on to it.

She smiled.

So did I.

12
Benson

Love is a curious thing. For the novice, like myself, one who had never experienced it, nor even got a glimpse of it, it was also very frightening. And wonderful. And confusing. And nauseating And... and... and...

With the thing I had going with Wendy, I was like a lion trying to stay downwind from her, the gazelle. Not that I was going to hunt her down and eat her, goodness, no, that's too Dr. Lecter for me, but I was being cautious. Taking my time, you know. Making sure that the conditions are perfect before I made my move. Pounced. Roared. Whatever.

Listen to me. I'm such a liar. I totally dived headfirst, crack-your-skull-on-the-bottom-of-of-the-pool, into love. It had been three months. Two months and two weeks longer than any other girlfriend I've ever had. Smitten is what my mother would have called it, but I was taking the high road to infatuation. And we'd only seen each other in person once.

During the week, Wendy and I texted each other a hundred times. I called her on Wednesday and Friday, further proof that the 'L' word might soon be in play because I detested talking on the phone. I even resorted to sending memes and emojis.

Ugh, what was happening to me?

On Sunday, I checked to see if Wendy had messaged me during the night. I knew she was on duty that afternoon, so the odds were she wouldn't have sent me anything, but love has wings, springs eternal, and all that.

I had planned on sleeping in, but Dave knocked on my door at 8:00. He had said something the night before about going to church. This held no appeal to me whatsoever, and I was surprised it did for Dave. I know he likes his crowds and his interesting new conversations, but church seemed like it was a little over the top.

When he knocked, I pretended not to notice.

'Benzebub, get ready. I want to take you to the holy land.'

When I didn't respond, he knocked again. 'It will be fun.'

'Not interested.'

'What if I bring along some cookies?'

Part of me wanted to ask the type of cookie, but sanity returned. 'Same answer.'

'Jellybeans?'

He knows I love them, but truly, I just wanted to play video games and wait for Wendy to wake up.

'Just go,' I said. 'You can tell me all about it when you get back.'

I thought I'd won the battle until a piece of paper slid under the door. I stood up with a groan, just to see what he tried to bribe me with.

Peanut Butter Cups?

'See you later, Dave.'

After he left, I tried to go back to sleep but eventually gave up. The frustration of not being able to drop off was too much so I hauled myself from bed, put on my slippers, and embedded myself in video games. Just before lunchtime there was a knock on the door.

'I'm back, Clarice. I think it would be quite something to know you in private life.'

'It's unlocked.'

He kicked the door open dressed in a Nirvana t-shirt and Wrangler blue jeans. I was taken aback because I'd never seen him in either. He strode across my living room and stood in front of the television screen which blocked my view of the video game. I leaned to the side, but he moved with me.

'Get out of the way. I'm almost done.'

Dave reached behind the TV and unplugged it.

'Hey!'

'You have other needs today, Benson.'

'I don't know what you're talking about.'

'Of the amorous nature. Fleshly delights.'

'Why do you talk like that? Did the sermon go into sex and stuff?'

Dave's lips pressed together as if he was perturbed, and he waggled a finger negating my question. 'Now, now, thou shalt not remember the Sabbath day to poke holes in it.'

'What do you want?'

He inhaled deeply and slowly through his nose. 'I want you to travel to far Mississippi and visit your Juliet.'

I put my gaming console down. 'Not gonna happen.'

'And why not?' His hands were on his hips which magnified the enormous John Deere tractor on his belt buckle.

'Why are you wearing that getup?'

Dave glanced down at the bullet hole in the smiley face and spread his arms. 'What these old things?'

'Yeah.'

'I've been to church.'

'Is that supposed to answer my question?'

Dave brushed the sleeves of his shirt. 'Letitia told me that people who go to church wear jeans and a t-shirt. Thus…' He spun in a circle and threw his hands out. 'Voila!'

'Did they laugh at you?'

'Not too much.'

'Next time wear a suit.'

'I'll think about that. Now, get up. It's time for you to do something with your life. Take the next step with Wendy.'

'It's Sunday and I have to work tomorrow. I don't have much gas in my car, and I don't feel like filling up.'

'Benson,' he said slowly, reproachfully. 'That's no way to treat the future Mrs. Buttknuckles.'

'Which part of 'I'm out of gas' isn't registering?' I felt my hackles raise as he pushed the buttons regarding the future I'd already dreamed about a thousand times. What would happen if Wendy and I got engaged? Slow the truck down, man. She and I have only met face to face once.

'I've got you covered. Where there is a will, there is a Lamborghini.'

'That doesn't make any sense.'

'Come, Clarice. Let me show you.'

Boy, he was acting weird. He reached out a hand, and, with a deep sigh, I grabbed it. It was smooth, unlined, and almost hairless. He pulled me up easily, and I followed him out the door.

The courtyard and sky above were bright, no haze. A plane descended into the airport floating lazily like an eagle about to grab a fish. Its descent left contrails of sound and smoke behind it. In the trees around the Palms, birds chattered noisily. Perhaps they were preparing for autumn already. Or maybe they were protesting the four squirrels perched in the maple trees along the parking lot.

Dave's head bobbed as he descended the stairs in front of me. The golden 'W's on his pockets swiveled side to side.

A few other Palm Apartment residents were enjoying the morning on their balconies drinking coffee or reading a book. Patricia and her husband were reading sections of the newspaper on the balcony. They were rugged up in sweatshirts because it was getting colder, but everyone wanted to enjoy the last pieces of summer while they were still available. Gladys waved to us as we walked past her office. She struggled to rise from her chair in which she was wedged.

When she opened the door, I greeted her, but I was curious why she had invested the energy to come outside.

It didn't take a rocket scientist to figure that out.

'Ta da!' Dave pointed at a purple Lamborghini in front of him.

'Yeah, so what. It's a Lamborghini.'

'No, it's not just *a* Lamborghini. It's *your* Lamborghini. Your purple chariot drawn by a raging bull.' He swiped his hand underneath the black logo of a golden bull.

'Ha ha.'

He reached out for me again, not pleadingly, but like a request to introduce two people. 'I rented her for the weekend so I could take Letitia and Meg to church. I've still got it for one more day, so you might as well use her.'

I have to admit, the sight of a purple Lamborghini was awe-inspiring, but there were multiple things working against Dave's plan.

A: I'd never driven one before, and my efficiency with manual transmissions was shaky at best.

2: If something were to happen to it, A.K.A. I wrecked it, I wouldn't be able to pay off the repairs and

Lastly: Nobody in Iowa drives a purple Lamborghini. Not even Mildred Day's grandkids. If you didn't know, Mildred was part of the pair who developed my favorite treats. Rice Krispy bars!

'That's really nice of you Dave,' I said as I enumerated the reasons above for turning him down.

'Please, Benson, your refusal is silly. I know you want to take her. Wendy will be impressed.'

'No, she won't. She'll think it's stupid.'

'I promise, you'll have fun.'

Oh, yes, it is most certainly fun to drive a purple Lamborghini. The engine sounds like liquid thunder. The leather seats are comfortable and contoured to fit even my generous proportions. The sleek lines make one think of a powerful bull or bucking stallion. It really makes a person quiver.

Thirty minutes after my automobilic seduction, I was behind the wheel of the sports car, adjusting mirrors, and trying not to look stupidly out-of-place. I started the car, and it roared to life. Even though I unintentionally squealed out of the parking lot, I felt powerful and in control of my existence. After he caught up to me in the street, Dave placed one hand on his hip and waved goodbye to me with the other hand while shouting through my open window, 'Go get her, tiger.'

You know what one of the best things is about driving that machine? Watching people watch you. They covet. We all covet pretty things, things we can't have and never will or never shouldn't.

Even Iowans.

When I left Des Moines, almost every person on the street gawked and pointed. Young men rubbed their chins while young women covered their hearts. Old men's jaws clenched with envy. Old women covered their ears and shook their heads. Ah, to really own one of those babies. Begrudgingly, I was glad Dave convinced me to take her for a spin.

When I was halfway to Davenport, I called Wendy on my cellphone. It connected through the speakers of the car. My car does not have Bluetooth.

'I wondered if you were going to call me today.'

'Where are you?' I asked.

'North of Davenport, in the boat.'

'When are you done working today?'

'2:00. Why?'

'I'm coming to visit.'

Silence. Uh oh, that's a bad sign. I slowed the car. 'Do you not want me to come over?'

'Sorry, I just had to stop a few kids from throwing rocks at ducks. What did you say, again?'

'I'm coming to visit.'

'Oh, that's wonderful!'

Relief. 'I should be there about 3:00.'

'Great. What are we doing?'

'I was thinking about taking you out for dinner. Any suggestions?'

'Yeah, I know a place.'

Because she had expressed excitement for my impending arrival, I felt on top of the world. Powerful, like a bull. The Lamborghini and I became one. I was the mighty Minotaur, half man/half bull. I stomped on the accelerator and surged forward past minivans and pickups. The speedometer quickly reached 95 miles per hour.

'What is that noise?' she asked.

'What noise?'

'It sounds like something growling. You haven't brought along a dog, have you?'

I leaned my head back and howled. 'No way, baby. I've brought along a bull.' I'd never called her 'baby' before, and probably never would again, just like I'd never drive another purple Lamborghini.

'Benson, are you okay?'

'Yes, yes, of course. Loving life. Beautiful day for a drive, and I'm coming to see you.' My eyes coveted the triple digits of speed, and I nudged it up just a fraction more. I was so powerful.

'Okay.' Her voice was hesitant as if wondering whether Dave had rubbed off on me too much.

'Where should I pick you up?'

'Call me when you're near the city and I'll guide you.'

'Sounds wonderful.' I disconnected the phone by pushing a button on the steering wheel.

While driving, I sang the song, Foxy Lady, by Jimi Hendrix. I didn't know all the words — actually, I knew next to none of them, but I knew how to shout out *Foxy* and *Lady*. For the verses of the song, I was limited to howling at the moon or pretending I was Jimi himself.

During one of my howls, I glanced in the rearview mirror and felt the record player of my life screech from music to reality. Though Wendy might be a foxy lady, I was not exactly Wolfman Jack. I took a deep breath and sighed, then slowed the Lamborghini to a more appropriate 85 miles per hour.

Unfortunately, I spotted the highway patrol five seconds too late, and before I knew it, the colored lights were flashing behind me.

I cursed and signaled to pull over. The cop pulled in slowly behind me, lights still twinkling on his front crash bar. He made me wait a good minute to marinate in my own sweat and stupidity. *Why did I let Dave talk me into this?*

With a hand near his sidearm, the officer approached the Lamborghini cautiously and rapped on the window.

'Good morning, officer,' I squeaked after finding the button to open the window. 'How can I help you?'

'Must be excited today.'

'I am.' I cleared my throat as the squeak continued. 'I am,' I repeated, this time with a voice more befitting a man in a purple Lamborghini. 'I'm visiting my girlfriend in Davenport.'

'She likes Lamborghinis?'

'I don't know. I've never shown her one before.'

'Looks like it's a rental,' he said, studying the iPad in his hands. 'Can I see your license and registration?'

'It is a rental,' I blurted out. 'My friend, Dave, let me drive it today.'

'Are you on the rental contract?'

My face turned red. 'Not that I know of.'

'Some pretty serious insurance ramifications if you're caught.'

'I'm a good driver,' I mumbled lamely, aware that I sounded like Rainman.

'Benson Bartholomew Olson. That's quite a mouthful.'

'I had no choice.'

'No priors. No speeding. No record at all. Sounds like you've had a relatively dull life.'

'You can say that again.'

'Tell me again why you're in such a hurry.'

I flipped through the Rolodex of excuses which might lead to a warning rather than a ticket. Maybe my girlfriend was sick, or she was having an anxiety attack. But that wouldn't necessitate renting a Lamborghini.

Thus, I blurted out the first thing that came to mind. 'I'm in love, officer.'

He covered a laugh with the back of his hand. 'That's nice.'

Red-faced, I felt the odd necessity to treat him as if he was my therapist. The words came out in a torrent, words that didn't really make sense to me, and even less sense to him. He stood there, statue-like, with aviator glasses reflecting my pleading face. I stared at myself as I babbled.

'I met this girl. Her name is Wendy. She's an officer like you, except in the Fish and Wildlife. She's gorgeous, blond hair, brown eyes, terrific forearms, and a great set of big toes. I've never been in love before. I feel squishy inside. That's why I was speeding. I didn't even know that my foot was, of its own accord, depressing the accelerator. Honestly, I didn't even think I was driving. I felt like I was floating.'

He laughed again. The mustache bunched up under his nose and he scratched it. 'More like you were flying.'

'I'm really sorry about that, sir. Any chance for clemency this time? As you see, I am a very cautious driver when I'm not in love.'

He studied me through the reflective lenses. I was just another rabbit pleading for its life while caught in the hawk's talons. The excuses were always plentiful. *I wasn't paying attention. Are you sure your radar isn't off? I'm positive that I was doing the speed limit.* He'd heard it all, but maybe not the romantic alibi.

'Well, Benson Olson, this is your lucky day. I'll give you a warning this time. But on your way home, make sure you control your love-foot, lil' Thumper.'

The sigh of relief was audible. My shoulders released the tension, and I had to control the howl rising within me. I was back on top. I was the bull.

He scribbled me a warning and I received it with thanks. The patrolman tipped his cap and retreated to his souped-up car, a Mustang, I think. He sat there waiting for me to take off, and with shaky hands, I started the car again. The engine revved, ready to roar, to blast off. I put the car in first gear, but I released the clutch too fast and peeled out back onto the interstate in a flying blaze of shoulder-gravel glory.

Twenty minutes later, after having been pulled over a second time within one hundred yards of the first, I was the proud recipient of a newly-printed pink ticket with a $105 fine and a court summons for reckless driving.

It's funny how life is sometimes. You avoid the boulder only to get mauled by the avalanche.

By the time I was three-quarters of the way to Davenport, I was in a foul mood. I had wanted that day to be perfect, and it would have been if only that stupid cop hadn't been so uncompromising.

Five minutes outside Davenport, I called Wendy again. 'Hello,' she sang happily.

'I'm almost there.'

'What's wrong?'

'Nothing.'

'Come on, tell me.'

'I got a ticket.'

'For what?'

Do I tell her the truth? Why should I not? 'Reckless driving.'

'What?'

'First, I was speeding. He let me off for that, but when I pulled away from him, I accidentally cracked his windshield.'

'That's rough.'

'Tell me about it.'

'Well, come find me and I'll make you feel better.'

'Okay.' The dejection in my voice was apparent.

'Benson.'

'Yes.'

'I like bad boys.'

I could hear the smirk in her voice, but it made me smile anyway.

Aaaawoooo! Foxy Lady.

'Where can I find you?'

'Take exit 67.'

I was quite nervous meandering through the smaller streets. When I finally spotted her, she was leaning against a lightpost. I assumed she was looking for Dave's car, so when I rolled down my window, she was taken aback when my face appeared.

'Wanna ride?' I tried to sound as cool and casual as possible, but my foot came off the clutch and the car lurched forward almost hitting a pickup in front of me. The Lamborghini stalled.

'What are you doing?' she laughed.

'Get in and I'll explain everything.'

She did, and I did.

After parking the car, I flipped up my door and escorted her to the path alongside the Mississippi. We walked hand-in-hand taking in the sights and sounds of the river. The September sun was warm on our backs in one direction, and even better on our faces during the return. I told her about Dave's church experience, the rental, the warning, and the ticket. All the while, I snuck glances at her and the way the sunlight played in her hair. Freckles dotted her nose and speckled her clavicle where the blue dress was pulled off her shoulders. One time she leaned in close and I could smell her perfume. Or maybe it was her shampoo. Either way, she smelled clean and summery, like a flower in full bloom.

As these words tumble out of me, I realize I sound very much like a Hallmark card, but that's what love does. That's what falling in love is.

I think.

Before that night, I would have said love was impractical, maybe even go as far as to say unnecessary, shoes for a snake, or headphones for a deaf person. From my rational perspective, we're animals. We eat, hunt, mate and raise our offspring, and die, just like all the other beasts. I'm not sure what the evolutionary advantage of love is, but by the time we finished our walk, my life had been transformed. I had mutated into a walking, bumbling, love-struck chicken. Never mind the bull. Everything about her was entrancing, and I was falling for her faster than I realized.

I wanted that night, that part of my life, to be played on repeat – us, we, my new favorite words, walking hand-in-hand as the sun set. I wanted to have people be jealous of *us*, the young couple, two little ducks paddling rapidly on the surface of life.

Those were thoughts that replayed in my head as we drove to the restaurant along the shores of the Mississippi. Eventually, she pointed to the venue, a restaurant with a front façade like an Old West saloon – *Wild Bill's*. It was hard to find a parking space, but we found one not too far from the entrance. I didn't want to park there, but Wendy insisted that we could fit. With great care, I wedged the Lamborghini into the space between two large pickups, a Dodge Ram and a Ford F-250. Through my windshield I could see an old couple watching us while they enjoyed ice cream. The old man had paused mid-lick, his mouth open, tongue extended. He had grizzled cheeks and a dabble of ice cream on his chin. His wife did not stop licking, but her blue, penciled-in eyebrows threatened to connect in the middle of her frown as Wendy's door flipped upwards, not outwards.

'It's pretty close,' I worried. I'd left enough room on her side for her to open the door, but I was not sure mine had room to flip up, especially with the Ram's side mirror above my head.

'You'll be fine.'

I stared up at the Ram beside me. It seemed an insurmountable wall of metal. I rolled down my window to study the minuscule fifteen-inch gap between the Lamborghini and the pickup.

'I think I'll find another spot.'

'Don't' be silly. Come on.'

I killed the engine and the community sounds took the engine's place. Muffled Country music filtered through the swinging doors from Wild Bill's. From somewhere up the street, people were laughing. The cars driving slowly behind me were all searching for a parking spot like mine.

'Why are there so many people here?' I asked Wendy.

'Cheeseball night.'

I tested the gap to find that the door would indeed not have room to flip.

'Just crawl out the window.'

'How will I lock the car if the window is open?'

'You won't have to. It's not like anyone is going to steal it. It sticks out like a sore thumb.'

I sighed before tilting the steering wheel up to make a first attempt which succeeded in nothing. With great effort on the second stab, I exerted more force and found purchase by pushing my body upwards first and then twisting. At least Wendy was happy. I could hear her laughter quite clearly from the back of the car. With great urgency, I cleared the next obstacle, that I could get one leg out the window, and if I grasped the steering wheel, the other leg might follow. Now, with both legs dangling out the door but my upper half still ensconced in the seat, I realized that I was stuck.

'I'm dying,' I declared as my chin was pinned against my chest.

Wendy reached in and grabbed my belt buckle.

'Whoa there Nellie,' I said. 'What are you doing?'

'Helping.'

I'd never had a girl place her hand there before. Even in my worst dreams, the first time would not have looked like this. I had to get out quickly.

She grunted and tugged on my belt. Again, I wrestled with the steering wheel. Thankfully, with her help, my butt was now up on the ledge of the door, but I was bent over backwards, my upper torso lying on the driver's seat.

'Almost there,' Wendy said as if she was trying to squeeze a proton torpedo into the Death Star.

'Use the force,' I suggested, which caused Wendy to explode with laughter, and she almost dropped me.

Like a cork from a bottle, I twisted sideways. Every part of my body was within shouting distance of being popped from the car. With one last tug, Wendy yanked me from the Lamborghini. Unfortunately, I remained wedged in the fifteen inches between Ram and Bull.

Thankfully, it only took a few more seconds to extricate myself from between the vehicles. At the back of the car, Wendy stared at me with humor and fascination. In that moment, she was more beautiful than ever because she accepted the limitations of my gracelessness with a grain of salt. She leaned forward and kissed me lightly on the lips.

It was our first kiss. Light, unexpected, a graze by all measures, and most likely done out of pity, the kind of thing you'd do with a kitten after un-stucking it from a hole, but my brain went into overdrive. My heart raced. My pulse pounded. I felt light-headed and on the verge of passing out which would deposit me back into the space between the vehicles.

'Wow,' I stammered. 'I wasn't expecting that.'

12 – Benson

'Get used to it.'
I'm a bull.
I'M A BULL!
Aaaawwooooooo!
Nothing could possibly have ruined that night.
How so very incredibly wrong I was.

12.27
Wendy

For those of you who haven't been to Wild Bill's, the restaurant is situated in the middle of a row of boutique shops. On one side of Bill's is a lighting store, and on the other is a carpet place. Achmed's Shag. Hardware Hank's and a small coffee shop flank those businesses, but Wild Bill's is smack-dab in the middle. It is the widest building on the street and the front sidewalk space, with large wooden beer kegs and stools, interrupts the flow of traffic between Achmed's and Hank's. Around the kegs and stools, peanut shells are strewn everywhere. This is part of the restaurant's allure. Once you enter (or stay outside), you're given a peanut-shaped plastic bowl of unshelled nuts which is your appetizer, and then you simply chuck the remnants on the floor.

The façade is fake, rustic wood to paneling to make the place seem two hundred years old. The visible front doors swing forwards and backwards, and every time someone enters, the waiters and waitresses are required to shout out 'Hey!' as if welcoming long lost friends.

Another part of the kitsch at Wild Bill's is the mechanical bull. I've only ridden it once, and that was enough. I'm surprised more people don't get hurt on those things especially as they surf the alcohol wave. A few customers have left with dislocations or breaks, but it's rare. Most who get up on the thing have at least done some time on a horse, albeit a docile one. Yet, there is always that one person…

A few patrons sat on the barstools near the front veranda. They were drinking beer and chasing them with margaritas. The women were wearing cowboy boots and blue jeans, and the men, seed-corn caps and western shirts. A few had hitched up their jeans with belts and overly-large belt buckles in the shapes of all sorts of things, but a few had gone all out with the longhorn bull's heads. I greeted a couple I had met before, but I couldn't remember their names. I smiled, waved, and said, *Hey, how are you?*

'Do you come here often?' Benson asked.

12.27 – Wendy

'Every few weeks. The cheeseballs are to die for.'

'Does everyone dress like that?' he asked as he surreptitiously waved his hand at the implied dress code, conscious that he was not dressed like they were.

'What do you mean?'

'All the country stuff.'

'We do live in Iowa.'

'Yeah, but it's Iowa, not Texas. Half these people wouldn't even know how to ride a horse, much less know what spurs are for.'

'Don't be so judgmental.'

For a Sunday night, Wild Bill's was hopping. Like squirrels busily preparing for the cold storing the last nuts for the upcoming winter, so too were the patrons of the saloon as they hoarded three or four beer mugs at every wooden keg. As winter was coming in the not-too-distant future, we all were storing up our happiness for the long dark days ahead when everything froze including our goodwill. Even Iowans get grumpy in the winter.

The doors swung inwards revealing a throng of similarly clad western-wearers. The waiters and bartenders were dressed in jeans and boots with cowboy hats tilted back on their heads. The only thing that distinguished the help from the customers were the bandanas around their necks.

As we entered, the staff and many customers turned to us and shouted, 'Hey!' Benson gave me a look. I smacked his arm playfully.

While journeying through the tables, I pointed out the dance floor at the back of the saloon with neon swirling lights and a smoke machine. Couples were line-dancing, fingers intertwined in beltloops or grasping buckles. Everyone seemed to know the moves except for a few on the fringe who either had no rhythm or were just learning. The dance floor was separated from the restaurant and bar area by a stall fence. The wooden slats held old ranch accoutrements hanging from wires: lanterns, horseshoes, and whips. To the left of the dance floor fence was the mechanical bull riding arena. It is the most popular place in the restaurant and worth the price of admission just to watch the macho guys straddle the headless bull and get tossed into oblivion.

As Benson was taking it all in, one of the waitresses noticed us. She tilted her head, dropped off some drinks from her tray onto other tables, and made her way over to us.

'What can I getcha?'

'Can we have a pitcher of margaritas?' I noticed the pained look on Benson's face. 'You don't like margaritas?'

'No, that's fine. I was… uh… just watching the dancers.'

'Are you sure?'

'Yeah, yeah. Bring it on.'

'Anything else?' the waitress asked.

'Can we get a large basket of cheese balls?'

'You betcha.'

She wheeled away from us, her blonde hair swinging happily. As she walked away, another patron reached up to tap her arm. She replied with the same *You betcha* and threaded her way to the bar.

'She sure is happy,' Benson said.

I swallowed hard. My heart was beating heavily in my chest. I wasn't sure whether he was excited or afraid. Technically, it was our first date, and I had chosen it. I felt a tug of fear. What if I'd made a mistake? It had been such a long time since I'd met a nice guy. I wanted to be as happy as the waitress.

'It's a good place to work.' I took a deep breath. 'Come on, let's find a table near the dance floor.'

There was a live band playing Country/Western covers. I recognized the artists and songs, but I couldn't tell if Benson was about to cover his ears.

'You don't like Country music?'

'You'll have to help me with the indoctrination process. It hasn't been part of my upbringing.'

'You're one of those.' I sighed.

'What do you mean?'

12.27 – Wendy

'One of those snobbish music-people who thinks Country is trash.'

'Isn't it all about divorce, trucks, Jesus, and shotguns?'

'Benson, I'm shocked at your ignorance.' I covered my heart trying to be upbeat, but his negativity hit me like a sledgehammer to the guts.

After noticing my expression, it finally clicked for him. This was an important place for me. This was where I found community and connection. This was where I sang songs, got happy. I didn't want him to ruin it for us, but especially not for *me*.

'Hey, I'm sorry,' Benson held up his hands.

With great relief, I leaned forward and gave him another kiss. Once again, he was surprised and probably a little mystified by the public display. While standing near the dance floor hearing a particularly cringey version of *Achey, Breaky Heart,* he placed his hands on my hips and returned the kiss.

We broke apart breathlessly. 'In this position, we might as well move onto the dance floor.'

His hands immediately dropped from my waist, and he blushed. 'Uh...'

'Maybe later,' I laughed.

A middle-aged couple vacated one of the kegs, so we took the stools around it. From this vantage point we could see both the dance floor and the bull riding.

'Have you ever done that before?' He pointed to the arena where the headless apparatus was about to be mounted by a grinning, cowboy-hatted twenty-something with large legs, a cask-like chest, and thick neck. He had rosy patches in the middle of his cheeks from excitement and/or exertion and/or alcohol. I wondered how many times he'd been tossed already.

'A couple of times,' I said as we watched the young man saddle up.

'How did you do?' he asked me as our margaritas arrived. The waitress placed the sweating pitcher in the middle of the barrel and then deposited our margarita glasses, rimmed with salt, in front of us. A lime was perched precariously on the edge of both.

'I only did the amateur version.' I poured the drinks. A beady line of sweat appeared on Benson's forehead. I ignored it as I took a sip. 'I was thrown off after about half a minute.'

The cowboy thrusted his hand into the rope around the neck. Both rider and fake-animal were about the same size. The crowd started to hoot and holler as the bull began to spin and buck slowly. The rider's face was alight. His cheeks glowed even redder. While the rider held on for dear life, the band struck up another line dance favorite. A few women streamed (and screamed) out onto the peanut-shelled dance floor and started kicking up their heels. The confrontation of two entertainment styles built the excitement, and I couldn't decide which to go to first. I downed the first margarita lickety split and refilled my glass. Benson watched me curiously.

'What do you think?' I asked him over the noise.

'It's... impressive.'

'Which do you want to try first?'

A panicked look crossed his face. 'I'm not sure either suits me very well.'

Emboldened by the drink, I tried to pull his hand toward me. 'Come on. Live a little.'

'This doesn't feel like living to me. More like dying. Execution-style.'

I fake slugged him in the arm. I was exhilarated. I saw that he had not touched his drink, so I motioned for the waitress to come over. When she appeared at our table, I was already jiving to the music. 'What would you really like, Benson?'

'Can I have a rum and Coke, please?' The waitress grinned and turned to leave, but Benson stopped her with a hand on her arm. 'Easy on the Coke, okay?'

'You betcha!' She danced her way back to the bar.

'I'm gonna dance.'

Benson froze.

'Do you want to come with me?'

12.27 – *Wendy*

'Most definitely no.'

The margarita rose to my lips again and I swallowed. After wiping the salt and wetness from my lips, I boogied out to the line. Heel. Toe. Shuffle. Shuffle. Spin. Lean left. Lean right. The music was intoxicating.

Engrossed in the dancing, I closed my eyes. When I opened them again, Benson was no longer at the table.

My heart dropped.

Suddenly, there was commotion in the bullring.

It was Benson.

Somehow he had been cajoled into mounting up.

Uh oh.

12.48
Benson

Looking back on that night, which I'll uncomfortably call 'The Tragedy of Wild Bill's', I wonder how I got into the bull riding situation in the first place. I could use the excuse of 'peer pressure', but to be brutally honest (and a little condescending), there's no way those flannel/belt-buckled/cowboy-hat-wearing yokels were my peers. As you have already noticed at this point in the tale, I'm a highly refined young man who…

Enough.

I was basically coerced by the gigantor who had just been thrown by the bull. Though he didn't use the word 'chicken', or 'coward', or 'lily-livered-gizzard-eater', the mere expression on his face made me feel ten inches tall and three shades of yellow. Maybe you've been in that situation. Delusions of grander, right? *This might be the moment my life changes. What if I'm actually stronger than I look or feel? What if they all adore me at the end of my amazing ride? What if Wendy notices my muscles and wants to run her hands over my biceps.*

As I watched the beefy cowboy get tossed, I had equal and opposite thoughts. *What a loser* and *There is no way I need to be wrecking my privates on that.*

Look, I'm good at video games. I've spent a reasonable amount of time building, destroying, fighting, running, and jumping, all in the company of distant 'friends'. When I play video games, we talk, we tease each other, we kill each other, and everything turns out fine, because when I turn the game off, I'm still alive, unbroken, un-dislocated, and bruise-free.

But those people at Wild Bill's, with their shouts and their clapping, and their yeehaws, and their boots – I don't know what came over me. I can only label it as a brief do-si-do with insanity. The strapping young lad with the same dimensions as the bull slapped his meaty hand on my shoulder after he had been thrown and said,

'You're next, Pardner.'

'Uh, I don't think so.' I rued the fact that I hadn't backed away further from the action. Frankly, I'm almost positive of the reasons he chose me: short, balding, tennis shoes, and no belt buckle. I was like a canary in a cage full of raptors.

'Come on,' he encouraged. 'You'll be fine.'

'No, really. There are plenty of other people in line who want to prove their mettle.'

'I promise, you won't regret it.'

Why is it that when people promise a regretless opportunity, you regret it almost immediately?

As he hoisted me onto the back of the stupid thing, you'll notice that I colored the facts a little bit ago. He didn't belittle me and there was no mention of cowardice. He was actually a pretty nice guy, but I don't want you to think I'm weak.

And the last thing I wanted to do on that night was to appear weak. It didn't really matter that Wendy had gone off to line dance. I had no desire to watch that. I only wanted to watch the bull riding while waiting for her to finish. Maybe just to get a little perspective on how the lower half of humanity lives.

'I don't know what to do,' I stammered as the cowboy strapped my hand onto the fake shoehorn.

'Just hold on.'

'How?'

He cinched my hand tightly to the saddle horn, and mimed what I should do. With his arm swinging off to one side and his head flailing around, he looked like an epileptic. I surmised from his seizure that I was to grasp the rope and move with the mechanical bull's movements. For some people, this might seem like an easy task, but the only thing I experienced that resembled this bull was my living room sofa, and that bad boy never bucked in any way, shape, or form.

I knew it was a bad idea as soon as I nodded. He had seen my clothes, how out of place I must have felt, how superior I had imagined myself to be to these people in their fake Country clothes. If Dave would have been there, he would have encouraged me just like this bullish young man had. He would have said, *Choose Benson. He's begging to do it. Look at him! His heart is pounding; his pulse is racing. Why, you can see he's almost licking his lips to give it a crack. Come on, big fella. Strap him on like Wile E. Coyote to the rocket.*

With morbid fascination, I felt like I was watching outside my body. My heart pounded in my throat and my skin was clammy. I was tempted to simply fall off the bull at first turn, but something inside my evolved, human self demanded that I stay pinioned to that stupid machine for as long as I could. And if I did somehow stay up on that thing, that idolatrous monstrosity worshiped by Country fans and Country fakes alike, in some miraculous way, Wendy would see me in a new light. A real man.

A bull.

Awhooooooo?

'Are you ready?'

'No.'

I felt the vibration between my knees as the bull moved slowly in a circle. I had watched enough of the others' rides to know that this was the prelude, kind of like rodeo foreplay. I had intimated to the cowboy that I only desired the amateur setting, but I didn't watch to see if he inputted that. The customers encircling the arena waved their hats above their heads. Above the din of shouts, I heard a 'Ride 'em cowboy' and 'Go get 'em little doggie'. One of the women tossed her hat to the cowboy leader and he slotted it on my head as the bull continued to move. The hat felt crusty and even a little sweaty, but there was nothing I could do about it; and to remove one of my hands from the rope (I did not feel qualified to free one) felt a little like cowboy suicide.

Even though the bull was not bucking or spinning fiercely, I could feel the muscles in my forearm begin to stand out. I felt only a sense of adrenaline-fueled, panicky trepidation. For me, grasping the rope with two hands seemed much more natural to the Darwinian model of evolution.

'Yeehaw!' the cowboy shouted. He was trying to move with me as the bull shifted into second gear.

Whoever thought, 'I think riding a bull-shaped machine would be a great change of pace from my exercise regime,' probably did not pass on a complete set of genetics to anyone else.

Within moments of the second gear's engagement, I felt my shoulder socket begin to ache. Multiplied by the attempts of my loins trying to grip the bull's back tighter, this increased the pressure on the nexus point between my legs. I began to feel lightheaded. And that wasn't the worst of it. The mixed drink I'd consumed far too quickly was being stirred with the cheeseballs in my stomach.

'I want to get off,' I stated quite adamantly to the cowboy.

'All's you have to do is let go of the rope.'

I tried. But I found with ultimate horror that my hand was stuck.

'I can't,' I said to the circling cowboy who was out of necessity my spotter.

'That's the spirit!'

'No, I mean, I can't let go.'

'We've all been there, man.'

The bull began to spin faster. Level three. Panic set in. With my free hand, I tugged on the other. At that point, there was nothing I wanted more than to be left in a dusty mess at the base of the mechanical bull, but I also knew, that with my hand stuck like that, if I let go with my legs, I was likely to dislocate a shoulder at best, or at worst, amputate my arm at the shoulder.

'You need to stop this, now!' I shouted at Mr. Cowboy.

'You can do it! You're doing great! Nobody makes it past level three on their first try.'

'You're not listening! My hand is stuck, and I can't get off! Where is the emergency ejection button?'

'That's funny! Give it a little more time and I'll stop it. I think you're getting the hang of it.'

The bull was really beginning to jerk. The crowd noise continued to rise to a frenzied pitch. If I could have looked around, I was sure that even the line-dancing troupe was leaning against the fence watching me.

'Are y'all ready for level 4?' the cowboy screamed to the gathered crowd.

The onlookers went wild as they circled their hats above their heads and stomped their feet.

'No, no, No, NO!' I shouted, but no one could hear me as the bucking bull suddenly went ballistic. I whipped forward and backward, sideways. I desperately tried to disengage my hand from the rope while simultaneously feeling the grim claws of nausea. I'd been on amusement park rides like this before and I knew that I had to get off or...

'Please!' I shouted. 'You have to sto...' As my mouth opened for the word 'STOP!', cheeseballs and a very mixed drink became a stream of lumpy, projectile vomit. What were shouts of encouragement became sounds of revulsion. Three members of the audience in the front row were left stunned by the remnants of my stomach splashed across their striped shirts. A semi-masticated cheeseball was deposited on the wide-brimmed hat of the very large man who was supposed to be controlling the mechanical bull.

They were stunned, and I felt worse than I ever had in my entire life. Finally, Wendy parted the crowd and grabbed the cowboy by the front of his shirt. 'Turn it off!' she shouted in his face. Her words brought him to life. In slow motion, he reached behind him and punched the red button. Mercifully, the bull cruised to a stop and finally, with immense difficulty, I freed my hand from the rope and fell to the ground.

Wendy rushed to my side. The world was spinning so badly, I felt as if death would be a welcome addition to my life. I wanted to stay there, curled in a ball, ignoring the rest of the world which murmured with disgust. The ladies whose outfits had been ruined by my vomit had already departed for the bathroom, and the cowboy was leaning over Wendy's back as she knelt by my side. A partially digested cheeseball dropped onto the floor near my face.

'Benson, are you okay?'

'No.'

'Where does it hurt most?'

'My pride.' She put a hand on my back, and I pulled away slightly. 'And my shoulder. And my... nether region.'

'Can you stand?'

'Maybe.'

With assistance from the cowboy, Wendy helped me from the floor. As I stood, she picked peanut shells and dirt from my shirt and hair. My shoulder ached fiercely, and my hand had some serious rope burns. As the crowd parted like the Red Sea, we staggered back to our barrel where the margarita pitcher had bled condensation onto the wood. Wendy's drink was half-finished.

I was never going to drink again.

'How are you feeling now?'

'About the same. Mostly embarrassed. Probably a little bruised.'

'You did really well,' she replied lamely.

'Whatever. Maybe we should go.'

'I'm sorry, Benson. I didn't mean for this to happen. I just wanted to have a good time.' She reached out and tenderly touched my cheek. In that gesture, despite the taste of vomit and cheeseballs, I felt something inescapably wonderful, something that surpassed the pain and shame I felt from the bull ride. Wendy is a beautifully complicated, soul. Perhaps we all are, just with different colors. The tenderness with which she touched me allowed me to recover not only my pride but my sense of fate.

'Would you be okay with going somewhere else for a little while. If you really want, we can come back later. I... did have fun... for part of the evening.'

'Maybe we can get a pizza and take it back to my place,' she said.

'I would really like that. But you might have to eat most of the pizza.'

She nodded and smirked. 'I'm still hungry.'

13
Patricia

The Palms were a big adjustment for me – for us. Gordon, my husband, never had a nickname, not in his entire life, until we arrived here. Dave called him *Gorgon*. Gordon didn't know why, and I hadn't the heart to tell him that a 'Gorgon' is a mythological creature – Medusa, you know – with snakes for hair and that simply seeing their face turns someone to stone. I don't think Gordon is quite that bad, even though he can be grumpy sometimes.

Gordon and I started our married life nearly forty-five years ago. It was on a family farm owned by my parents. Gordon's parents were farmers also, up there in northwest Iowa, not too far from where I grew up. We raised corn and soybeans year in and year out on 700 acres near Emmetsburg, saving enough money to retire to the city and winter in the south. We never thought we'd get that old to be snowbirds, but life has a funny way about it.

It went fast – all of it. We met at a gun club when he was 23 and I was 19. It was a beautiful, early summer evening. The lights were on at the range. The moths were bouncing off the bulbs. The sounds of 'PULL!' and gunshots could be heard sporadically across the acres. He was so handsome in his jeans and camouflage hunting shirt. I was serving non-alcoholic drinks to the shooters. I watched him for a while as he 'pulled' and shot. He knew I was watching him. After a few shots, he turned to me and smiled, took off his safety glasses and removed his noise canceling headset, and said…

'Do you want to have a try?'

Little did he know that I was a better shot than him. 'Sure.'

I set my tray down, took his glasses, headset, and 12-gauge. Five minutes later, after hitting twelve consecutive clay pigeons, he took his objects back with dropped-jawed admiration.

'Will you marry me?' he laughed.

'Not yet.'

13 – Patricia

It took three years.

Hunting was just an amusement. Gordon's one and only focus was the farm, and I liked that. I never wanted to leave the land either.

So we didn't. Not until we moved to the Palms. We rented out the land, sold the farmstead (that was a horrible day), and bought an apartment in Des Moines. Yes, there are many other places in the city we could have afforded, but the Palm Apartments felt like home the first second we walked onto the grounds.

During our time here over community meals (that took some getting used to, but we love it, now), Gladys, like most of the residents with their problems, has opened up to me about the details of her struggle with her daughter. We know firsthand about children and struggles. We have two kids, a boy and a girl, and our son has issues with dependency – not the drug-related kind, but depending on us to support him financially. We've had to curb his allowance now that he has turned forty. He tried desperately to get us to give the farmstead to him, but knowing his history of tenancy, it would have been wrecked in months.

Anyway, Gladys welcomed us on that first day, showed us the demo apartment which was clean and well-taken-care-of. She introduced us to some of the other tenants, mostly younger professional people, a few retirees like us, and then the oddballs, Dave and Benson.

At first blush, they seemed like replicas of our Jimmy, but after a while, they kind of grew on us. More like mold than anything. Not killer mold, just regular, old, stick-to-everything mold.

Gladys seemed to love them both, though she especially doted on Dave. I'm kind of partial to Benson myself, which is why I was worried when he arrived on that Monday morning driving a purple sports car and wearing a sling over his shoulder.

I was sitting on my balcony drinking my morning coffee. It was about 9:00, cool, not cold. The roar of the engine came from nowhere, and as it parked in the street, far away from every other car, Benson emerged. Even from that distance, I noticed that his hair was a mess, and he had deep bags under his eyes. It looked like he'd slept in the front seat.

He trudged slowly past Gladys's door, through the open part of the 'U' in the complex, and made his way to the steps on the opposite wing of the apartments to us.

Gordon was on his computer reading the news. His reading glasses were situated on the end of his nose and his index fingers were poised over the keyboard. 'Gordon.'

'Yuh?'

'Come out here.'

'I'm busy.'

'Look at Benson.'

'I don't care about Benson.'

'He looks like he's been in an accident.'

'So?'

'He's driving a purple sports car.'

'What?'

'In the street.'

I heard the clacking sound of the recliner leg being closed. Gordon made his way out the door and stood by my side. 'Over there,' I pointed to the car.

Gordon's whistle was low, impressed. 'That's a Lamborghini.'

'Is that expensive?'

He frowned at me. 'Does it look expensive?'

'Yes.'

'You answered your own question.'

Benson continued his ponderous walk to the steps near his second-floor apartment. His shirt was undone and his pants dirty.

'Are you all right, Benson?' I called out.

He stopped on the stairs and turned carefully. 'Yes, Patricia. I'll be fine.'

'What happened?'

'I don't want to talk about it.'

'Is that your car out there? The Lamborghini?' Gordon asked loudly.

13 – Patricia

'No.'

'Whose is it?'

'Dave's?'

Gordon and I turned towards each other and mouthed Dave's name. 'Why do you have it?'

'Like I said, I don't want to talk about it.'

'Were you in an accident?'

'No. Yes.'

'Which is it?' Gordon asked.

'The car is fine. The accident is of my own making.'

'Benson,' I called out, 'I'm coming over.'

'Please, Patricia. I'll tell you about it later.'

Gordon's brain had already gone technical. 'How did you drive a five speed with a sling on your arm?'

At this, Benson stopped at the top stair and rotated towards us. 'I have a high pain threshold, obviously.'

'Benson!'

With a rueful smile, he spun away from us without responding. He turned right at the top of the stairs and shuffled the last thirty feet to his apartment. Moments later, Dave's apartment door opened, and Dave went into Benson's without knocking.

'He looks like he got lucky,' Gordon said.

'Lucky? He's in a sling?'

Gordon smirked and began to walk back into our apartment.

I sat back down at the patio table. After a half an hour of trying to imagine what Benson had been doing for the weekend, my coffee turned cold, and the crossword puzzles were only half-finished. Why in the world was he driving that car? What was with the sling?

There just aren't that many things for us retirees to do other than poke our noses into other people's business. About the only thing I've got is questions, and the only thing I want is answers. I guess that's the difficult part about sliding down the back side of Aging Hill.

Anywho, we found out soon after what happened. I think it's romantic, but Gordon thinks it's laughable.

I guess after you're married as long as we have been, we can get along with differing perspectives.

14
Benson

'So, how did it go?' Dave rubbed his hands as if preparing for a meal. I didn't want to talk to him. This was all his fault.

'Do you have eyes?'

'Yes, can you not see them?'

'According to the doctor, I have a subluxed shoulder. Dislocated, in the vernacular. My right hand is rope-burned, and I still have vomit on my pants. And,' I stressed with particular vehemence below the belt, 'I've got peanut shells in my underwear.'

'Sounds like a true Greek tragedy.'

I growled as I threw my keys into the bowl on the kitchen island. I just wanted a shower, some ibuprofen, and some sleep. It was Monday, but a sick day was on tap.

Fortunately, the night did end well. We ended up at Pizza Hut and ate from the buffet rather than take it back to her house. It was cheaper that way. Wendy had a big appetite, which was admirable, but, due to the fact that my gut was still roiling, I mostly just watched her eat. After the meal, she took me to the hospital to have the shoulder checked out. She said she loved driving the Lamborghini, to which I responded, 'You probably shouldn't get used to it.' We went to her house and stayed up until 3:00 in the morning. Just talking. Unfortunately, the drive home was miserable after only three hours of sleep.

'Go away. I want to clean up and lie down.'

'Give me the deets, though. How was the car?'

I told him about the warning ticket and the real one. He was impressed. I left out most of the details regarding the amorous moments, but went into full recollection when telling him about the mechanical bull. He seemed greatly interested in how it worked.

'I'll have to try it sometime.'

'I think you should,' I responded spitefully.

'When do you think you'll see her again?' he asked as he stuck his fingers into his belt loops.

'I have no idea. Not this week, for sure.'

Instead of leaving, Dave plopped down on my sofa which sent puffs of dust into the air. He stretched his long arms out along the back and crossed his legs.

'Please, go back to your own apartment.'

'It was an interesting day while you were gone yesterday.'

I continued in the kitchen touching my pockets for anything that couldn't go through the washing machine.

'It seems that there are new developments here in the Palms. A few relationship issues. Some people are talking about getting rid of the fishpond, something about animal rights, which I agree with, but our fish are very happy. Don't you think our fish are happy?'

I didn't respond.

'And then, Gladys.'

'What about her?'

'I think she still wakes up hearing the screaming of the lambs.'

'I realize you want me to say, "What?" but I'm not going to give in. Do you hear me, Dave?'

He nodded slowly. 'There are many people in this complex that hear the lambs.'

'You're so weird.'

'I know.'

I didn't really want the conversation to continue, so I went into the bathroom to shed my clothes and stuff them into the washing machine. They still reeked, but it wasn't overwhelming. As I stood there in my underwear and socks, Dave rounded the door. I saw his face in the mirror. Shadows had formed around his eyes and cheeks where the light from my medicine cabinet illuminated the pointier parts of his appearance.

'I'm not in the mood, Dave. Please, go back to your apartment. We'll talk later.'

Instead of leaving, he crossed his arms and leaned against the doorframe. 'I met another interesting person.'

'Great.'

'You don't want to hear about him?'

I grabbed the clothes detergent and fabric softener, poured them into the dispensers, then cranked the dial. 'No, I don't.'

'Why not?'

I wheeled on him. 'I haven't had much sleep, Dave. Thank you for the use of the Lamborghini. Thank you for letting me take it to see Wendy. Those are things I really appreciate, but what would be better for me is if you would just… go.'

After grabbing my phone, I flipped the light switch sending the bathroom into darkness. Moving past Dave, I turned right into my bedroom. There were clothes everywhere. I probably should have filled the washing machine, but it was already running. The room smelled of cheap cologne and dirty socks, not a great combination. If Wendy was ever going to stay here with me, I was going to need to professionally clean and disinfect it.

I flopped onto my bed. Then, with a brief thought of work, I rolled over and texted my boss to tell him that I'd be taking a sick day.

Once the message sent, I rolled onto my back, stuck my feet under the covers, then realized I still had peanut shells in my underwear. Sighing, I rolled over to the side of the bed and rifled through the treasure chest to rid the jewels of any crusty doubloons that shouldn't have been there. While I was at it, I felt the bed shake. Dave had lain down on the other side of the bed.

'For Pete's sake!' I shouted at him. 'Get out of my bed! Go home!'

'I wanted to tell you about the fascinating person I met.'

I covered my head with pillows. Despite Dave's presence, I began to fall asleep. The last thing I heard him say through the muffled pillows was…

'…*Marty. He's a gun dealing alcoholic.*'

15
Marty

Sorry, I'm late to the party. You haven't met me yet, but my role in this whole thing coming up was delayed by the fact that I hadn't met Dave until the meeting.

Dave always said I was a fleshy sack of contradictions. He might have been right.

I'm probably the handsomest man you'd ever meet. No tattoos. I eat well, take care of my body, or I do now.

AND... I'm also a gun dealer.

AND... an alcoholic. Barely functioning, as purported by my ex and her family, but able to run my shop, nonetheless.

The gun store is located in a rundowny part of Des Moines surrounded by derelict buildings with old bricks peeling white paint. The front doors of my shop are gated at night, and, at the end of every day, I make sure that none of the merchandise is missing. I've got an eye for detail... and an eye for tail.

I know, I'm a misogynist. I can't help it. Another one of my predilections inherited from a father who treated the women in his life with open condescension and aggression. When I'm not drinking, I am able to look women in the eye. Unfortunately, until two years ago, sobriety was a real struggle. At the insistence of my ex (and law enforcement), I entered Alcoholics Anonymous with a closed mind and a generous chip on my shoulder. Eventually, the mind opened, and the chip became kindling for something better in my life. Thanks to AA meetings, and my fortuitous meeting with Dave, I felt like a new man.

Still handsome and a *wee* bit chauvinistic, but much better than I was.

Now, you've just about reached the part in the story where life was going to change for Dave, Letitia, Benson – even me – but that's the point of stories: change is necessary and often painful.

15 – Marty

Benson and me have had our run ins, especially during the upcoming parts of this narrative. He was a decent sort of fellow, a little high-strung and wildly paranoid, somewhat autisticky for my likes. Him and Dave were closer until Dave met me.

We won't go there quite yet. You'll hear from me in a little while as my part, though smallish, is imprinted painfully in the bigger picture of Dave's life. Be patient with Dave – with all of us – if you can.

I'm heading down to the shop now. I have to change the signs in the windows. It's not long until the Christmas-buying season, you see, and people buy guns even after Christmas. Sounds strange, doesn't it?

What did you get for Christmas?

A semi-automatic shotgun. New Year's bargain.

Oh, that's nice.

Though this is what I do for a living, I wish the world was different. I really do. But there's too much money to be made. And I need money to survive.

I hope someone like Dave will be at the shop today.

Nothing like having weird conversations over Sig-Sauers.

16
Gladys

Eleanor was twenty-two when she moved out of the apartment at the Palms. We had lived here for ten wonderful years, or at least they were for me. As my only child, she fulfilled my needs for comfort and support. I hired her as part of the cleaning team for the complex, though she never really took a liking to scrubbing the public spaces.

Eleanor's father never lived here, thank God. In fact, he's never even seen the place. Though his own daughter grew up at the Palms, he never made an attempt. Never called. Never even tried. Maybe that was part of the reason why she left. I think there was some small part of her that wanted to find him, to be successful, and to shove it in his face. I know I would have liked to do that myself, but instead, with my degenerating body and physical inabilities, I have had my hands full just managing the Palms. Anyway, I don't want him here. I want Eleanor with me.

When she left, she was so excited. Her hair had been pulled up into a high ponytail on the back of her head. Her brown eyes were impatient, and her hands fidgeted with the car keys. After finishing packing, she squirmed beside her open car door, bouncing slightly on the balls of her feet. I walked slowly wanting to draw out time, to keep her little – with me. Much to her embarrassment, I couldn't control the tears from streaming down my cheeks. So, when she finally chucked her last bag into the back seat of her car, she gave me a quick squeeze and a promise, *I'll call you soon.* The promise turned into dust as I didn't hear her voice for two months. She texted me when she got to college, but that was about it. Just a few messages about grades, and food, and a few brief stories about classes, but no information about friends or love interests, or even her health. It was a very difficult time for me.

What had been a very close connection in early days, maybe too close from Eleanor's perspective, was severed by adulthood and a desire for adventure. Eleanor was my trembling thread to sanity and the last of

16 – Gladys

my close relationships, except for some of the residents. She was my source of conversation and amusement. She was everything to me.

And then, she was gone.

That was six years ago. I know, I know, enough time has passed that I shouldn't be sentimental and emotional about it, but I can't help it. I still go into her room to breathe the air, to smell the memories of her childhood, and to remember. When she was young and she needed me.

But her room gets me every time.

Nobody tells you about the stuffed animals.

They are neatly positioned on top of her bed staring at me with beady glass eyes, mouths fixed in permanently happy grins. They are stuffed full of memories and reminders of different times when she was little, my baby, and now they sit as guardians of my grief. When I look at them, I am taken back to the bouncing, curly-haired girl, gap-toothed and boisterous, who pointed out everything to me, as if I'd never seen a squirrel, a large floating cloud, a daisy, or a black and white puppy straining at its leash. The stuffed animals remind me of how lonely I am.

Eleanor is a graduate of Wake Forest and now a lawyer in Charlotte, North Carolina. She got close to a serious relationship, once – Michael was his name – but Eleanor had a couple of things going against her: my failed relationship and her love of work.

She calls me every couple of months but I know she doesn't enjoy it. My life reminds her too much of failures. And this little apartment is a shadow of an old life she doesn't want to revisit.

I went to Charlotte once. I flew. That was an amazing experience, let me tell you. I held onto the armrests for dear life. It felt like a rollercoaster and a bus ride at the same time. The woman sitting next to me kept looking at me out of the corner of her eye as if waiting for me to puke or scream or something, but I was very proud of myself to keep everything in. When we landed, my legs felt wobbly, but I was already ruing the return trip.

Well, they say that what doesn't kill you makes you stronger, but with regards to air travel, I'd rather not get any stronger.

I told Dave about my trip to Charlotte once. He smiled and nodded, you know that Iowa nice nod where you lean your head backward, bob it a couple of times, and pinch your lips together and say, 'Ya, ya, I know what you mean.'

'Have you ever been on a plane before, Dave?'

'Nope.'

'Then why did you say 'I know what you mean'?'

'Because I, too, have felt like puking and screaming at the same time.'

'When?'

'It was an IMAX and the screen was all around you, over your head, to the sides, I mean really weird feeling. It was this water adventure where they take you through the water cycle. The cameras simulated evaporation, rising from the ground, and then cold air currents, and the seats shook you. A real sensory experience. Then came the wind and storms and for Pete's sake the camera was blown all over the place. Plenty of people were screaming, and even though they told us, 'If you feel sick or dizzy just close your eyes,' you forget that piece of advice when you're scared. So we're falling to the ground, it's rushing up at us, and just when we're about to splat onto a tree or something, we land in a river which, of course, rushes us down the current to a waterfall. Yup, that's where I started screaming. I remember the lady next to me covering her ears.' Dave patted my shoulder. 'I sure know what you mean.'

'Dave, that's nothing like riding on a plane.'

'Okay. I don't know what you mean then.'

'But it was so nice to see her, Eleanor, that is.'

'Why?'

I know it was Dave's way, but the question caught me off guard. Why was I glad to see her? *Was* I glad to see her? Or, was I just glad to get out of Des Moines?

Eleanor had changed. She lived in a big house and had a fancy blue car. It had a screen that allowed you to see behind the vehicle, so you didn't run into things. And she kept telling me about all the stuff she was buying, and all the places where she was traveling, and taking pictures – oh, the pictures. I saw some of them on Facebook and such, but she wasn't really great at telling me about them.

'I don't know why, Dave. I guess it's just something parents say.'

'It doesn't sound like you like your daughter very much anymore.'

'That's not very nice, Dave. I love her.'

'There's a big difference between loving your daughter and liking who she's become.'

'I'm proud of her.'

'Hmm… Yes, well, I can be proud that I found a penny on the road, but that doesn't exactly make me better off.'

'You're not making any sense.'

Dave was quiet, then he took a breath, stopped, and started again. 'Being proud of someone's accomplishments sometimes just means you're proud of yourself, that you had a role in the process. It's more about you than it is about the person who did the job.'

I felt stabbed to the heart. Was I proud of Eleanor's lifestyle so that people would say to me, 'Oh, you must be so proud to be the mother of a lawyer,' or was I proud of Eleanor who worked so hard to become who she was? 'Oh, Dave…'

He touched me on the shoulder, not in condescension, and not really in an apologetic way. 'Why did you go to Charlotte? To see Eleanor, or to see how Eleanor lives?'

I felt my lower lip trembling. 'I don't know.'

'Why do you love Eleanor?'

'That's so unfair, Dave. I don't even know her anymore.'

'Aha!' He shouted exultantly. 'And therein lies the problem.'

I took a tissue from my bra and blew my nose. 'What problem?'

'Gladys, you can't really like someone you don't know, not really, anyway. You haven't seen her for what? Two or three years?' I nodded and held up two fingers.

He pointed to one of the pictures on my wall, a senior photo of Eleanor in a pretty blue dress which emphasized her eyes. 'In your mind, you picture her as that eighteen-year-old, or maybe even younger, when she relied on you for everything. She needed you, which is what *you* needed. You don't know her anymore because she doesn't need you like that, and when you try to make her need you, or make her *feel* that way, she doesn't *want* you.'

'It feels like you're being mean.'

'Truth is more like tobacco than chocolate.'

'But I don't like feeling like this.' My eyes glistened with tears. 'What do I do?'

Dave leaned back in his chair and ran his fingers through his sideburns. 'Get used to the French kiss of disappointment.'

'What?'

'It's when two people kiss open mouthed and their tongues…'

'I know what a French kiss is, Dave, but what does that have to do with disappointment?'

He stopped rubbing his sideburns. They were standing straight out from his face. 'People like to think if they act a certain way, or if they live a certain way, life is going to be paved with emeralds, and nobody is going to fart. But let's be honest here, Gladys, every once in a while, you meet that person you don't like, and for some reason you end up making out with them in spite of it. When you move in for that special, non-magic moment, your lips meet, and then part and sure enough, he's had Doritos, a morning coffee, and smoked half a pack of cigarettes. That, my friend, is DISAPPOINTMENT. You don't want to be kissing him, but you put yourself in that place just by being alive.'

'That's disgusting, Dave.'

'Yes, so is disappointment.'

'So, what do we do about it?'

'We need to figure out how to get you to like your daughter again. Never mind being proud or loving her – ya gots ta like her.'

'How do I do that if I never see her or talk to her?'

16 – *Gladys*

'I've got an idea.' His index finger shot up into the air. 'We have to get you used to the idea of Eleanor being an adult. We've got to change all the photos in this house. Take down the baby photos and the coloring photos and the cute-as-a-furry-rabbit photos. Eleanor is a woman, and a highly successful one at that. If you ever want her to come back here, or if you ever want to really interact with her again, change your perspective.'

'I change the photos?'

'That's a start.'

'What do I do with them?'

He shrugged. 'Either give them to her or throw them away?'

'What?'

'They're holding you back, Gladys. If you were doing well and handling all this, and not staring at stuffed animals in a bedroom that hasn't changed in nine years…'

'Six.'

'Whatever. Then you could keep the photos up there with the new ones of Eleanor who is now a beautiful, successful, mature woman.'

'How about I just put them in a box? I really didn't want to get rid of all those memories.'

'Dadgummit, Gladys, do you want to like your daughter or not?'

'Okay, okay, I'll… I'll put them in an envelope and send them to her.'

'No, no, no – not through the mail.' He pounded his fist on my sofa and dust bunnies flew in the air. 'Just hold on to them until she comes to see you.'

'She won't come back to Des Moines.'

'After I'm done with you, she will.'

I looked into his eyes and saw a strange determination that I hadn't seen many times before. 'And after that?'

'We're going to renovate the apartment.'

'I can't do that, Dave. I don't have the money.'

'I guess we'll have to get you a raise, then.'

'And how are we going to do that?'

'I'll take care of that. Don't you worry about it.'

'Anything else? Jenny Craig? Should I lose fifty pounds?'

'What the heck do your looks have to do with anything? If your looks were what mattered to Eleanor, she would have left long before she did.'

I looked down at my clothes.

'It's not your clothes, either,' he said, reading my mind.

'Then what is it?'

'We have to get you used to speaking to people the age Eleanor is now. Mid-twenties.'

'Who are you thinking of? Letitia?'

'No,' he snorted. 'She's black. You need someone white. Someone you don't know, too. Like Eleanor. You don't know her either.'

'Dave,' I rolled my eyes, 'if you were a normal person, I'd have thrown something at you by now.'

'Wouldn't hurt. You're probably a terrible pitcher.'

'Wow. Anything else you'd like to offend me with?'

Dave leaned forward on the edge of my tattered sofa. 'Do you want to like your daughter or not.'

I nodded. 'Like.'

'I've got an idea of someone who would be perfect. Someone you don't know. Someone who will engage you in conversation.'

'Who?'

17
Wendy

I felt like I was meeting Benson's parents or brothers and sisters for the first time, but he had assured me that everything would be just fine. Don't be nervous. They're normal people. Except for Dave.

Don't worry.

Have you ever had anyone tell you that before? *Don't worry. I've got everything under control. You'll enjoy yourself, I promise. Everything will be...*

Invariably, everything is not *just fine*. It borders on atrocious, and you walk away from the event thinking, 'I don't know if I'll be trusting that person any time soon.'

At that moment, I had a sneaking suspicion that the event was all a set up and somehow Dave was pulling the marionette strings behind the scenes. Ugh.

Since our semi-disastrous first date, bull riding/dancing night, we had talked almost every day. Benson is surprisingly verbal. I assumed that because he spent so much time online he would only like to text, but not so, thankfully. He's got an opinion about most things – uninformed opinions, yes – but at least he's willing to carry on the conversation and let me have my opinion also. Makes me feel like I'm in a relationship of equals rather than what I've been used to.

It was a strangely wonderful thing to be nervous. The fingers gripping my stomach meant that what Benson and I had going was more than just infatuation. I was old enough to be thinking about the future. Unfortunately, I was worried about Dave being the wild card in everything. Benson had a tendency to carry on about him. So many unnecessary details about Dave's habits and daily events. If that was the worst thing about Benson, I was golden.

I was thirty miles from Des Moines when my phone rang. I answered it through my car's Bluetooth. Benson's voice came out too loud and I turned him down.

'Benson.'

'Wendy.'

'Is everything okay?'

'Sure it is. Absopositively perfectamundo. How far away are you?' He asks.

'Colfax.'

'Hurry.'

'What's the rush?'

'I just want to be near you.'

Hmmm. 'All right, what's going on. Give me the real truth. What aren't you telling me?'

Silenced shrouded the cab of my car. At first, I thought I'd lost connection, but then he spoke, and it sounded like he'd been holding his breath because everything spilled out quickly.

'You're right. I should tell you.'

The sense of doom rose like a mushroom cloud. 'Tell me what?' I took my foot off the accelerator and the pickup slowed to sixty miles per hour. Cars began to pass me, cars with rusty fenders and dirty panels with bumper stickers about politics and football teams.

'Look, Wendy, I don't want you to think I've invited you on false pretenses, because I really do want to see you. I really want you to see where I live, and the people I hang out with. But there are a few more people than originally planned. They all want to meet you.'

'Uh, what are we talking about here? Fifteen or twenty?'

'North.'

I frowned. 'Forty?'

'Uh-uh.'

'Just tell me!'

'I think the reservation count was eighty-four.'

'RESERVATION COUNT! What is this, a frickin' wedding reception?'

It seemed like Benson almost choked on my use of the word 'wedding'. 'No, no, really, it's just that… well, Dave can get a little out of hand when it comes to community gatherings. I know, I know,' I could

17 – Wendy

tell he was holding up the hand that wasn't holding the phone and he was probably pacing, too. 'I probably should have left Dave out of this, but he likes you. And I want him to like you.' A pause. 'And I want you to like him too.'

I knew it.

Frickin' *Dave*. Bull hockey.

In the end, he was going to ruin everything.

'That's not the way it works, Benson.' I pulled off onto the shoulder of Interstate 80. 'When you want someone to trust you, you do trustworthy things. Tell the truth and stuff like that.' I glanced at the time. It was 5:20 on a Saturday afternoon in late September. Cool, already. Getting dark. Most farmers were half-done harvesting and preparing for their trip south.

'Yes,' he whined, 'but this is different. It was supposed to be a surprise, like a surprise party. You like surprises, right?'

'Does the sound of my voice give off the impression that I like this surprise?'

'No, not really.'

'Benson, how much am I going to hate what is about to happen?'

'Like on a scale of one to ten, one being a checkup and ten being a root canal without Novocain?'

'Sure.'

'Well… maybe a 4.8.'

'Crap.'

'But,' he stated loudly into the phone, 'I'll be right with you the whole time.'

I rolled my eyes, tapped my hands on the steering wheel, and started driving again. 'So now it's at a 4.7.'

'Don't be like that, Wen.'

I swear, I thought I'd never put myself at the disposal of another guy again, but dammit, Benson is so sexy and lovable, especially when he calls me 'Wen'. He's kind and courteous. He makes mistakes and apologizes. Those are all the things I find attractive in a man.

'I'll be there in twenty-five minutes.'

'Yay!' He hung up before I could rethink my decision. I wanted to ask him what the lineup of the 84 people was, but what difference would it make? I'd only met Dave once, and the stories Benson tells me about Dave's girlfriend, her daughter, and clingers-on don't fill me with restless anticipation. Benson had mentioned something about all of them, but I hadn't seen any photos. Benson's not great with photos.

One mile from his apartment complex, I checked my appearance in the mirror. Same old face, same hair. I'm not sure what he sees in me, but love-blindness can't be all bad.

Love.

We hadn't said that word yet, but it was coming. I could feel it, like a zit. It was gonna hurt, but when it was over, I'd be relieved. Just a scar that would fade.

I rechecked my complexion in the mirror for any zits. Thankfully, no.

I took my hands off the steering wheel and brushed the crumbs from my clothes. I was wearing jeans and a nice shirt with a sweater over the top. I'd spent some time on light makeup, something I never did. It's not necessary in my line of work. I did it for Benson.

My GPS guided me the half-mile to the Palms and suddenly, almost dangerously, I was greeted by people holding placards saying, 'GREETINGS, WENDY!' and 'CAN'T WAIT TO MEET YOU!' 'TIME TO GET YOUR PARTY ON!'

I had to give it to Benson (or more likely, Dave); it did feel kind of nice to be greeted so royally. They appeared joyful and cold. Many were wearing sweatshirts and earmuffs. A few of the older ones had their winter coats on, not the full downy ones, but the ones they sit in to watch football games.

I turned into the parking lot across the street from the apartment complex, pulled into a spot, and stared across the road into the courtyard to see that a marquee had been set up in the middle. Standing heat lamps were erected sporadically underneath and half a dozen grills sent black

17 – Wendy

smoke into the air. A young Hispanic woman approached my car and mouthed the words, *Are you Wendy?* through my windshield. When I nodded, she shouted exultantly to the others behind her that I had indeed arrived. She opened the door for me, and after I got out of the car, she led me towards the throng of well-wishers. The crowd parted like the Red Sea until finally Benson greeted me with a kiss. The Hispanic woman issued an 'Awww, isn't that cute?'

'You made it.'

'Miraculously, yes.'

Benson led me by the hand towards the marquee. Its peaks were roughly ten feet high and decorated with flags fluttering in the breeze like pennants on the spires of a castle. They whipped in the wind, snapping yellow and red against the dull gunmetal sky. Even though I wore my sweater, I shivered. Benson noticed and wrapped his arm around me.

On the way to the marquee, he introduced me to so many people, I was overwhelmed. I thanked them for the wonderful welcome.

I came to find out that it was a tradition at the Palms for people to gather to celebrate each other. It's strange and romantic and revolutionary. To celebrate people simply because they live near you; that's something from a different time and a different planet. Most of the people on my street in Davenport stay inside their own castles, surrounded by their moats of indifference, jousting with their boredom and lack of productivity.

We moved between braziers, and I felt the heat cake my skin and warm it almost immediately. I thanked Benson for his chivalry. He dropped his arm, but he didn't move away.

Beneath the marquee, a hodgepodge of tables had been set up stretching from one end to the other. The length of the connected tables was about fifty feet and was a cornucopia of color. An assortment of tablecloths and napkins, some from children's parties long ago – an Elsa face peered up at me with questioning eyes as if I was an imposter in her world. There were bowls and plates and silverware, all Corningware and ceramic. Lots of dishes to be done afterwards. Because the sun was setting, someone had strung lights through the crossbars above – Christmas lights which illuminated the eating area below. The entire gathering was bathed in a rainbow of happiness. People milled about with either warm drinks or cans of beer. More and more people approached me, including a woman in her fifties who introduced herself as Gladys. She seemed very, very nervous, as if somehow I was about to bring down the fist of doom squarely on top of her head.

At the far end of the marquee was an inflatable swimming pool/fish pond. Inside it were a dozen goldfish being fed by a handful of children. One of the boys threw a rock at the fish which brought about the wrath of his mother. She grabbed him by the arm and gave him an earful. Her index finger was pointed at the end of his nose. I've done that to some people on the Mississippi before. I've never thought of it as mother-ish, but I can see how it might be interpreted that way.

Dave stood at the far end of the tent by one of the grills. He was talking to two young African American men. Dave wore an apron with the image of a bare-chested weightlifter. On his head was a floppy Chef's hat with some writing on it which I couldn't read from that distance. He saw me and raised a mug of steaming something or other. Knowing Dave, or what Benson had told me about Dave, it was probably hot apple cider which he brewed himself. In the basement. In the dark.

The sun kissed the western horizon carefully. Cold descended upon those who were outside the marquee forcing them closer to the braziers underneath. Conversation filled the space.

'How did this all come about?' I asked Benson.

'It's Dave. He loves parties. Let me amend that – he loves to throw parties.'

'Why is that?'

'Maybe he never got to have them when he was younger. He was fostered, you know.'

'How could I possibly know that?'

'Sorry.'

17 – Wendy

I placed a hand on Benson's arm. 'You don't have to apologize. What's the story?'

'He doesn't talk about it much, but every so often Ignatius stops by. That's Dave's guardian – er, kind of.'

He pointed to an elderly gentleman on our right close to another one of the barbecues. He was a black man of medium height and build, unremarkable in many ways, but his eyes were wide-set and intelligent, framed by horn-rimmed glasses. He wore a dark coat with a green scarf. He had curly, salt and pepper hair and a wide face.

'Dave's parents died when he was little, and his aunt and uncle 'took care of him.' I use quotation marks because what little he says about them is that they wanted 'to take care' of his inheritance.'

'Is he rich?'

'It's hard to tell. I don't think so. But, he seems to be able to buy or rent whatever he wants at a moment's notice. The things he owns…' Benson motioned to the surrounding buildings, dirty two-story domiciles, endless stucco, and staircases. The connected roofs were splotched and the walls chickenpoxed with wasps' nests. There was no car in the parking lot younger than ten years old, other than the Mercedes, which I assumed belonged to the judge.

'When Dave's court case came up, it happened to fall on the day that the Honorable Ignatius Stackworth was sitting on the bench. Dave must have impressed him so much that the judge decided to follow his progress. That was a long time ago.'

'Does Dave have this impact on everyone he meets? What is it about him?'

We both stared in Dave's direction. He and the boys had been joined at the barbecue by another older gentleman and his wife. She clung to her partner's arm and glanced around nervously. 'That's Patricia and Gordon.' Dave shook Gordon's hand and then tapped his cheek.

'He's one of a kind, that's for sure. I don't know, Wendy, it's like… Words escape me. Dave is part Teflon, part fly paper. He experiences everything and yet nothing sticks, nothing phases him, but he remembers all things.'

We were joined by Gladys who held a red Dixie cup. There was a nervous energy radiating from her that I found strange.

'Hi,' Gladys said. She slurped from the cup and then began to chew a piece of ice.

'Hello.'

She cleared her throat and tapped her chest as if choking on the ice cube.

'I've heard a lot about you. Um, Benson says you're wonderful.'

Benson's face crinkled up, and he tilted his head at her.

'Thank you.' I spoke to Gladys, but stared at Benson.

'I'm making such a mess of this.'

'Gladys, are you okay?' Benson asked.

'Mm hmmm, yes, just fine, thank you. I'm nervous.'

'About what?'

'Uh, I get that way around new people. I'm so happy for you both.'

Gladys had fleshy cheeks and a thin, transparent moustache under her nose. Her eyes had been shadowed sky blue, and her eyelashes were mascaraed within an inch of their lives. Gladys's hair was thin and fake blonde, recently dyed. Her outfit was retro – a designer sweatsuit, puffy jacket and Birkenstock sandals with white socks.

'I'm happy for me too, but what are you happy about?'

Gladys had difficulty swallowing and sucked in her cheeks to get the moisture at least near the back of her mouth. It made a strange noise as the swallow started – a *crrrking* sound and then, with relief, the saliva passed down the tube.

'That you're so happy! I've always wanted my own daughter to be happy like that. You know, from what Dave tells me, I think you and her are about the same age.'

Gladys launched into a lengthy saga about her daughter in one of the Carolinas, a lawyer who doesn't really care that much for her mother. The longer the story went, the more I could almost identify with the

17 – Wendy

daughter. I felt Benson tensing next to me. His eyes were wide, his jaw was clenched, but his lips were moving. He was mouthing some kind of words at Gladys like, *What are you doing?* He caught me catching him and he smiled guiltily. I felt sympathy for Gladys because she had no idea what she was doing, only that her voice was overfilling a conversational balloon that was about to burst.

'I'm sorry for the pain you're feeling,' I said.

Suddenly, as if wakened from a dream, Gladys finally noticed us. Her face turned red.

'Oh my. I'm such an idiot. Will you both forgive me? It's just… Dave told me this might happen.' Our eyes followed hers to Dave where he lifted his glass again.

'What do you mean,' Benson asked, 'that "Dave told you *this* might happen"?' What is '*this*'?'

She looked startled by the question. What had Dave told her to do?

'I'll… well,' she stammered, 'we'll talk about it later.' She turned with a flourish, her sweatshirt billowed outwards flashing a bit of belly skin, and was out from under the canvas canopy before we could say, 'What?'

Benson was completely flabbergasted by what had just occurred. 'Do you want something to drink? A beer?'

'Yes, but what was that all about? That might have been the weirdest conversation I've ever had in my life?'

'I have no idea.'

With my wildlife-Spidey senses (I can usually tell when someone is lying to me), I scanned his face for deceit. He was telling the truth. 'Benson, we didn't bring any beer.'

'It doesn't matter.' He reached down into the nearest cooler and grabbed two cans of beer, handing one to me.

'You just take anybody's drinks?'

He shrugged and popped the lid. It shushed out over the rim, and he covered it with his lips trying to corral the foam. Once he had tamed the brew, he licked the opening. 'Every Saturday we fill these coolers, and anyone can grab from anywhere. It's not like we're putting out Dom Perignon.'

I prised open my beer and took a sip. The acrid liquid burned my throat, and I wanted to belch, but I couldn't because Ignatius had moved in beside us. He was taller than both Benson and I (which was not really saying much). His mug was steaming. Apple cider, by the smell. I glanced at my beer and felt odd, like I'd done something wrong. I always feel that way when I'm drinking and someone else isn't. It's like being caught by my parents with a liquor bottle in the barn.

'I'm Ignatius Stackworth.'

'That's quite the name.'

'If I could go back in time and talk to my parents, I'd ask for something like 'Joe' or 'Luke'.'

'No, I like it.'

'Ignatius is a judge...' Benson announced abruptly.

'Was...' Ignatius corrected.

'*Was...*' Benson said, 'when Dave's case came up all those years ago.'

'Yes, you told me.'

Ignatius pondered us over the rims of his glasses. 'It was quite a deal. He had been living with his aunt and uncle, but preferred his foster parents.'

'So why did he go with his aunt and uncle?'

'He had no choice. They were the last resort. Kids fall through the cracks, and the court system simply wants to fill the cracks with the easiest possible solution.'

'What happened to his parents?' I asked.

A very uncomfortable pause ensued. 'They died tragically.'

'How?'

'You'll have to talk to Dave about it. He is very private about that information.'

'Okay,' I responded slowly.

17 – Wendy

'His case was abnormal.' He glanced over at Dave who was flipping hotdogs on the barbecue.

'You mean Dave is abnormal?' I asked sarcastically.

A grin played at the side of his mouth. 'Well, yes, but not in the way you might have meant it. Dave's abnormality is that he lives *beyond* things. I don't know if that makes sense.'

'It doesn't.'

The judge scratched his jaw. 'I have followed Dave's journey over the years, from age thirteen until now, and I've finally come to understand Dave's personality is *beyond* me. He cares about everyone, but he doesn't care what they think.'

'What is he, a saint?'

Both Ignatius and Benson held up their hands at the same time. 'No, no, no,' Ignatius said good-naturedly. 'Dave is anything but that. I've had to pull him out of trouble more than once.'

Suddenly, Gladys interrupted again. She tugged on my arm daintily, and when I turned, she offered me another beer.

'Thank you, but no, I've already got one.'

She appeared crestfallen, like a child who had offered her parents a hand-colored self-portrait, and they declined to put it on the fridge.

'Can I talk to you for a few more minutes?'

This was not at all how I felt like spending my afternoon. Granted, I could see she was struggling with self-confidence and probably needed some psychiatric help, but it's not my job to…

'Thank you so much,' she yanked my arm even before I could agree. We walked slowly toward the corner block with the word OFFICE stenciled on the front glass. The wind had picked up slightly and she shivered. I, too, felt the cold.

'Maybe we should stay under the tent near the braziers?' I suggested.

'Soon.' Gladys produced a key to open the office door. 'Do you mind?'

'No.' *Yes.*

The office was warm and dark. When the fluorescent lights flickered above us, I noticed worn, upholstered furniture took up most of the room. None of it matched in color, only in decade. 80's, I guessed. On the far side of the room, the front desk cordoned off another door which read APARTMENT 1. The desk was chest high with a chipped, faux-marble laminate top. A small metal bell squatted in the middle with a curled Post-it note that read, *Ring if unattended.* A faded old telephone, yellow, replete with curly cord, clung to the back wall alongside an ancient swimsuit calendar. A hairy-chested man with beach bunnies on each side smiled lasciviously at me. I cringed. I was thankful that Benson did not have a hairy chest like that. I wasn't into Magnum P. I. at all.

Gladys unlocked the APARTMENT 1 door. Before entering, she glanced back at me questioningly. I frowned and followed. If she had been a man, I had a feeling that was how serial killers behaved. You know, getting them to help you move furniture into the back of a van, and suddenly you become another person's suit. As it was, it felt like I had as much to fear from Gladys as I would have from Benson. Probably less, other than an assault on my ears.

Her voice was high-pitched, whiny, like a giant mosquito with nasal issues, and it sounded like she was perpetually discontented. As we walked through to her connected apartment, she used it to describe parts of her life that I didn't really want (or need) to know. Where she went to school; how many years Eleanor had braces; a fight she and her husband had before Halloween. There was so much narrative, I felt the apartment constrict.

Moving further inwards, halogen lights flickered as she flipped switches. She only gave a passing reference to her living area, one with an old television set, a large, threadbare beanbag in the corner, and a dusty coffee table with women's magazines scattered across it.

Instead of remaining in the living area, she led me down a short hallway to a bedroom on the left. It was at this juncture where I began to feel completely uncomfortable.

17 – Wendy

When we turned into the room, I almost took a step back out. The room was a shrine. I can't describe it as anything else. It was visual overload, and my brain whirred like a computer with too many tabs open.

The walls were completely full of photos of a young girl at various stages of development. Obviously, this was the Eleanor, the daughter and the lawyer who Gladys was babbling about outside. On one wall was the journey from birth to school. On the opposite wall from where I was standing were elementary school years with every school picture. There were gappy grins with lost teeth. There were three with her hair parted directly down the middle. Another with a bowl cut. There were two where the smiling stopped. Teenage years, I suspected. On my right, were other pictures from high school. Lots of cheerleading and a few from parties or celebrations. In none of those was she smiling. Black seemed to be her color on the outside, and it wouldn't have surprised me if that was the same on the inside. From this gallery, I could deduce that Eleanor seemed to have had a joyless adolescence and early adulthood.

The full-size bed was covered with a yellow, downy quilt, and dozens of stuffed animals. Teddy bears and rabbits, a buffalo, with a few dogs and cats. Each one looked well-used. Patches of overuse showed the batting beneath the quilt cover. Next to the bed was a nightstand with two books: *Runaway Ralph* and *Aragon*. I read those when I was younger, too.

'This is her room. Eleanor's.'

'Do you have any other children?' I asked.

'No. I never wanted another one. Because my ex was out of the picture so quickly, it wasn't a possibility anyway.' Her voice rose at the end of the sentence. Another sore spot.

'She's very pretty.'

'She didn't get that from me.'

I wanted to contradict her, but she would have known I was lying. 'What's she like now?'

If I could have known the well of grief I was opening, or even the mere fact that Dave had presupposed this question, I may have asked something else. Unfortunately, surrounded by the visual representations of Eleanor's history, Gladys broke. The wailing began even before she collapsed onto the bed sending dust motes scattering in every direction. She covered her face in shame. Her body writhed with emotional pain and contorted her. My discomfort mounted, for I had no idea what I should have been doing. Sit down beside her? Reach out? What could my consolation, if any, have looked like?

In retrospect, I did the only thing I could think of doing. I remained silent and let her cry. What seemed like hours, was only a minute. Finally, the tidal wave of her sobbing broke and she retrieved her handkerchief from inside her shirt.

'I'm so sorry, Wendy. So very sorry. I didn't mean for that to happen, and yet I did.'

'I don't know what you mean.'

'Dave. He said…'

'Dave?'

'We… he said it would be good for me to meet someone Eleanor's age. I could practice getting to know her through you.'

'I don't understand.'

'It all sounds so confusing, I'm sorry. Eleanor left here six years ago. This was her home…'

To be frank, it was patently obvious why Eleanor ditched her mother and this freakish room. I couldn't even begin to imagine how weird it would be if every time I returned to my parents' home, they had done this to my old room.

'Gladys, do you think that maybe you haven't exactly moved on from Eleanor being a child?'

'That's what Dave said, too. It's just so hard to move on. She was so beautiful.'

It was a good thing that Gladys was not looking at me because I was starting to feel a little bit cranky about Dave's manipulation. The whole set up made me grumpy. I shouldn't have had to be doing this

17 – Wendy

while everyone outside was having a party. Benson was going to get an earful when I got out there.

'Maybe you should not listen to Dave.'

Startled, she glanced up. Her face was splotchy and her eyes gingery red. A small streak of snot was lodged in her papery-thin mustache. 'That's not possible. Everyone listens to Dave.'

'Why?'

'Because he's always right. And he does so many things for me. For us at the Palms.'

'Like what?'

A shadow crossed her face. 'That's between Dave and I.'

'What exactly would you like me to do for you, Gladys?'

She looked down at her hands, at the hanky, then to the bedspread underneath her legs. For a moment her eyes wandered the walls, sweeping the pictures, the static moments of her daughter's life. 'Can you help me clean out her room?'

'Right now?' *Good God, no.* That would have been one of Dante's circles.

'No, of course not,' Gladys responded quickly, but obviously she meant the opposite. 'There's a party going on outside. And… you've been kind enough to come with me.' She paused. 'How do I look?'

'Like you've been crying.'

She laughed and thankfully wiped the snot with her hanky. 'I haven't cried like that in a long time. Not since Eleanor left.'

'Let's go outside anyway,' I suggested. 'The fresh air and company will be good for you and we can leave this conversation for another day.'

'So will you?' she asked hesitantly, expectantly.

I breathed deeply smelling the girlish scents, as well as decay and oversized expectations. It would take a while, and I would be ruthless. I told her that.

'That's okay. Maybe that's what I need most is some female companionship to help me through the next stage of life.'

The sigh which threatened to escape my lungs remained bottled there. Instead, I reached my hand out to her. She took it and stood with effort to lead me back outside.

We were just about to leave the hallway when my attention was arrested by a photo on the wall.

It was Dave. He was standing on the balcony overlooking the courtyard. He didn't know the picture had been taken.

Gladys had drawn a love heart around him.

18
Meg

My mom brought me to the party, but I didn't really want to go. My tummy didn't feel so good. I wanted to stay home and play with my Barbies and watch a video. I wanted to sit on the sofa and dangle my feet over the edge and bounce them. That's fun. But Mom says that Dave wanted us to be there. I don't think Mom wanted to go either. Her eyes were dark and puffy. Sometimes she says they get like that when she cries, but I don't know. I hadn't seen her crying. I guess it was because she was talking to AnTwerp.

Sometimes when my mom goes to sleep at night, I can hear her in the living room tapping away on the computer. It makes a funny sound, like mice crawling inside the walls. I am not afraid of mice or anything because I am almost a grownup. My mom tells me she is not afraid of anything, but I wonder about that sometimes. She jumps when there are loud noises, and other times when she can't find me, she will run around outside the house screaming my name. But I'm not lost, I'm just hiding. I like to hide where nobody can see me or hear me. When I play hide and seek with Dave, he pretends that he doesn't know where I am and he looks in the weirdest places like on the ceiling or under rugs – like I'm going to fit under a rug, duh. Dave always finds me, though.

I got a bloody nose this morning. It was gross and sticky. Mom asked me if I was picking it, but I said no, even though I was. It bled for a long time, longer than normal, and Mom wondered if she was going to have to take me to that place. Going there gives me the shivers. One time I had a really bad cut on my finger after I opened a knife and then shut it on my finger. It hurt a lot, and Mom drove me super-duper fast to that place. As we were sitting in the Merjency Room, there were a lot of people moaning and crying and 'carrying on'. When Mom says 'carrying on' she makes a little motion with her fingers. I don't know what that means.

The moaning and 'carrying on' sounded like what Mom sounds like sometimes at night. There was a man in the Merjency Room who was leaning against a lady. She was patting his head like my mom does sometimes, but the scary part was, his shoe was all bloody and gross and it looked like it had got caught in something. My mom told me not to look at it, and when I asked her what happened, she looked away and said something like lawn blower, but I couldn't figure out why a lawn blower would do that to his shoe.

'Meg, sit still!' I was sitting on the chair while she tried to do my hair. It is very curly, she calls it 'gnarly' or sometimes 'ratty', but she won't shave it off like hers, even though I want her to. It's better than her trying to pull a comb through the 'rat's nest'. That hurts a lot.

I whined. I couldn't help it. Everything hurt. 'I am, Mommy.'

'We... have... to... get... to... the... party.' Between each of the words, she pulled the brush through my hair and my head pulled back. I knew that her teeth were clenched because it's hard to make my hair soft.

'You can go to the party and I'll stay home. Barbie will keep me company.'

'That's not going to happen, Meg.'

'But why?'

'For one thing, you're five years old and I would get in trouble if I left you home alone. For another thing, Dave really wants you there and you know what Dave wants, Dave gets.'

'I like Dave.'

She sniffed and placed her hands on the sides of my head and then kissed the top. I like that sound. 'You feel a little bit warm.' Mom touched my forehead with her hands and then with her cheek. 'Do you feel okay?'

'I'll be all right, Mommy.' I climbed off the chair and onto the floor. My legs hurt a little bit, but not that much. I'm a big girl.

We drove to Dave's house and Mom turned on the radio. I didn't know what the song was, but it was hop hip and Mom knew the words. There were a few bad words that got beeped out and every time there

18 - Meg

was a beep, Mom looked at me and smiled, but I was in the back seat and she couldn't see all of me. I saw her eyes in the mirror. There were crinkles around the sides when she smiled, but it didn't seem like she was very happy. Just moving. Always moving. I couldn't see much of her head from where I was sitting because she's so short. The top of it is like black sandpaper. I guess she hadn't had time to shave it.

For a little while, I dangled my feet over the edge of my car seat and bounced them, but it hurt. It hurt even more that I wanted to hum along with the radio, but it felt like I was too tired to do it. The song stopped somewhere in the back of my throat. I didn't have enough air to push it out, but maybe it was just 'cause we were in the car. When we get to Dave, he would make everything feel all right. He always does. He'd find me.

My mom looked around the street and sweared. She apologized to me, and then told me all the parking spots were full. We had to walk. When she opened the door, the car made that ding ding noise until she turned off the lights. I copied the sound with it. *Ding ding ding ding.* It was like an alarm when something was wrong. As she unbuckled me, she leaned over and I could smell her perfume. She smelled pretty, like a flower or a piece of fruit. The smell reminded me of the grocery store when we walk past the flowers in the plastic wrappers which are for women whose men care about them.

I touched her cheek as she pulled me out. She liked that. As she set me on the ground outside the car, I told her I wanted her to carry me. For a little while I wanted to be a baby again and feel her face on mine as she rocked me side to side. She used to sing to me, make up songs with words like, *Meg is my treasure, my beautiful gift,* but she doesn't do that anymore. Probably because I'm a big girl now. But I'd like her to sing to me again sometime. That would be nice.

We walked the sidewalk together hand in hand. Because Mom is so short, I didn't have to reach up so high, not like when I walk with Dave. He's a giant, but he usually carries me anyway. His hair is much softer than my mom's shaved head.

The big open space of the apartment complex was full of people: tall white people, tall black people, tall brown people, fat ones, skinny ones, some had bright coats on, but most wore black or gray. There was a new lady standing near Benson. She had blondey hair and red cheeks. Lots of people were standing with them under a tent. I like tents. We used to go camping in the backyard when I was a baby, just me and Mom, but not for a long time now. Underneath the tent were heaters on legs. They were glowing orange. Mom said they were very hot, but I didn't know. The heat never seemed to get down to where I was.

Gladys was talking to the blondey lady. I wanted to ask the new lady who she was and tell her my name. Gladys was talking very fast and loud. I could hear her all the way over where we were walking. Mom (what is that word?) tolerates her because Dave says she is necessary. That's what he says about everyone. We're all necessary.

Dave saw us and waved. He had a can in his hand. I looked around at the rest of the people and saw that there weren't many kids. Just a few by the fishpond. I wanted to go join them, but I was just too tired. Maybe next time. Jeravious and Duwayne were on the other side talking to some brown-skinned people. Jeravious's pants hanged down below his butt. I thought that was funny. His underwear had smiley faces on it.

We walked over to Dave and he introduced us to someone, Patricia, I think her name was, and then he turned back to the grill and flipped a hotdog. Normally, I'd have been really hungry and asked if I could have the first one, but not today. When Dave turned around again, he leaned over and said really close to my face, 'What's happenin' Megmalion?'

I smiled and wanted to say something funny, but I couldn't. My head was full of the ouchey. I touched his cheek and then stuck to Mom's leg.

'She's not feeling very well.'

'I can see that.' Dave's furry things on his cheeks had grown longer and the hair over his lip moved like a fat caterpillar.

18 – Meg

'She had a very bloody nose this morning. It went all over the place. It lasted for an hour. I almost took her to the emergency room.' Mom's hand was on my head, but by the tension in her leg, I could tell she wished I would let go.

'Hmmm…'

'Maybe she needs a hotdog,' Jeravious said as he grabbed a charred sausage from the grill. He placed it in a bun and handed it in my direction, but I curled even farther into Mom's backside and hid my face. Eating a hotdog would make me feel gooey inside.

'You go ahead and eat that thing,' Mom says.

'Well, Meggie, would you like to take a little ride with me?' Dave asked as he opened his hands. Normally, I'd jump at the opportunity, but I felt weird. He picked me up all the same and carried me on his hip. It was good to be close to him and I laid my head on his shoulder. 'Come on, Letitia, let's go meet Benson's girlfriend, Wendy.'

I heard my mom mutter something like, 'That's the whitest white girl name you'll ever hear,' but I thought Wendy's name was beautiful. I've watched Peter Pan before, and I wish that I had a sister like her.

Wendy was talking to an old black man. His glasses were pulled down on the end of his nose. His nose was big and looked like a chocolate-colored lightbulb. I wanted to touch it but decided not to. I had seen him before. Somewhere. Where was that?

'Hello, Letitia,' he reached out his hand to my mom. I couldn't really understand what his name was. It came out kind of mumble-jumbled: Ingrayshus Stackwords. My mom reached up to shake his hand, and they started to talk about her work at the college.

'And I'm Wendy,' the blondey, white girl said. Benson was standing close beside her as if afraid someone was going to take her away.

'How are you?' my mom asked, and Wendy said that she was nervous about something – meeting new people, maybe. I'm not nervous about meeting new people. It's fun. Wendy pointed at me, and I got introduced. I looked at her from Dave's shoulder. They were all very nice, but I was glad Dave was holding me. His arms were strong, and he smelled nice – not like food or anything, but like something I know. A memory. He smelled like a memory.

They talked small for a while, and I could feel myself falling asleep. The sounds of voices, low and high, the wind whipping under the tent blowing the hot air around. Because I was up higher, I could feel the heat and it made me sleepy. People began to eat, grilled meat, some salads, something sweet made with marshmallows and Snickers bars. I hoped I felt better afterwards so I could try some of that.

Another voice. I tried to keep my eyes open to see who it was, but it was hard. He was tall – not as tall as Dave, but close, and he had big brown eyes. He was wearing a Hawkeyes sweatshirt with a gold cross on a chain sticking out the front. His voice was low, like a cow. *Moooo.* I wanted to giggle, but I couldn't. So I turned my head to just listen.

'I'm Marty.'

'Letitia.'

'Marty and I have been spending a lot of time together, my sweet pumpkin,' Dave said.

'Interesting. What kind of things do you two do together?'

'This and that.'

'We're just getting to know each other. After one of the meetings, we went bowling. One time we went to a Drake football game.'

'You went to a Drake football game and didn't tell me?' My mom's voice got kind of high the way she talks when someone is making her grumpy.

'Letitia works at Drake, Marty.'

'Oh.'

'We probably should have brought them along.'

Marty didn't answer right away, but when he did, I could tell he was ready to leave, too. 'Maybe I'll go find someone else to…' His voice kind of faded out. *Moooooooooo.*

When he left, Mom must have got closer to Dave because her voice was louder. 'Do you even want me to be part of your life?'

18 – Meg

I felt his arm move and he must have touched Mom's head. When I turned my head to look, she pulled back. 'My sweet joy muffin, you are my everything.'

'That's not an answer.'

My eyes were getting heavy and my brain felt clunky like it was bouncing around inside my head. For a few moments, it felt as if I was floating – maybe that was Dave, maybe it was just life, but then suddenly, Dave pulled me away from his chest and I jerked my eyes open.

'Oh, Dave, I'm so sorry,' Mom said and grabbed me away from him. My face was wet, and I rubbed my mouth. When I pulled my hand back, it was full of blood.

'It's okay,' Dave reached for some towels to hold on my face.

'I'm going to take her to the hospital to see if we can get something done about this.'

'Do you want me to come with?' Dave asked.

'Would you?'

Dave nodded and untied his apron. He followed me and Mom, but then Mom stopped him. 'You should probably change out of that shirt,' she nodded to his shirt. 'You look like you've been shot.' He looked down at his chest. Other people were staring at us. They were disappointed that Dave was being taken away from them, especially Gladys.

Dave ran up the stairs to his apartment and Mom took me to the car. As she buckled me into the seat, she wiped off the excess blood on my coat and then pushed the rags back onto my face to stop the bleeding. She got into the middle seat in the back next to me. There was a weird look on her face. She was not unhappy with me, more like frustrated that we went to the party in the first place.

Dave ran to the car. Various people called things out, things I couldn't hear, and he turned to wave while running towards us. He was smiling as if we were going for a ride to the park. Mom muttered under her breath. I don't think she was happy with Dave.

Dave tapped on the window and got into the driver's seat. He reached his hand back over his shoulder where Mom dropped the keys.

The drive to the scary place was quick. My nose was still bleeding. It pooled into that little hole in my upper lip, you know that place? Mom wasn't holding the towel hard enough so I took it. I was still a little scared though. I wished this part was done so we could go back home and I could play with my Barbies.

Dave stopped at an entrance with a roof over it. It felt like we were going to stay at a hotel. Mom yanked me out of the seat, and we hurried through the whooshing doors. My head was on Mom's shoulder. A few people stared at us. There was blood on her shirt now as well as mine. We made our way up to the front and the nurse, a big lady with white hair, was sitting behind the desk.

'Ooh, what happened here?'

'She's got a nosebleed.'

'How did that happen?'

'It just started. It's the second one today.'

The old lady was checking back and forth between my mom and me. 'It's not abuse, if that's what you're thinking.'

'That's not my job to think about those things.'

'Don't you judge me,' Mom's voice was rising. I moaned. She was squeezing me too hard.

'Ma'am, I'm not judging you. I was just ascertaining how the injury happened so that we can treat it.'

'It's *not* an injury. It's a nosebleed.'

The nurse didn't say anything, but she handed Mom a clipboard and asked her to fill it out. We sat down. There were a whole bunch of other people sitting in the plastic chairs. Some of them were staring out the windows into the darkness but most were playing around on their phones. I like to play on Mom's phone, but she doesn't let me do it very often. She says it will rot my brain. That's silly, I think.

Dave entered the room with all the sick people and saw us. As he made his way over, a brown person called out to him.

18 – Meg

'Dave.'

'Carlos. Mi amigo.'

'Dave, I need you to hold Meg while I fill out these forms.'

He was torn between Carlos and my mom. She gave him a look. *Listen to me now, or pay the penalty for living.*

Dave sat next to Mom. He cuddled me in his arms, and he was not even frustrated when I started bleeding on him again. Mom finished the homework and took it to the nurse. This time they didn't say anything to each other.

'How are you feeling, Megatune?'

'Not so good.'

'You feel like you've got a fever.'

I've had those before. You feel hot and then cold and then you shiver even though you're hot. It felt like that. And my tummy felt balloony too.

I must have fallen asleep because then I was in a room where it was just me and Dave and Mom and a guy with blue pajamas on. He was wearing a mask so I couldn't see his face, but his skin was very dark, kind of like Mom's, but his voice was funny. Like he was from somewhere else. He introduced himself as Dr. Bujabi but said I can call him Booji.

Dave sat me on the hard bed on top of some kind of funky paper. It was crinkly and sounded too loud in my ears. Booji took the towel away from my face. Thankfully the dripping had slowed some, but it felt like there was more in there. I was dizzy, though. Booji peered into my eyes with a light thing, and then he bonked my knee, and then he looked up my nose. He took my temperature. It had four numbers on it which caused my mom to look at Dave and shake her head.

Dr. Booji's face scrunched up when Dave said something about Dr. Lecter, and Mom didn't seem happy, but I didn't really care about them right then because Booji was pushing on my tummy and it hurt bad. He asked Mom where all the bruises came from and she shook her head once and then twice. She hadn't seen them before when he pointed them out on my arms and legs. They were dark, purplish circles. Some were as big as Dave's fingers and others seemed small, like a ladybug had landed on my arm.

'We'll have to get a blood test, just to check a few things off the list,' Booji said.

'What kinds of things?'

'Judging by her temperature and the slight swelling in her abdomen, and her lymph nodes are slightly swollen, I would guess she has an infection of some sort.'

'What about her bloody nose? Do we need to be worried about that?'

Booji frowned but then smiled to cover it up. 'Kids get them all the time. We'll keep an eye on it though.'

On the way back to Dave's apartment, Dave and Mom didn't speak many words. Mom had picked up some antibiotics from the drug store, some syrupy stuff that tastes better than the tablets, and easier to swallow, too. I like the cherry ones that make my throat feel furry. After we dropped Dave back at the apartment, he kissed Mom on the lips. His big head filled up the whole front window. Mom thanked him, but she still sounded kind of upset. Either she was still worried about me, or she was disappointed about missing the party.

We went back home. It was very dark, and I was sleepy again. I wondered what everyone else was doing. Was Benson having fun with his girlfriend? What about Ingrayshus? Marty? I would have liked to have talked to him a little while longer. And Jeravious and Duwayne. I wondered what the kids were doing at the fishpond?

Oh well. I took my medicine and went to bed early.

Sometimes that happens.

19
Patricia

Gordon and I were sitting in front of the television a few hours after the party. Gordon was tired, maybe a little tipsy, too. Although it was Saturday, we were not generally prone to drinking alcohol in the afternoon. Everyone else was doing it, so Gordon decided to indulge, thus leaving him in the vegetative state he was in. His eyes were still open (as well as his mouth). They were fighting the good fight against the deceptive tiredness of old age, but the war had already been lost. By the time suppertime rolled around, he would have had a nice long nap.

That left me time to reflect on what happened at the party.

As I write a few things in my daily journal, I'm confused by the event itself. Was there actually a purpose? Or, was this just another thing in a long line of other things that I'm still getting used to at the Palms. Yes, it's quiet most of the time, but I was thinking retirement was supposed to be a little less socially exhausting. I'm still of an age where physical interaction is necessary for good mental health, but old enough to know when enough is enough.

Judge Stackworth was an interesting character. He's a few years younger than Gordon and I, but definitely has a different life experience. Though he didn't share many details, some of the stories were heart-wrenching. Kids in court. Kids in trouble. Parents in court. Parents were the trouble. He was fascinating, and his demeanor was that of a wise one who had been dented by life. Gordon only spoke briefly to him, but lost interest in the horror stories. He left shortly later to speak with some other older residents, like Doctor Vinson, while simultaneously supervising the children's fishing expedition in the goldfish pond.

I met Marty. I am not normally one to swoon, per se, but the man exudes testosterone. A woman my age should not be thinking such things, but my journal is a repository for all life's experiences, so I'll catalogue even this one – one that my loving husband shall not see, and even if he did, he probably wouldn't care. It took all my will power to keep from fanning myself.

'Hello,' I said as he stooped beside me to retrieve a Coke from the cooler beside my leg.

'Hi.'

'I'm Patricia.' I extended my gloved hand, and he shook it.

'Marty.'

'Are you a friend of someone's?'

'Dave's.'

'Isn't everyone?' I laughed and put a hand over my chest. *Was I actually flirting with a man nearly half my age. Call me Cougar. Mereow.*

'Seems that way.'

'How do you know him?'

He frowned as I batted my eyes. Did women even do that anymore? 'We were at a meeting together.'

'I didn't even know that Dave had a job.'

His frown deepened. It was obvious that he did not want to be talking to me, but I certainly wanted to appreciate his yumminess for a little while longer. 'Not that kind of meeting.'

I waited for him to elaborate, but he did not. Instead, he popped the top of the soft drink and tilted it to his mouth. After swallowing, he burped behind closed lips.

Sexy.

'How do you know Dave?' he asked.

'He lives over there.' I pointed at Dave's apartment and Marty's eyes followed my hand.

'I know.'

'You've been to his apartment before?'

'Yes.'

Not a man of many words.

'Where are you from?'

'South of here.'

19 – *Patricia*

Inwardly, I sighed. Why do we have to get old? I used to be quite a looker when I was younger. The boys lined up to dance with me. And now?

'What do you do for a living?' I asked.

He cleared his throat, suddenly looking very uncomfortable. 'I run my own business.'

'What's the business?'

'What is this, twenty questions?'

I blushed. 'I'm so sorry. I wasn't being nosy. It's just a party, and you're new.'

Sighing, he ran a hand over his hair. I could see his bicep bulging through his shirt. 'No, it's not you. I… well… My store causes a lot of consternation in people.' He waited for me to ask the inevitable question, and when, after a short pause, I did, he responded. 'I sell used firearms.'

'Oh.' I was torn. He was both more attractive and less attractive after pronouncing that last sentence.

'You see what I mean?' He took another drink of his Coke and prepared to leave.

'You don't have to leave. I'm curious. Does it bother you?'

'To what?'

'To be part of the gun control issue?'

His cheek muscles bounced as he clenched his jaw. 'I'm not part of the problem. I sell guns, but I don't fire them. I can't control what people do with them.'

'But…'

'Look, lady. I can see that you're nice enough and you're trying to make conversation. But we don't have to pretend anything here. You can go be a moth, flutter away to all the other liberals here who want to shut me down.'

'That's not what I was going to say.'

He frowned. 'What were you going to say, then?'

'I used to be a pretty good shot. I won a few ribbons at the local clay pigeon competitions in northwest Iowa.'

Marty's expression changed. Somewhere behind those lovely green eyes was a man trying to look behind my age at the woman I used to be. Suddenly, I felt like a young woman again. And that was wonderful.

'My husband said that's one of the reasons he married me. If I could handle a gun, I could be responsible with anything.'

'Sounds like you married a wise man.'

I glanced over at Gordon who was standing beside the fishpond. He had a hand in the back pocket of his gray jeans. He used to have a nice butt, but now it looked like he'd had his glutes amputated. I sighed. 'Yes. Very wise.' I touched my throat. 'What I was going to say, though, was that I wished we lived in a world where we didn't need guns. What you do may be necessary, but unfortunate.'

'Yeah, I guess so.'

'Are you married?'

At this point, the discomfort was his. He looked far more squeamish about the matrimonial topic than the munitions one. 'Uh, not anymore.'

'I'm sorry if it seemed like prying.'

He bobbed his head and glanced around the courtyard.

After a few moments, I got the hint that he was done with this old lady. 'I guess I'll see you around,' I said.

He took this as his cue that he was released from the bondage of our conversation. 'Nice to meet you,' he mumbled as he struck off under the marquees ducking beneath the white crossbars.

I watched him go feeling like I was seeing the boat of my youth drifting away, too. Dear diary, would it be possible to purchase another life?

Changing subjects.

The new woman, Wendy, apparently Benson's girlfriend, and Gladys went to the office for some reason. When they returned, Gladys appeared to have been crying. After reconnecting with the party, they separated to opposite ends of the gazebos: Gladys with some of the new

19 – Patricia

people off the street and Wendy, to Benson. She looked relieved and reached for a beer. They put their heads together. She didn't seem happy.

From my brief conversation with her, she seemed very nice, very down-to-earth. It's nice to have women doing men's jobs. It's not like I'm a women's libber or anything, but there's a little too much testosterone in the world.

We chatted about her work on the Mississippi, the wildlife, her interests. I tried to extract more information about her relationship with Benson, but she was tight-lipped. Either she doesn't like him that much, or she can see me for who I am – a nosy neighbor.

Much later, after the party started, Letitia arrived with Meg who seemed very despondent. Tired.

And bruised.

I had an inclination to wander over and check her out, but I wasn't sure how Letitia would have taken that.

I worked for thirty-five years as a nurse, and I might have seen a lot of things – worse things than even Judge Stackworth has. Those bruises would have caused questions. And those questions wouldn't have been pretty. I didn't get close enough to see the entirety of her skin, but if I had two nickels to rub together…

Anyway, after the nosebleed, they took off in a hurry. At least Letitia and Meg did. Dave straggled behind saying goodbye to everyone. Benson looked distraught about having a Dave-less party.

I am going to bed early tonight.

I hope I'm wrong about what they will find out about Meg at the hospital. Maybe she's just got an infection.

I doubt it.

20

Benson

It had been a long, dreadful day, one which I would have exchanged for any other in my life. So would Dave, I think, but much to the chagrin of the others, he had a different way of dealing with what happened a few days after the party.

As Dave took Letitia and Meg to the hospital in the middle of the party, I thought it was an overreaction, the whole go-to-the-hospital-for-a-bloody-nose thing. But what do I know? I'm not a father and probably won't be for a long time. Dave told me that they were going to keep Meg overnight for observation.

That was three days ago, and she was still there.

Even though I questioned why Dave was not at the hospital, he said he couldn't tell me. Instead, Dave and I went to Lefties to try out one of their new recipes – pickle and hamburger strips (interesting stuff if you're interested and want to stop by) when Dave's ancient flip-phone rang.

'Hello. Dave speaking.'

He held the phone away from his ear, as if the voice on the other end was too loud. I followed his expression as the one-sided conversation took place. In the rare event that Dave listens without speaking, his face does most of the talking. In that case though, Dave's face transformed from inquisitive to blank. I mean absolutely nothing. He went dark like someone had unplugged his television.

'I don't understand…'

Only half a minute later, communication ceased. At that moment, it was like Dave was stuck in suspended animation. The phone, still held an inch from his right ear and sideburn, was silent. I couldn't tell what was going on in Dave's head, but there was a strange dimness about his expression. He wasn't even blinking. He just sat there in slack-jawed shock.

'What is it? What happened?'

He didn't, or couldn't, respond.

'Dave? Are you there? What's going on?'

As if revived from a heart attack, Dave coughed and blinked rapidly.

'Dave,' I said his name loudly causing other Lefties patrons to turn suddenly to us. 'Are you okay?'

Finally, he spoke. 'That was Letitia.'

'And?'

'Meg has leukemia.'

The words didn't register immediately. Leukemia. Cancer. 'What?'

'I can't say it again, Benson.'

'She has leukemia?'

'Don't say it a third time. That will make it true.'

My mind whirred. With heart in stomach, I began to pack up our half-eaten lunch. After depositing the remnants in the brown and green plastic trash can with a swinging door, we walked quickly to the car. Dave was still in a trance, and after he settled into the passenger seat, he fiddled with his phone as if somehow trying to activate an erase-message app.

'What are you thinking?' I asked.

'Have you ever heard of the Mothman?'

'What?' I held out my hand for Dave's keys. He wrested them from his pants pocket and deposited them in my hand.

'Mothman. From the Appalachians.'

'I have no idea what you're talking about, or even why you're thinking about that rather than Meg and Letitia.'

'You asked me what I was thinking. I told you. If you don't want to know, don't ask.'

This was a new revelation – irritated Dave. 'I apologize if I've offended you, but what does Mothman have to do with anything?'

Dave stared up over the dash and through the windshield as we left the parking lot. It was a brisk, sunny day nearing October, very discordant with the news we'd just received. Normally, on a day like this, Dave and I would be on a quest somewhere, maybe south to Missouri, or west to Nebraska. Quests had been rarer with my Wendy-fixation and my replacement named Marty. Unfortunately, the quest for the day would be to the hospital, and I would be driving faster than normal.

'Somewhere in West Virginia, about sixty years ago, some gravediggers were preparing for a funeral when they saw a man with large wings and glowing red eyes lift off from a tree.'

'A few days later, a couple was driving, and they saw the same winged figure with red eyes chasing them down the road. They drove a hundred miles an hour to get away from it, but they couldn't seem to escape. It just followed them until finally, it broke off. The couple was unhinged — they couldn't get the vision of those red eyes out of their minds.'

'What happened?'

'Some other locals said it was just a sandhill crane.'

'Flying a hundred miles an hour?' I checked the rearview mirror for traffic and the sight of a man in a moth costume. I stopped at a red light.

'I know. And there were other witnesses, too. But there's always doubters. People who can't deal with what's right behind them, chasing them.'

'What do you mean?'

'That's how I've always viewed cancer. The Mothman. A winged, genetic mutant, red eyes, chasing me. And the doubters coming later, questioning everything…' His voice went silent.

'You scared?'

He didn't respond.

The Emergency Room reception area was filled with frightened, forlorn, and upset people. After the doors shushed shut behind us, Dave and I sanitized our hands and strode quickly past a young mother cradling her feverish child. Another man in the latter stages of drug addiction had passed out across three cushioned chairs underneath the television. An elderly couple paged through magazines while waiting to either get in or get out.

20 – Benson

As we approached the desk, a man called out from the back right corner. 'Dave!'

Marty.

With a full head of hair, and a large grin, he could have doubled for a Hollywood actor. His strong jaw jutted out as he tried to smile and rise from his seat.

'Mar-tay. What's happenin', my brother?' Dave responded with his own smile, transforming instantaneously to the Dave we all knew and loved. They man-hugged, tapping each other on the back, then pushed each other away. I was flabbergasted. There was no way Dave should have been laughing and smiling with Marty when we'd just been told the horrendous news. What in the world was wrong with this man?

'My daughter is in to have her appendix out. Her mother is with her right now and she kindly asked if I'd wait in the reception area.'

'Your daughter Monica?'

'No. Cameron.'

When I offered Marty my hand, he shook it hard. He had a fist of iron which I found irritating, and the fact that he was closer to Dave's height than mine left me feeling like a Munchkin in the land of the Philistines. I tried to squeeze his hand harder, but mine had still not recovered entirely from the bull riding episode, so I released it and slunk back to my metaphorical corner.

'Do you want to come with us?' Dave asked Marty.

I was flabbergasted. We needed to get up to Meg's room pronto and he wanted to bring his alcoholic friend.

Marty looked back and forth between Dave and me. 'I'm not sure that's such a good idea. What are you guys here for?'

'Dave's future stepdaughter is receiving some treatments. It's probably best if you don't come along.'

Holding up his hands, Marty took a step back. 'Meg? Oh, man. I'm sorry. When did this happen? Wait, you don't have to tell me anything. I completely understand.'

'No,' Dave insisted. 'I can use the support.'

201

'What?' It was a stab to the heart, for sure. I, Benson Bartholomew Buttfinger and all the names he had called me over the years was the first person to his side, and he wanted to bring this… this… taller version of Tom Cruise to 'support' him? Of all the slaps-in-the-face…

'Are you sure?'

'Yes, yes, please.' *What a Benedict Arnold! Dave, you're Batman, and I'm Robin. You're the Lone Ranger, and me, Tonto! Get rid of him!*

'Let me grab my jacket.'

As Marty stalked back to the corner to retrieve his jacket from the crowd of emergency misfits and defectives, I grabbed Dave's upper arm and gripped it tightly.

'Ouch.'

'What are you doing?' I hissed. 'Letitia is not going to be happy about having a stranger in the room. And to be brutally honest, they probably won't even let him in there anyway. You can only have a couple people in the room at a time. Letitia's vote is going to count more than yours. They might not even let *me* in.' The stress of the word *me* was heavy with meaning. *I* was his best friend. *I* was his support. *I* was the one who had been there for all the adventures. Not this good-looking faux-friend with his wavy hair and million-dollar smile. No, me, Benson and my thinning hair and fifty-cent grin.

Marty returned with his coat and checked both our faces for en – or discouragement. 'Listen, Marty,' Dave started.

'Oh,' his voice fell, 'Yeah, I get it, well… It's probably for the best anyway. I should probably wait for my own daughter's results.'

'That's probably a good idea,' I said.

'You know what?' Dave stepped closer to Marty. 'Just come for a walk with us and we'll see where it goes from there.'

I was angry – furious, really.

With a swift motion, Dave grabbed both of our arms and pushed us in front of him like mismatched bodyguards towards the Emergency Room desk where a frazzled nurse in her blue scrubs typed into her computer. Dave stood behind us and urged me to talk to the nurse at the station.

She was younger, though perhaps a little older than me, but her befrazzlement made her appear a decade older. When she peered up from her typing, she seemed irritated. 'Yes?'

'We're here to see Meg Collins. And Letitia.' Dave stood stock-still behind us holding his hands in front of his waist.

The nurse checked the register. 'She's in the third room.' The nurse pointed over her shoulder and buzzed the door.

Once again, Dave used us as human shields to walk to where Meg was being kept. Along the hallway, where doors were opened, each room contained four or six beds, each shrouded by cloth curtains on plastic rings and was filled with hospital-gowned sick and injured people, some moaning, others unconscious. Machines blipped and bleeped and hissed. The stench of disinfectant, as well as something more heinous, feces and blood, wafted in currents throughout the ward. In one room, an elderly man sat beside his wife's bed. He was staring disconsolately out the window. The glow from outside revealed a lonely, devastated human being trapped in a nightmare from which there was only one escape. His sadness was palpable, even in the flash we saw him as we walked past.

The door of Room 17 was ajar. I turned to look at Dave, but the wildness had returned. If given half a chance, he would have run screaming back down the hallway.

'Are you okay?' I asked.

His nod was short and curt, uncertain. Marty placed an arm around his shoulders and opened the door further. Just as they were about to enter, a nurse called out.

'Excuse me! Only two visitors at a time.'

As a unit, we all turned. The nurse, a graying woman in her late fifties, had stood behind her desk and leaned forward on it.

'Yes, I'm talking to you three. She already has her mother and two visitors in there, which is one more than allowable, but in this case…' She stopped. 'Dave?'

'Yes.' He was still shielded by Marty and me.

'Are you here for Letitia?'

He nodded.

'Okay, but don't stay long. When you get in there, just send the other two out. Maybe if one of you three...' Her pantomime suggested that either Marty or I remain in the hall.

'Thank you,' I said. I glanced at Dave in bewilderment. Did everyone in the world know him?

Dave slowly broke away from us, like a calving iceberg, and approached the nurses' station where he engaged in a brief, quiet conversation with the woman. Marty and I stood awkwardly in front of the door waiting, mute, each one wondering which of us would be going with Dave into the room.

Finally, he returned. I looked behind him. The nurse was cradling her cheek in one hand and blushing.

'She said we could all go in for a little bit.'

'What did you say to her?' I asked.

He didn't respond but set his eyes firmly and nudged Marty through the door.

I followed last.

It took a few steps inside the hospital room for our eyes to adjust to the semi-darkness. The shades had been drawn and what little light that threatened to enter was caged at the window. Though Room 17 had been set up with four beds, it was surprisingly empty except for Meg and her visitors.

Our feet quietly shuffled across the floor, as if sound would break things. Dave suddenly stopped me. I turned to look up into his face. His eyes were wide and frightened, like a startled horse, and his nostrils were flared.

What in the world was wrong with him?

Then, I saw what he was staring at.

Nothing in the room could have prepared us for the sight of Meg, her face illuminated by a dim overhead lamp, pale, with dark bags under her eyes, curled up in the hospital bed. She had an IV leading from her little left hand. Running up the arm from the line were a series of small and large bruises. She looked so vulnerable. Dave whimpered beside me, unable to move further into the room.

'Why is he here?' Letitia's voice croaked from beside the bed.

'It's Marty,' he said. 'Marty, Dave's friend.'

'I know who you are, but why are you in this room. I don't know you and you don't know Meg.'

Marty looked to Dave for backing, but Dave didn't say anything.

Intuitively, Duwayne and Jeravious knew it was not their call as whether to bounce Marty from the room, but they definitely seemed relieved to see Dave and I. They both stood at the same time, quick and desperate. They wanted to get out as fast as they could, not to abandon Letitia and Meg, but they felt completely unqualified to be grief supporters.

Jeravious bypassed Marty and went to Dave. Though a few inches shorter, Jeravious seemed to dwarf Dave then. He put a big hand on his shoulder. 'Hey,' Jeravious said, 'glad you could make it.'

Dave's eyes were locked on Meg. Just a month ago she had been laughing and riding on his shoulders. Duwayne lightly punched me on the shoulder as he moved past me to leave the room.

'Are you guys going home?' I asked.

'Yeah, we've been here for a few hours. We've got to get to work.'

'Thanks for being here,' I said, feeling frustrated that Dave was not the one doing this. He should have been the thanker and the comforter.

As Jeravious and Duwayne closed the door behind them, we turned our attention to Letitia, whose exhaustion was palpable. Her head was bowed, and she held Meg's right hand in both of hers; her thumbs were busy and restless rubbing her daughter's soft skin. Letitia did not look *beside* herself in grief. She actually looked *beyond* it, as if existing on a different plane. The crisis was something a human body and psyche was never prepared for.

Marty crossed to the far side of the bed where he stood opposite Letitia. 'Dave asked if I'd come to be with… him, er you.'

She did not look up, but her jaw twitched. 'It's surprising that Dave couldn't come by himself.' She spoke as if Dave was not in the room.

'I… don't know how to respond to that.'

'*Why* are you in my daughter's room?'

'No, I…' Marty struggled to find the right words, so again he glanced to Dave who still had not said anything.

'He's here to help if he can,' I said lamely.

'Can he cure cancer?' she asked.

'No,' I stammered.

'Then he's useless. Get him out.'

I watched Marty's face crumble. Dave's mouth had dropped open slightly, and his eyes were wide as if witnessing a horrific accident in real-time.

Marty nodded slowly and realized that Dave was not going to add anything. He looked embarrassed and sad. As he turned to leave, Letitia stopped him.

'I'm sorry, that was rude of me.'

Marty raised his hands. 'Of course, no offense. It's a difficult situation. I'm very sorry for…' his hands spread over Meg like a blank accusation.

'You can have a seat if you'd like,' she said without indicating where.

'I won't stay long. I have to get back to work.'

According to what he said downstairs, that was not true, but I hoped he would leave soon. 'How is she?' he asked.

'She's struggling,' Letitia murmured to us, or no one, maybe to God.

'What happened?' I edged closer to her – them – leaving Dave where he was in the center of the room. I didn't want to stand next to Marty, so I sat on the edge of the bed near Meg's feet.

20 – Benson

'Last night, Meg cried out in her sleep. She had another bloody nose, and when I woke her, she said her bones hurt.' Letitia's face started to crumble. 'Benson, I don't know if I can take it.'

I touched her on the shoulder and she flinched. It was the wrong person's hand.

'It's too much. No one should have to go through this. Especially not alone.' For the first time, she turned her full attention on Dave. Her words should have signaled to him that he was being called to come closer, but they did not have the effect she wanted. She sighed, closed her eyes, and resumed her vigil.

I mouthed the words, *Get over here*, but he either didn't see me, or he just couldn't move. Instead, Marty moved one step closer to Dave.

'What are the doctors saying? Can they treat it?'

'Yes, thank God, it's treatable. Chemotherapy begins tomorrow, but the doctors say that she'll probably need a marrow transplant.'

I don't personally know anything about these treatments, but images of lost hair, vomiting and weight-loss immediately came to mind. I couldn't even begin to imagine what chemo would do to a five-year-old.

'What does a marrow transplant look like?'

Surprisingly, Marty spoke up. 'There are two ways to do it. My sister had a transplant, and they told us a donor would have it taken from the marrow of the hip bone, or directly from the blood. Obviously, the blood one is easier and less painful for the donor, but it all depends on the can…' he stopped, unsure of what to say next. 'I mean, it's not about the donor, really…'

Letitia kissed Meg's hand and leaned back in her seat. 'Are you in the medical field?' she asked without looking at either him or Dave.

'No, I, uh… I own my own business.'

'And what is that?' I asked.

'I allow people to purchase firearms.'

'You're a gun dealer?'

'I prefer arms and munitions distributor.'

It could not have gotten any worse. The tension in the room built as Dave's choice of emotional support, a frickin', handsome-as-hell warmonger, stood awkwardly between all of us, holding his metaphorical hat.

'Do you know anyone who could be the donor?' I asked her.

'No, not yet. The doctor said that in general, family members don't tend to be the correct match, which is unfortunate.' Her jaw clenched. 'Meg's father has declined to come to the hospital, so they can't check him anyway.'

'I'm sorry,' I responded lamely.

'Not as sorry as I am. It would be nice to have a father in the picture…'

The not-so-subtle stab at Dave would have hurt him, and I winced when she said it. But when I looked to see how he was taking it, the room was empty. Both he and Marty had left silently.

Letitia briefly glanced up. When she saw he was absent, the unsurprise registered quickly. 'Figures.'

What was he thinking?

I was outraged on Letitia's behalf, and after doing my best to comfort her for an hour, I awkwardly said goodbye. After briefly touching Meg's arm, I left the way I entered. Letitia thanked me and went back to her lonely vigil. Just her and Meg.

After leaving the room, I checked my pockets. Thankfully, I had the keys. I didn't know whether Dave had taken the bus, or if he would be waiting for me in reception.

As the doors reopened to admit me back to the Emergency Room, it was immediately apparent.

Dave had taken the bus.

But Marty was still there.

I didn't want to talk to him at all. What a low life. How could he possibly have agreed to accompany us into Meg's room?

He waved discreetly and approached me as I was about to exit the hospital. 'Hey.'

20 – Benson

'It's probably not a good time,' I said.

'That was a hard one.'

'Yes.'

'What do you think is wrong with Dave?'

For some reason, his question rubbed me the wrong way, and I felt my nerves, which were already irritated, firing my response. 'How can you not know. You're his best friend, right?'

Marty held up his hands. 'Look, Benson, I'm just trying to help here. If you don't want me in the picture, that's fine. But pushing people away because you feel a little jealous is not…'

'Jealous?' I wanted to punch him in the face. 'You think this is about me? And Dave? Geez, man, this is about Meg and Dave's inability to be the father that she needs.'

My voice had caused the commotion for everyone in the emergency room to stop what they were doing and stare at us. 'Take it easy, Benson.'

'Tell me how to do that, Marty? How do I *take it easy* when a five-year-old girl is fighting for her life in Room 17? Tell me. How?'

'Go find him. Help him understand.'

'Understand what?'

'The only thing that will help is for him to be with Letitia and Meg.'

I shook my head angrily and left him. *How in the world could anyone force Dave not to be Dave?*

On the drive home, I fumed about Dave's cowardice. Letitia was as close to a wife as he ever would have, and the minute he encountered difficulty, he ran away. I tried to imagine what Letitia was feeling. Probably something similar to how she felt when Meg's father ran out on them, too.

I half-expected to see Dave standing on the balcony outside our apartments leaning over the railing and waving to other residents. It was his normal time of day to stand above and greet the peasants like royalty, granting blessings upon those who might pass below. But he wasn't there, which, if to be honest, was a relief.

I entered my dark, silent apartment, dropped the keys on the kitchen island and went to take a shower.

At six o'clock, the television was on, and I'd just finished my chicken pot pie frozen dinner. I'd stewed while streaming a new series on television. Eventually, I called Wendy to fill her in on the strange and infuriating details. She wasn't as upset about Marty's appearance (which really annoyed me), but she was curious about Dave's departure. After we disconnected, I tried to eat my chicken pot pie in peace.

Then, there was a knock at my door.

I knew who it was.

'I don't want to talk to you now.'

No verbal response, but he knocked again, this time more insistently.

'No!' I shouted. 'Go away.'

Silence ensued, but then I heard the familiar sound of a key in the lock. *Of course he had a spare key with him.* Before I could reach the door to block it, he had shoved it open. I was startled by his appearance, and even more by who was with him.

21
Marty

Are you getting a glimpse of who I am?

Well, you've found out what I do, a little bit about my personality, and at least a small portion of my relationship with Dave. You may or may not be startled by some of life's twists and turns, but there it is. I was part of Dave's and Meg's story, so I suppose you'll have to put up with me for a while, even if you may not like me yet.

To be brutally honest, it's been a few years since I've done something completely altruistic. Please believe me, I don't think altruism is beneath me, far from it, but in my line of work distrust is a far better character trait than the alternative, and waking up the next morning to see that my business has inadvertently allowed a bunch of kids to be killed at a school is extraordinarily painful.

Now don't go getting your panties in a bunch. I don't sell to psychopaths, dope addicts, or weirdos. Most of my patrons are decent, law-abiding citizens who feel a deep respect for their country, their protection, and a desperate need to feel the calming presence of a sidearm on their hip or on the bedstand. For those desires, I'm willing to fill the void and absorb people's abuse. I have a license to sell firearms and ammunition, but I'm also a regular attender at Alcoholics Anonymous and Grace Baptist Church. Dave met me at one and took me to the other.

Dave was not an alcoholic. It surprised me that they allowed him to attend the meetings, but I think our facilitator was under the impression that, though Dave was not an alcoholic, he made the attendees feel better about themselves. At the very least he brought a modicum of humorous distraction.

At the first AA meeting where I met him, Dave strolled in ten minutes after the meeting started. We'd said the oath, had an opening prayer, and were just getting into the nitty gritty of how people were riding the wagon, clinging to it, or had been run over by it, when the sound came from the entrance. As Jamie was speaking about walking by his favorite bar three times per week just to smell the cigarette smoke and hear the tunes, he was interrupted by a man who definitely looked like he belonged at AA. He opened the door and stepped through in checkered pants, a striped shirt, and a tie. His hair was standing up on end like he'd just gotten out of bed.

He held a flask in his hand.

'Excuse me,' Vaughn, our AA facilitator, said. 'You can't bring *that* in here.' Vaughn was a pretty straight-laced fella who'd been alcohol free for almost twenty years. He was just about ready for his anniversary party (full of cheap canapes and soft drinks) scheduled for later in the year. He was about fifty-five and rail thin. He ran a lot – traded one addiction for another – and used running metaphors all the time; stuff about finishing strong, knocking down the wall, getting out of the starter blocks with speed. Although he was gracious and patient, he was also intolerant of outsiders and protective of us who had fallen prey to what he called the Devil's Saliva.

Dave turned to look behind him, then pointed at his chest.

'Yes, you,' Vaughn's irritation bespoke a man who did not suffer idiots lightly.

'I'm here for the meeting.'

'Not with that flask, you're not.'

Dave studied the object in his hand. We'd all had one before. Real shiny, twist top, holds a good eight shots of whatever pain-killer you wanted. 'It's my water bottle.'

'I've got dozens of good water bottles here you can use, but that's got to be put away.'

'Why?'

'Because bringing that in here is like walking a sugar addict past Dunkin' Donuts.'

Nodding his head slowly, Dave unscrewed the cap and tilted it at his mouth. The rest of us watched the movement as if our entire, beautiful past was slowly being poured out before us. Many of the others'

21 – Marty

mouths opened. Chase licked his lips. Flo's hands lifted slightly, muscle memory from the same activity.

Suddenly, and without warning, Dave spit the entire contents onto the floor. It was dark and syrupy, more like watery chocolate than anything else. He wiped his mouth. 'Who put balsamic vinegar in my water bottle?'

The attendees cringed and every nostalgic memory was suddenly transposed into a visceral nightmare of drinking the acidic vinegar.

Vaughn rolled his eyes. 'Are you finished yet?'

'Quite.' After he had finished wiping his tongue with his arm, Dave motioned toward an empty seat. 'Do you mind if I sit here?'

Vaughn, not impressed in the least, but unwilling to throw any newcomer out, nodded hesitantly.

Dave sat down with a huff, crossed his legs, and adjusted his checkered pants. Once his arms were situated, he smiled. 'Now, where were we?'

'Why don't you tell us who you are, why you're here, and what all that was…'

Eyebrows arched, Dave pondered the seven of us in a circle of plastic chairs arranged so we could all see each other – we were equals, even Vaughn. Alcoholics Anonymous took place in an old school gymnasium on the southwest side of Des Moines. The building did not get used much anymore and smelled like it. Old wooden bleachers were our backdrop along with pennants of long-ago conference championships won by the Raiders in 1964, '69, '72, and '80. The gym smelled of dust, sweat, and faded memories.

'Do I just spit it all out then?' He smiled. His teeth were still brown from the balsamic.

'However it works for you,' Vaughn replied.

'Okay. Hi everyone. My name is Dave.'

As through rote repetition, the attendees welcomed him robotically. 'Hello, Dave.'

'I'm from the southeast side and I read that you were having a little shindig and thought I might pop over.'

'You do realize what the purpose of Alcoholics Anonymous is?' Vaughn asked.

'Of course! You want to drink a lot and do it without people knowing who you are! No more public displays of drunkenness; no more urinating on your parents' peonies. In this place, surrounded by other amazingly anonymous people, you can drink to your hearts' content and find Nirvana in not knowing each other's names.'

Vaughn's anger raised ten notches. 'Listen, Dave, I don't know who you think you are, but this is a serious meeting. Your flippancy is not appreciated.'

'Flippancy?' Dave echoed. 'Flippancy? You mean there's no drinking here?'

Colin snickered. 'No. We've come here to keep each other accountable, so we *don't* drink.'

I knew he was being sarcastic, so did the rest of them, but it wasn't often that AA had a personality like that enter the sacred circle.

'You can stay,' I suggested, willing him to remain for the mere fact that he seemed to offer more color and life than the other six combined, who, for the most part, were pleased about their recovery, but homesick for the previous past of inebriation and the blessed forgetfulness at the bottom of a bottle. 'Can you tell us a story?'

'Can I tell you a story?' he repeated incredulously. 'Absolutely.'

Much to Vaughn's dismay and repeated attempts to interrupt, Dave launched into a convoluted dream about cows living on the planet Saturn who had eyes on opposite sides of their head and ate Snickers bars instead of grass. Just as he was rounding the corner to 'And they lived happily ever after,' Vaughn clapped his hands loudly, just once. Immediately, the rest of my fellow used-to-be-alckies stopped smiling. They hadn't had this much enjoyment in ages. Usually, we bemoaned the fact that being in withdrawal was hell on earth, or our spouses were leaving us, kids hating us, or all those things that come with our disease.

21 – Marty

'That will be enough, Dave. As amusing as that story was, I think we'll move on to Flo. Last week you were telling us about...' Vaughan turned to Flo to put the train back on the tracks.

'Oh, yes, I suppose.'

A stifled groan filtered from the group.

Dave stayed for the whole meeting. He listened intently and asked pertinent questions, questions without pretense (nor tact). We loved his openness and weirdness. By the end of the meeting, Vaughn had unwillingly abdicated his leadership to the bearded wonder. It was almost 10:00 when we finished.

'Well, this has been fun,' Dave uncrossed his legs and slapped his thighs with his hands. 'Same time next week?'

'No, Yes. No,' Vaughn said. 'I think it best if you resist the urge to come. Really,' he said, his hands indicating seriousness, pushing back against Dave's questioning look, 'we need to get some hard work done next week. The interruption, while amusing, cannot happen again.'

'Okay,' Dave responded, not with dejection, but with a simple acknowledgment of facts.

'Let's huddle up for the prayer.' Vaughan circled his arms. Everyone got together in the middle, put their arms around each other, and said the Serenity Prayer. *God, grant me the serenity to accept the things I cannot change, courage to change the things I can, and wisdom to know the difference.*

Dave listened, his head above all of us, and when we were finished, he put his hand in the middle. 'On three. Screw alcohol!' We didn't, but I thought it was funny. Vaughn did not.

We broke the circle and collected our things. Dave stood behind me as I grabbed my coat from the chair. 'What can I do for you?'

'The word on the street is that you're a gun dealer.'

I rolled my eyes. We all had to share who we were and what we did for a living – if we wanted to. 'Yes?'

His voice dropped to a whisper. 'I might be in the market.'

Vaughn was watching us intently, his expression less than pleased. Thankfully, Dave hadn't announced his intentions loudly. 'I'm not working now.'

'But you can get me something, couldn't you?'

'You'd need a background check. That might take a while.'

'No problem.'

'What are you looking for?' I asked as I wrapped the scarf around my neck which covered my military tattoos.

'I need a semi-automatic BB gun. Preferably with scope.'

I couldn't help but burst out in laughter. 'I don't deal in that kind of weaponry.'

'But could you get me one?'

'What do you need it for?'

'Pesky grasshoppers. They keep eating my plants.'

'Why don't you just go to Walmart?'

'I don't go there. It's against my religion.'

'And what is that?'

'Baptist.'

Again, I couldn't not laugh.

'Would you like to hang out a little longer? Maybe we could get a drink?'

Who was this guy? Did it not click with him that we were at an AA meeting? 'I don't think that's such a good idea.'

'I know this great place. Lefties. Have you heard of it?'

'Pickles and hamburgers?'

'That's the one. They have an excellent Pepsi machine. Get me some Diet Mountain Dew.'

'I'm not sure you need any further caffeination.' I waved at Vaughn as we exited. Vaughn was already shaking his head as the door slammed shut behind us.

'Mountain Dew has caffeine?'

'A lot.'

'I'll get decaf, then.'

21 – Marty

'Good luck.'

'Does that mean you'll go?'

I checked my watch. I really had nowhere else to be. I was no longer married. My daughters lived with their mother. My apartment didn't need my noise. And Dave might prove to be an interesting diversion.

'All right.'

'Great. You can drive.'

I stopped. 'You didn't drive here?'

'Nope. Rode the bus.'

For the first time, I had a slight twitch of... not necessarily fear – I can handle myself pretty good... but wariness. Still, he looked about as dangerous as the gum attached to his shoe which was leaving a long string of stretchy goodness behind him.

Lefties was good, and they stayed open late. The staff obviously knew him and called him by name.

'What's your last name?' I asked.

'I don't have one. What's yours?'

At that time, I didn't know Dave preferred not to have his last name known. I just thought he was being secretive. Don't worry. You will find out eventually. It's important to the story.

'My last name is Gifford.'

'You must be from the Frank Gifford line. Why, if I could count on my fingers all the Giffords I know, there would be at least two.' At this point he sipped on Diet Mountain Dew in an enormous red-plastic cup. He drank half of it in one breath and then panted.

'What's it like selling guns?'

'I suppose like selling pants or groceries. People have a need, they select what they want, and I fill their order.'

'Except people buying milk don't have to get a background check and wait, how long?'

I didn't want to tell him that it would probably take thirty seconds. 'Long enough. Even for a semi-automatic BB gun with scope.'

'How did you end up an alcoholic?' he asked quietly.

For some reason it was easier to retell my story to Dave than to anyone else, even the other members of AA. He was earnest in his listening, and he asked stunningly pointed, sometimes slightly offputting, questions, but I wasn't put off. I had had a hard life. Too many incorrect decisions, not much courage in battling my inner desires, and a wife who made life miserable for me. I now know it wasn't her fault. I'm able to understand that, even retell it to Dave, but it's easier to blame someone else when life is holding a gun to your head. Now sober for almost two years, life was finally getting back on track. Business was booming, pun intended, and I'd purchased some land on the west side of Des Moines, a nice little acreage with a farmhouse. Quiet. Maybe I'd get some chickens.

'Sounds like an idyllic end to your life.'

'I'm not dying,' I laughed.

'Not yet. Everybody does, though.'

'Thanks, Socrates.'

'You're welcome.'

We gobbled up our pickles and hamburgers, sucked down our drinks, and Dave paid. That was nice. He looked like he couldn't afford a bus ticket, but he extracted a thick, Velcro wallet from his back pocket. It was full of twenty-dollar bills. I ground my teeth. 'You shouldn't be carrying that kind of cabbage around.'

'What? The money?' He rolled his eyes. 'Just useful paper.' Dave plopped a sixty-dollar tip on the table.

'Whoa,' I was astonished. 'You aren't a drug dealer, are you?'

'The only thing I deal in is awesomeness.'

'You're one weird dude, Dave.'

'Thank you.'

We stood to leave. Dave waved to the young waiter behind the counter who shouted back at the staff who was closing shop. When we reached the door, I offered to give him a ride home.

'Won't be necessary, my good Marty. I live just around the corner.'

'All right.'

21 – Marty

If I would have known 'around the corner' was fifteen city blocks away, I would have insisted, but I didn't know then what I know now. I stuck out my hand. 'I guess this is goodbye, Dave. It's been very interesting. I hope I see you again someday.'

He shook it gravely and bent over slightly so that his eyes were nearer mine. They had golden flecks in them, and he didn't blink. 'How would you like to go to church with me?'

22

Jonathan

For some reason, the floral display on the altar was memorable the morning I met Marty Gifford. One of the ladies on the decorating committee had brought in some late summer roses. We aren't normally a rosy kind of church, instead sticking to much more subdued decorations like old King James Bibles and shepherds' crooks. But that day, the ladies outdid themselves and sprayed the altar with reds and yellows making it looking like a summery sunset at the front of the church. When I entered from the side, three of the ladies' guild members were stationed, hands cupped below their chins, eyes wide, expectantly awaiting my assessment. When I nodded and smiled, they clapped daintily, and turned as one, like three-headed Cerberus, and walked down the far aisle, past the band which was gearing up for the first hymn, a slightly out-of-tune rendition of Blessed Assurance. I really wish they would get their act together.

Anyway, as I followed the ladies' movement to their seats, my eyes alit on a now-familiar figure.

Dave.

Letitia and Meg were beside him, thank God. At least Letitia would eventually draw him away from me after the service. On that day, though, a stranger was sitting next to Dave. He had shoulder length, wavy dark hair, parted down the middle. His brown eyes swept the sanctuary. He was having a pretty decent conversation with himself, or it appeared that way, and he fidgeted in his seat as if something underneath was biting him. I'll have to do penance for what I thought that morning (not that Baptist's really give that much thought to penance, but it's a good turn of phrase), but I wondered if Dave hadn't brought a possessed man to church. I'd never cast out a demon before, and I didn't want to start the service on a low note.

Dave waved at me and then nudged his friend in the ribs. I could read his lips. *Jon Nathan*. Ugh. I hate to say this, but every time Dave came to church, I was a little more self-conscious. Letitia shushed him.

22 – Jonathan

Thankfully, I somehow navigated the service successfully without too much interruption from Dave.

Afterwards, Dave introduced me to Marty and proclaimed just a little too loudly that he had purchased a premium sniper air rifle with complementary scope. 'I've picked off seven grasshoppers this week alone, one at fifty feet.' Dave tapped his chest theatrically while Marty glanced around nervously.

It had become my habit to ignore Dave's first salvos of commentary knowing that they were intended to shock and disarm me, much like a stun grenade.

'Hello,' I held my hand out to Marty, 'I'm Jonathan.'

Marty stared skeptically at my offered hand before eventually shaking it quickly and firmly, releasing it like a wet fish.

'Is this your first time at Grace?'

'What?'

'Here, in this church.'

'Uh, yes. Dave invited me.'

'Did he?'

'Yes.' Marty frowned, still deciding if I was safely ignorant or just unintelligent.

'Where did you two meet?'

'At Alcoholics Anonymous,' Dave interjected in a whisper. He covered his lip with an index finger as if it was a secret.

'I… didn't know you attended those meetings,' I said to Dave.

'It was my first one. But I met Marty, we hit it off. I bought a sniper rifle. He came to church.'

'How long have you been in recovery?' I asked.

'Oh, I'm not an alcoholic,' Dave answered.

'Then what were you doing there?'

'When the Fox hears the Rabbit scream, he comes a-runnin', but not to help.'

'What?'

Even Marty seemed perplexed by Dave's response, but I think we'd both known him long enough to let that one go into the net.

On another morning, already October, Dave was back at church with Marty. I am embarrassed to say that I was thankful that Dave hadn't come back very often, but I knew why he was there that morning.

Meg.

When Letitia called me from the hospital and told me the terrible news, she asked if I would come to sit with them. I asked where Dave was, and she told me he had abandoned them. Although I was confused as to why Dave had turned his back on them, I said I'd come. I told my wife what I was doing and drove as quickly as I could to Unity Point where I found them in the children's ward. I stayed for the afternoon praying with them and consoling Letitia. When I left, Letitia was on the verge of sleeping, but they were just about to move Meg to a different, private room.

Thankfully, Meg had been released home now, but she was due to undergo chemotherapy treatments. They were also looking for a marrow transplant.

So when I saw Dave that morning, I wasn't sure how to react. Should I go strong and tell him he needed to pull his head in, or did I listen first? Maybe he had a decent excuse?

Because of Marty's presence, I decided on the latter.

'Good morning, Dave. Marty.'

'Hello.' Dave answered. He looked terrible. Deep, dark bags bunched under his eyes, and he had lost weight. He had been thin already, but now he looked gaunt, as if it was he who had cancer, not Meg.

'How are you doing?'

'I see the Mothman…'

I had no idea what he was talking about, but apparently Marty did. Marty frowned and checked the surroundings to see if anyone else was listening.

22 – Jonathan

'His wings are growing and the red eyes... The red eyes, Jonathan.' Dave's tone frightened me. Never before had I come so close to viewing utter despair, or horror, or fear, or whatever it was. Was he speaking of a demon?

'Are you alright?' I asked.

'How could I be alright,' he hissed. 'He's after her. Right behind her.'

'Who?'

'The Mothman.'

'I don't know who that is.' I tried to place a hand on his forearm, but he flinched.

Suddenly, a light came into his eyes. It was like a candle being lit, and he blinked a few times, then scanned the sanctuary until finally setting his gaze on Marty and me.

'I need your help.'

'Of course. How?'

'Will you come with me today, to the apartments? Both you and Marty. I need to convince Benson. All of us, we'll find them.'

He wasn't making any sense at all.

'Marty, maybe you can explain it to me.'

Marty was hesitant but eventually spoke. 'Dave is looking for a donor for Meg. A marrow donor. He wants to scour the neighborhood, the apartments, maybe even this church, for someone who's a match.'

'Letitia isn't?'

Marty shook his head.

Dave's eyes were wild again, unfocused. He stared over my head toward the sound booth and beyond, back into the indoor café where congregants were lining up in front of coffee urns to fill their ceramic cups and grab a tasty morsel from the server's window, then settle down for some Sunday morning gossip.

'I'll see what I can do,' my voice was unsure. 'Maybe if I put something in the bulletin...'

Dave grabbed me suddenly by the front of the shirt and turned it over in his fist tightening the collar around my neck. 'This doesn't call for an announcement,' he growled, his teeth clenched. 'You need to talk to them. Round every one of these entitled, rich people, and get them to test. You always talk about the church being the church. Well, *be* it.'

He released me, and the fear I felt was replaced by righteous indignation. I straightened my shirt. 'You need to leave, Dave. We may tolerate many of your eccentricities, but assault is not one I intend to. Thank God it wasn't one of the parishioners.'

Marty stepped in between us. 'He didn't mean it, Padre. He's just overwhelmed.'

'Get him out of here, Marty.'

Marty grabbed Dave by the arm and tried to turn him, but Dave stubbornly resisted. 'You owe me this, Jonathan. You owe this to Meg.' His voice was getting louder. 'Your God owes this to her. DO SOMETHING!'

The church went silent, even those in the café. Everyone turned to stare at Dave, the man they had tolerated for much of the year. Even though they avoided him, they believed their allowances to the holy building were crowns in heaven.

His words struck me to the core. Was this the church's opportunity to put flesh on the creed?

As Dave and Marty walked slowly down the middle aisle towards the back, I watched them speak to each other, Dave leaning towards him, Marty doing his best to calm his friend. They were an odd couple, a real pair of misfits.

At that moment, I made a decision.

I'd be visiting a lot of people that week.

23
Benson

They stood there at my door, Dave looming, Marty guarding the entrance, peering side to side to see if anyone was watching. In another life, this would have appeared like a robbery, but not then. It was just Dave and his new best friend Marty.

'I'm still angry with you,' I said to Dave.

Weirdly, he waltzed into my apartment, astonishingly carefree and unburdened. In fact, his face was alight, as if he'd just had a vision. Marty followed behind, at his heel, like a slightly shorter and handsomer version of Dave himself without the sideburns.

'I'm not angry at you, though.'

'Why should you be? I'm not the one that ditched my girlfriend and her daughter at the hospital.'

'I've forgiven myself for that.'

'Jeez, Dave. Do you even listen to yourself sometimes?'

He paused to think about it. Instead of responding, he switched topics. 'I've got an idea.'

'I don't want to hear it.'

'Would you rather Marty tells you?'

'No, I would not rather have Marty do it.' Suddenly, I realized Dave had a Meerschaum pipe in his hand. It was intricately carved into the shape of a hawk's taloned foot holding an egg with a hole in the end of it. 'What do you have that for? You don't smoke.'

'Not yet, but I'm going to start.'

'Why?'

'They say smoking is relaxing. I thought maybe we could sit on the balcony and share some 'bacci' one night. Doesn't that sound romantic?'

I turned slightly to Marty. 'Does this sound normal to you?'

Marty shrugged but didn't reply.

'That's really beside the point, Bensonian. I've figured out what to do?'

'About Meg?'

'Over this odd world, this half of the world that's dark now, I have to hunt a thing that lives on tears.'

'Is that a quote from the movie.'

'Yes.'

'How does it apply?'

'Were you not listening? The Mothman. I've been created to kill the Mothman.'

'That's crazy, Dave. The Mothman is a myth, a figment of someone's imagination meant to scare people. The Boogeyman or Bigfoot. What you need to do is find a donor.'

'We're on the same wavelength,' he motioned back and forth between us. 'I've come up with a plan.'

'What is it?'

'In solidarity, we shall all smoke pipes together, then shuffle off to the hospital to get tested.'

'What?'

'A pipe smoking ceremony on behalf of Meg's recovery.'

I rose from my seat to confront them both. Marty took a step back, but Dave didn't. I noticed that his hands trembled slightly as they carefully held the pipe. It was a beautiful piece, delicate in structure, and the curvature was exact. 'When is the last time you slept, Dave.'

'It doesn't matter,' he responded forcefully shoving the pipe towards my face.

'I think it most certainly does. You're not thinking clearly. Mothman, pipe smoking, forcing Marty into this.' I held up my hands to Marty in apology. 'No offense.'

'None taken,' he replied.

'I don't feel tired,' said Dave inching the pipe closer.

'If I do this, will you go have a nap?'

'Most assuredly. We three amigos and whoever else wants to get in on the action.'

'Let's keep it lowkey. It's against the rules to smoke on the property.'

'Gladys won't care.'

'Yes, she will.'

'Come on, Marty. Let's get this circle set up.'

After they left, I called Wendy.

'Is everything okay?'

'No.'

'What happened?'

There was a tension between us – there always had been – when it came to Dave. He was like that perpetually glowing light on the smoke detector, a red-eye hovering over everything. If I wanted to speak to her privately, I often had to draw away from him, or he'd orbit, casting in bits of his own opinions, unwanted and unnecessary. That was his way of exerting his power over me. That's why he found Marty, I think, so that my attention was diverted from Wendy. He wanted me to be jealous. One eye on him, and one eye on her.

As our conversation continued, I could hear it in her voice, a vibration of resentment. I knew she wanted me to sever ties with him, but once he had his beautiful claws in – everyone said it – it was very hard to dislodge them. Gladys. Gordon. Marty. Letitia. All the wonderful people he had brought together were also entirely dependent upon him for their social bedrock.

'And so he's circling up some people to do a smoking ceremony. Supposedly it will draw us together to find a donor.'

'I don't think that's how it works.'

'Would you like to speak to him yourself?'

Wendy cleared that idea up in no uncertain terms.

'I wish you were here,' I say.

'Mmh hmm.'

Her response was not the ringing endorsement I hoped for. 'You don't want to be here?'

The silence hung between us like a ghostly force. Fear gripped me. 'Wendy?'

'Benson, we need to talk.'

Those are the words every human being in a relationship never wants to hear. There is something terrible and final, a decision already made, unconsulted, unquestioned. That phrase simply means, *Your life is about to change for the worse, and for the lonelier.*

'Don't say it, Wendy. Please don't break up with me.'

She sighed. 'I don't want to break up with you, but I can't continue the way it is. *You* have to break up with Dave. It will be so much easier for me.'

'But how?'

'You have to figure that out on your own, I guess.'

My gut began to churn. I had called her for support and encouragement. Oh, how I wished I never would have picked up my phone. 'I'll tell him right now. I'll go down there, step into the circle and tell him I'm not doing anything for him anymore.'

'Sure you will.'

She was unconvinced, and frankly, so was I. Just this one more thing. I'll do the smoking ceremony, find a donor for Meg, and then I'm done with him. Wash my hands of him. Move to Davenport, maybe.

'I'm off to do it now. Please be patient.'

She disconnected the call without saying goodbye. I stared at the phone. It was a dreadful thing to me now. She had severed me from her future, and this was the tool of her amputation.

Full of willpower, I stomped to the door. I'd show him. I'd tell him exactly how it had to be.

I threw open the door to find thirty other people standing on the balcony. It was cold outside and many of them had wrapped blankets or jackets around themselves to stave off the bitterness. They were staring down into the courtyard, so I stood at the railing and found Dave and Marty with a few others, circling the fishpond. Dave was on one end, Marty opposite him. Gordon and another resident, Miriam Deng, a

23 – Benson

Vietnamese resident, were on the edges of the circle. Dave turned and saw me on the balcony. He asked me with his eyes without verbalizing, *Are you coming?*

Yes, yes, I had to. Dave needed me. He was in a bad spot. I couldn't let him down in his greatest hour of need.

I hurried down the stairs, feeling the cold prickle on my bare arms. I should have put on a coat, but there hadn't been time.

When I reached the circle, Dave moved Miriam aside to make a place for me. Miriam was grumpy about this, but did as he asked.

'Today,' he said loudly enough for the entire apartment complex to hear, 'we bond in an ancient ceremony. You who are witnesses are invited to take part as well, but the ceremony works by proxy, too.' He held up the Meerschaum pipe. 'This is no ordinary pipe, but one from our ancient elders from the Appalachian Mountains. To share smoke from this pipe signifies that each one of us will go to the hospital to be tested for genetic matching to Meg.'

There were a few grumbles of disapproval. 'If you have questions, I will be available afterwards.'

'That doesn't look like one of the pipes the Indians used,' I said. 'I've seen *Dances With Wolves*.'

He gave me a dirty look. 'The important parts of the ceremony are the words and actions, not the object.'

'Tell that to a professional photographer being asked to use a Polaroid.'

'You don't have to do this, you know.'

It should have been so easy to walk away, but he caught me with his will. I felt like a dog in a basket.

'I'm sorry. Go ahead.' And with that, I promised myself to him for the foreseeable future. Surely, Wendy would understand. Eventually.

He lifted the pipe again, then lowered it. From a pouch at his waist, he took pipe tobacco and stuffed it. Saluting the six directions (the four cardinal ones and the sky and earth), he put the pipe to his lips and lit the tobacco with a plastic, long-stemmed lighter. The sight was confusing –

the ancient with the contemporary; the claw and the click. He drew smoke into his mouth, puffing it slowly, mesmerizingly, like a chain chugging up a hill. 'The smoke cleanses us, draws our spirits together. One of us will be chosen. One of us will be able to help Meg.'

His eyes were closed, and I felt sympathy and frustration. How could this possibly help the situation?

Dave handed the pipe to me. It was warm in my hands. 'You cup the bowl with your left hand and the stem with your right.' He instructed me with a mime. 'Go ahead,' he encouraged. 'Pass it around.'

When the smoke filled my mouth, I felt a strange sense of wonder. I've never smoked anything in my life. Never had the urge at all. And yet sharing this with him, and with the people around me, I sensed the bonding that he had spoken of. In sharing that, I was connected to the ancients – the ones who made the pipe and the ones who carried on the tradition. When you smoked, there was no speaking, only you and the others in shared peace. I pulled on it four or five times, and each time I felt calmer, more connected.

When I opened my eyes, Dave was transfixed. *Well?*

I nodded and blew out the last smoke before handing it to Miriam who accepted it cautiously. She made it look easy, and when she finished, passed it on around the circle. I took a moment to study the balcony ringed with people we knew and cared for. They were agnostic about what was happening, and yet they accepted it. Whatever was going on around the fishpond would be talked about for weeks.

With an anticlimactic sigh, Gordon returned the pipe to Dave.

'Thank you, friends,' Dave whispered and then spoke above him. 'Please, residents of the Palms, my smoke brothers and sisters, will you follow me to the hospital to be tested? Not for our own sakes, but for the life of a young friend, a spirit ember that has yet to completely burst into life. It will only cost you time, but if you are a match, you could save her life. And Letitia's.' *And his.*

It was too much for some of them – most of them. Dave's freakishness had finally caught up with him. Even Gladys. Maybe if he wouldn't have gone overboard with the smoke ceremony, he would have gotten more buy-in, but as it was, Gordon's wife Patricia called out, 'It's time for dinner, Gordon!' Apologetically, Gordon patted Dave on the shoulder. Perhaps it was not even that they didn't want to do it, but the mundane called. It was dinnertime, or Jeopardy was on; maybe they were in the midst of cleaning the bathroom. They would go to the hospital the next day or the week after. Surely someone else would be a match and they could put this whole thing to rest. Things would finally get back to normal.

And so would Dave.

That's what they all hoped.

I wasn't so sure.

24
Patricia

'It's time for dinner, Gordon!' I shouted.

There are limits to tomfoolery, obviously, and whatever Dave was trying to do in the courtyard was pure lunacy. I realized he was struggling with Meg's diagnosis, but counseling seemed to be a better idea than whatever that was.

Looking back on it now, I feel a deep sense of guilt because of the way things turned out. Maybe if each one of us would have dug a little deeper and…

After Gordon got back to the apartment, I closed the door behind him.

'What are you trying to prove?'

'I was helping,' Gordon said as he removed his coat and draped it over the kitchen chair. The smell of roasting chicken had filled the apartment, and I could tell his stomach was rumbling.

'Helping? How was that going to help anything?'

'I don't know. I thought I was supporting Dave.'

'He needs serious clinical help, that's what he needs.'

Gordon took a seat at the table and adjusted his silverware. 'I feel sorry for him.'

'We *all* feel sorry for him, dear, but this kind of weirdness can't continue. Someone is going to do something crazy.'

'I think you might be exaggerating a little bit.'

I placed the chicken and potatoes on the table, wiped my hands on the apron, and served up the dinner. 'I suppose you'll be wanting to get tested?'

'Don't you?'

I pulled out the chair across from him and sat down. 'Yes, I suppose, but we've got so many plans for these upcoming weeks. It's almost Halloween, then Thanksgiving – Christmas is around the corner.'

'Excuses.'

Gordon wasn't normally so short with me. 'Gordon!'

'You're using holidays as excuses for doing what is right. Technically, Thanksgiving and Christmas are the perfect times to do it.'

'Is this really that important to you?'

'I can't understand why it's not that important to *you*.' Gordon pointed a fork at me. 'We're a community. A family. We eat together. We talk together.'

'That's enough, Gordon. We're not a family. This is an apartment complex. Our family is in northwest Iowa, remember? A son. Cousins. Blood relatives.'

Gordon sighed and took a mouthful of chicken. 'Blood relatives,' he repeated. 'Imagine if it's our blood that would relate us to Meg.'

As my husband chewed quietly across the table, I pondered exactly why it was that being tested posed such a philosophical problem for me. Was it because I felt that Dave was taking my husband's attention? Was I playing the odds? Maybe I just didn't need the interruption in my routine. That's what retirement was supposed to be about – routine.

'When would you like to go?' I asked softly.

He shrugged. 'Tomorrow. The next day, maybe.'

We didn't go that tomorrow or the next day or even the week after. Eventually, we just fell into the rut of everyday life – coffee in the morning on the balcony, a walk in the afternoon, then a nap. Some time online. It was just easier not to help.

I still feel guilty about that.

25

Benson

Over a month had passed since the smoking ceremony. Besides me, a few others had taken up the challenge to get tested. None were a match. I had hoped I would have been, but alas, no.

Even though it was Thanksgiving, the Palms residents attempted to fight through the conflicting emotions of being thankful for the blessings they did have and reconciling it with the difficulty of Meg's reality. It wasn't that there weren't others suffering at this time. Tania's sister was living through the aftermath of a horrific house fire. Doc couldn't seem to get over his wife's passing. Gladys desperately wanted her daughter to come home. And I, with every part of my being, wanted to be with Wendy. I could still be thankful, though. It just seemed emptier, like being grateful for a pot roast when you really wanted a ribeye.

That Thanksgiving, not only was Meg sick, but the weight of that difficulty had affected Dave and his interactions with everyone. Even though we still gathered for our community meals, everything felt misaligned. Dave wandered around the complex in a fog. For four weeks, while Meg suffered through chemotherapy, he plodded along the balconies and mumbled up and down the stairs. If we didn't know who he was, we might have thought him a homeless man; but we did, and his actions were worrisome to say the least.

Many residents had gone out of their way to attempt conversation, but even that dropped off. Some stood on their balconies and watched him, arms crossed, shaking their heads muttering, *Poor Dave*. Most of them thought it was all about Meg, but I had my suspicions it was bigger than that. I broached the subject with Ignatius last week, but he was unwilling to share anything. His eyes looked pained and clouded – he knew something.

I exited my room and padded down the lined porch past the apartments of friends. Outside each room was a small table. In the middle of each was a picture of Meg. It felt kind of demented, you know? How do you eat when Meg's healthy face was staring at you?

At Thanksgiving, Dave was supposed to ring the bell for a progressive Thanksgiving dinner. Different rooms had prepared various parts of the meal; a few of the older residents had volunteered to cook turkeys. I volunteered to make a salad, which, in essence, was to buy one from HyVee. It didn't matter if they judged me, but I wasn't going to eat it either.

I smelled the turkey, biscuits, gravy, mashed potatoes, and my stomach started to rumble. At 11:55, Patricia climbed our stairs and stood next to the dinner bell. I frowned because that was Dave's thing – not Patricia's thing – he was the Thanksgiving muezzin calling people to eat.

'What are you doing?' I asked. 'Where is Dave?'

'He asked me to do it.'

'Why?'

'You're his best friend. You should ask him.'

If I *was* his best friend, I *would* have been first on the list of bell-ringers. There I was, feeling like a first grader being picked last for kickball.

Patricia checked her watch and took a deep breath, grabbed hold of the clapper and began to jangle it violently. It hurt my ears, and I ducked out of the way. 'What the heck!' I shouted above the sound to which she smiled.

Doors opened, people shuffled out and shouted across the courtyard, across and below, like a very strange Brady Bunch, 'Happy Thanksgiving!' They put their prepared food on the tables and then held bowls or plates in preparation for the food wander, a buffet-style odyssey around the Palms, loading up on the best foods. Turkey, stuffing, gravy, cranberries would create an island of goodness while mashed potatoes were heaped like white volcanoes. As people shuffled from table to table (leaning over, and sometimes, if you're like the Lee's, taste-testing before scooping) I noticed that no one had taken any of my salad.

I didn't blame them.

Staring at Dave's room, I waited for his door to open. It was always his favorite part. He loved seeing the residents grin. He loved seeing them laugh and joke with each other. He loved every part of these get togethers, and to see him absent felt as if the body was missing a limb.

I knocked on Dave's door. As usual, it was unlocked. He had made it abundantly clear, much to Gladys's chagrin, that anyone could use his place at any time.

'Dave?' I called out and opened the door a crack.

There was no response, so I pushed it open further and stuck my head through the gap. The apartment was draped in darkness, and it took a second for my eyes to adjust. When they did, I was shocked to find Dave slouched on his maroon sofa, hands on his thighs, staring at the ceiling.

'Dave?' He turned his head, but his eyes were empty – dead. 'You okay? What's going on?'

'I heard the bell. I wanted to help. I wanted to help. But that would hurt.'

'Hurt what?'

The ticking clock in the background was either a metronome or a time bomb. *Tick tock, click clock, pit pot*, endless and unceasing. There was no stopping time, and no hurrying the discomfort in the room.

'The pain of...' he couldn't say it, but he tapped his chest three times. It thudded in the empty room in time with the clock.

'Do you need to see someone? You know, like a psychiatrist or counselor or something?'

Dave leaned forward slowly clasping his hands between his knees, head bowed. 'You know what they'd say? *You know what you look like with your good bag and your cheap shoes? You look like a rube. A well-scrubbed, hustling rube with a little taste. Good nutrition has given you some length of bone, but you're nothing more than one generation removed from poor white trash. And that accent you're trying to hide – pure Pennsylvania.*"

His response irked me. 'This is not the Silence of the Lambs, Dave. This is real life.' I moved closer to him. 'Real. Everything about this situation is real, and all those people are out there eating together in whatever place they feel like, that's because of you. *You're* real to them. This community and this sense of togetherness – you did that. You brought them together and made them feel valuable.'

'I can't save them...' Dave's voice trailed off.

'Nobody needs you to save them.'

'But Meg...'

I clenched my teeth. 'You can't save Meg. That's not your job. The doctors... they're very good. We have some of the best medical facilities in the world. They'll do everything in their power to make her healthy again.'

'People die, Benson. People you love.'

'Meg isn't going to die.'

Dave rubbed his eye. 'Everybody dies. Some are old, some aren't, but eventually we all get there. It's the river that keeps flowing, keeps taking us with it. We fight against the current, but it does no good.'

'Meg is going to make it,' I state adamantly.

'YOU DON'T KNOW THAT!' He shouted into the semi-darkness. I was startled. He had never raised his voice to me before. 'There is only *one* Meg – one, Benson. And if she dies, it will be my fault.' He pulled himself from the sofa.

'Dave, you're scaring me.'

He pointed a finger in my face. 'Someone has to save Meg. And I mean to find that person.'

'That doesn't make any sense. What are you planning to do?'

Dave roughly shoved past me and out the door. He sidled to the balcony and began ringing the bell. It clanged loudly breaking the tranquility of the Thanksgiving meal. Like bears staggering out from their pre-hibernation, the people stood in their open doorways, napkins still tucked into shirts, greasy fingers holding turkey legs, buns, or bowls of cranberries.

He kept ringing it, and ringing it, as hard as he could. It did not surprise me when it dislodged from the beam and fell at his feet. The bell was now dented and the clapper lolled like the tongue of a dead animal. Dave's face was a mask of confusion, rage, and sorrow. He gripped the railing, and his voice reverberated in the courtyard, bouncing and echoing, the same emotions amplified by the acoustics until he was silent, and so were his people.

'I need you to do this thing for me. Please. I realize the last effort was not helpful. I'm not crazy. Just needful. I believed that begging your good natures, or appealing to the Midwestern values of 'help your neighbor at all costs' would be enough motivation for you to get tested. But I know for a fact that most of you did not.'

The pause between sentences was frightening – eerie. Guilty faces stared at him from around the balconies, above and below.

'Tomorrow, instead of shopping or baking or wrapping presents, or any of the things you normally do to distract yourselves from the fact that life is going to end at some point, I need you to go with me to the hospital to be tested. I'm begging you.'

All eyes were focused; all mouths had stopped chewing. All brains whirred furiously at what Dave was demanding of them again. It was not just that they would donate their time, but what he asked of them would interrupt their plans. No shopping, no football, no drinking.

'For maybe the first time in your lives, you can do something good and noble and unselfish. Among you, there might be one person who is a match for that trembling life waiting for a donor so that she can live well beyond her fifth year.'

The last echoes died out and I glanced again at the bell, lifeless and silent. It felt odd to think about the bell at a time like this, but the pleasant memories that had rung out before seemed to be fading in the midst of the current crisis.

'Please,' Dave shouted, 'do this for her!'

They looked guilty. Most of them had made reservations at restaurants, planned to meet up with friends at the cinema, even taken a day off work to burn holes in their credit cards, but none of them had probably given the first thought to helping someone else.

A few hands dropped to their sides, turkey legs grasped, stomachs suddenly un-hungry.

I wondered what would happen the next day. I was supposed to travel to the Quad Cities. Wendy and I were going to spend the weekend together, but now...? Did I need to stay even though I'd already been tested?

Dave's eyes turned towards me accusingly as if he had just read my last thought. Then, with slow deliberation, he turned back towards his room, stepping over the bell and its lifeless clapper, and entered. As the door closed behind him, it felt like a tomb had been rolled shut.

26

Jonathan

For every pat on the back, there are a dozen body blows that arrive out of nowhere. In my pastoral role, I get to see the best of people and the tragic wrestling match that accompanies their incessant desire to ignore impermanence.

Since Letitia brought Dave to worship that first Sunday morning, I'd been reevaluating exactly what was important in life, not just my own, but the life of humankind as well. My eyes had been opened, as the Good Book says, and I'd begun to notice all of life's nuances. Once was blind, now I see, and all that.

I had conversations with people in my congregation, comfortable and content in their slow, gradual descent into the meaninglessness that King Solomon was wont to express, about what it meant to be alive, not just living. They stared at me with glassy eyes, smiles hidden behind expressions of, *I have no idea what he's talking about*, as they pondered which golf course they were going to play during that afternoon, or which football game they needed to watch after church. It sounds like I'm denigrating them, and I don't mean to, but sooner or later there are terms which need to be grasped regarding the delicate balance between the time we have and the time we don't.

We get used to marking events that occur on weekends. The weekdays spill into a bucket of routine. But on the Tuesday that Letitia called me again from the hospital, I dropped all the meetings I had on my calendar (a staff meeting, a home visit, a trip to the nursing home to lead a worship service) and left right away. On the way to the hospital, I prayed a prayer I reserved for special occasions. Like the sharpest arrow in my quiver notched for the largest of beasts:

Dear God, wherever you are and doing whatever it is you do, can you pause for a little while and take care of Letitia and Meg?

Maybe I have a skewed understanding of God that he'll only respond to never-cry-wolfers, but the older I get, the more I get it, that

26 – Jonathan

you either pray or you don't, and whatever answer comes back is probably the right one even if you don't like it. Which is why I don't like to pray that prayer because it opens up a whole world of body-blow possibilities.

After walking to Meg's room, I rapped lightly on the door hoping not to disturb Meg in case she was sleeping.

Benson sat on the far side of the bed. He saw me and breathed a sigh of relief. I've seen that look many times before. In moments of grief, tumultuous difficulty, conflict, or whatever trauma that might be occurring, many people desire to see the 'professional' insert himself or herself into the middle. Take the pressure off the amateurs.

If sickness, the presence of a nurse; In despair, the presence of a counselor; In death, the grateful release of authority to the hopemonger – the spiritual person. End of life moments are the hardest. Shuddering, struggling inhalations, like the last gasps before diving under water, the death rattle, as it's called. I've seen them far too many times. Those moments are not easy and eminently pitiable in the presence of people who believe that there is nothing else – just an abyss of darkness and silence. Some believe this is the blessing of death – to be released from pain and suffering – but very few would whisper those words in the presence of a mother whose five-year-old daughter was fighting for her right to live.

'Pastor Jonathan,' Benson said, 'I'm glad you're here.'

'Thank you, I'm honored to be called.'

Benson moved backwards and allowed me to move past. I faced Letitia and noticed the dismal bags of worry under her eyes.

'Have you seen Dave recently?'

I nodded. The memory of Dave and Marty at church still played on my mind. I knelt down beside Meg. I frowned. This moment was not about Dave. 'You should go find him.'

'Right,' Benson said. He left with scarcely another word other than a goodbye to Letitia and a head nod to me.

We sat in the preternatural stillness of the medical world. The passing nurses whooshed outside the room; the noisy visitors spoke into their phones as they attempted to locate their own life-interruptions in the hospital. Meg was covered by a small blanket. Someone had brought her a purple unicorn. Its head was uncovered, and the horn was nestled near Meg's right ear.

'Why?' Letitia whispered into that stillness. 'Why? What did she do to deserve this?'

If only I had that *one* correct answer, the one that would help all sufferers to understand life's hardest question. All the others I'd gladly give up, if only God would upload the big picture of everything so we could finally see all the pieces of the puzzle moving around and together. If only there was a red phone line with direct access to the highest heavens which didn't have call waiting or even an answering machine, not even a heavenly messenger in God's office taking messages. Attempting to dig God out of the suffering holes is theological folly. I can only offer a small hope that God is indeed in those holes working to reconstruct things.

'She didn't do anything, Letitia. Nor did you. It's not your fault.'

I could tell I'd struck a chord, for she had been wondering that very thing – if there was something she could have done, a sign of sickness that she had missed. We all do that, I think. To understand the unpleasant realities of life, we try to change the past and our part in it. But it doesn't work. It only delays the process of dealing with the present.

'I should have paid attention to the bruising and the bloody nose and that nurse who implied I was beating her!' Letitia's voice rose and broke into a sob. It was a long keening wail, a razor blade on a chalkboard; truly life's worst sound, that of a broken mother whose existence was scuppered by the platitudes of the healthy. At that moment, I could only let her vent her imagination, her misplaced anger at the absurdity of a sick child. This tragedy was not a weight to be placed on herself, or Dave, or even the nurse, but transferred to someone tangible to help us stay upright.

26 – Jonathan

She cried for what seemed an eternity. A worried nurse poked her head in the room. She, too, was relieved that I was there. She retreated into the arterial vessel of the hospital hallways, a white blood cell fighting infections in other rooms.

When Letitia's sobbing finally sank, its keel ripped out by the reef of grief, she wiped her eyes.

'I thought I was strong. I thought, 'I am woman, hear me roar,' but when it comes to being a mother, I… have nothing.'

I remained silent.

'I feel so guilty,' she said, staring at her daughter. 'I can't stop thinking of all the times in the last five years when I wondered silently why I had to be a mother, why I had to pay the bills, buy the clothes, spend countless sleepless nights wondering how we were going to make it. I blamed him for knocking me up, creating this endless tension called a child and child-rearing. Sometimes I blamed her for disrupting my life, or at least my dreams. You know, travel and meeting exciting people, and all that stuff. Successful things. I looked at Meg as an interruption, but now that she is here…' her face cracked again, and the last squeeze of tears appeared in her eyes, '… in this room, with pins and needles stuck into her dripping chemicals into her veins, I feel like punching myself. She's my everything.'

'You're a good mother,' I said lamely.

She held up a hand. 'Don't patronize me. I have enough to work through without that.'

'I'm sorry.'

'When we rode over in the ambulance, I stared down at her and she smiled at me. She was trying to take care of me. But you know where she got that? Dave. He takes care of everyone.'

I nodded.

'And yet when I need him most, when she needs a father – or at least the closest thing to a father she's ever had, he's absent. Just like her real dad.'

'There's no comfort I can give you now, only that we'll do all that we can to be with you.'

Her lips pursed. 'That's the thing religious people say. "We'll walk with you during this time of suffering," or worse, "Our thoughts and our prayers are with you," or even, "Here's a nice casserole to tide you over." She choked out a sardonic laugh. 'But what does religion actually do?'

'Are you asking that as a non-rhetorical question?'

'Yes.'

I took a deep breath and held it, sighing as it came out. 'The only thing that faith can do – as opposed to religion – is give us hope that there is something better.'

'What good is hope?'

'That's a hard question, and I'm not sure I can answer it well, but hope is that small glimmer at the end of a tunnel, or that thin wafting scent of food when you're really hungry. Faith fans hope, so that we can live.'

'But if people have faith, then why does God do this?' She motions with her hands at Meg again. 'Why doesn't God pick on someone his own size?'

I've pondered that question many times in my life, and I've only come to one realization.

'Because Meg *is* his own size. As we grow older, we grow smaller; our hearts shrink, and our faith tends to get moldy because of all the stress and pain in life. But when we are children, we are immense! God isn't picking on Meg, nor is he testing her. The God I believe in is… Ah, it all sounds crumbly when we sit here like this.'

'No, please,' Letitia pleaded. 'Don't stop there. You believe God is…?'

'I believe that God is with us every step of the way, in sickness even much more than health. We don't often think about God when we are healthy. But kids – they do. Because their faith is larger, and they experience God in a different way.'

26 – Jonathan

'But what happens if...' She couldn't finish the unutterable sentence.

'What happens if she lives? Is that what you were asking?'

Letitia's head bowed.

'We'll figure out the celebrations when that happens.'

'And if it doesn't?'

Here was the crux of everything. 'Then we will fight the desperate battle against despair. You, me, Dave, everyone.'

Bowing her head, Letitia seemed to be praying, but she was thinking. 'It's amazing how many people we've met over my time with him.'

'Dave's doing?'

She nodded. 'It's been a whirlwind. Every day he introduces me to more and more people. I can't keep up with names, and I certainly can't keep up with him. It's like he's trying to make up for something.'

'What do you think that is?'

'I don't know – I think it has to do with his parents, but I'm not sure.'

'Have you ever met his parents?'

She shook her head. 'No, they've passed away. And he never talks about them. Well, once, when we were talking about Ignatius. He slipped and mentioned something about a court case when he was younger, when he was staying with his aunt and uncle. But when I pressed him about it, he gave me an obscure reference to Silence of the Lambs.'

'What is it with that movie? Why that one?'

'I wish I knew. I wish I could break him of the habit.'

'So what do you know about his past?'

'Not much.'

'Can I ask why you stay with him?'

Letitia turned her full body toward me then. 'When you've been where I have, abandoned and kicked to the curb by a serious grade-A jackboot, you get selective with men. Dave is the polar opposite of my ex. He is kind and considerate. He is over-the-top generous. He is great with

Meg and adores her. Those are all the best traits to put on your checklist for partner in life. Whether or not he tells me about his past or parents is beside the point. He is a good man – just different.'

'What will you do now?'

Letitia turned back towards Meg and grabbed her small hand. The little girl stirred and cried out with pain. 'We'll do what we have to do. Beyond that, who knows?'

She asked me to pray for them, but it felt empty and devoid of the hope I was trying to instill. It's like that sometimes. Maybe it's not the words that God listens to. Maybe it's something more.

I heard about Dave's Thanksgiving stem cell adventure and the call out to the hospital for testing. It was the same distress call he gave at church when Marty was there. Benson called me and asked if I'd come along. Guiltily, my first inclination was to say that I had plans, which I did, but I agreed out of duty. Hoping that it wouldn't take too long, I drove to the hospital in the cold.

When I arrived at the clinic, I was shocked at how many of the Palms residents had shown up. We each took a number. The nurse appeared slightly overwhelmed, but she smiled bravely. Having been placed on holiday work, maybe she was grateful for the busyness. She brought us in one at a time. She and Dave seemed to know each other. Once he was done talking to her, he stood in the corner, arms crossed, mumbling and chewing his fingernails, then staring disconsolately up at the television hanging in the corner of the room, which broadcast masses of shoppers purchasing things, credit-cardy things, stocking up on retail distraction.

Because of his strangeness, there was little interaction in the room. Many residents scrolled through their phones; others stared out the window or pondered the number on their ticket. When they entered the room for testing, I could see the relief on their faces. Then, after exiting, they bid the others goodbye, pulled up the collars on their coats and stepped into the freedom of the crisp fall air.

As the line dwindled, I wandered over to where Dave was.

26 – Jonathan

'How you're doing.'

There was something embedded deep within his gaze, but I couldn't figure out which emotion it was – fear? Anger? Irritation or discomfort? 'I'm not sure you get wiser as you get older, but you do learn to dodge a certain amount of hell.'

'That's… interesting, Dave. Can you tell me why you quote from that movie? It doesn't seem like it always fits the circumstances of life.'

He turned back to the TV. At first, I thought he was going to ignore me, but he didn't. He recrossed his arms and spoke away from me. 'When I was younger, I tried to care for people, but that doesn't always work out so well.'

'Tell me about that.'

He pursed his lips. 'I'm not supposed to give you that kind of personal information, Dr. Lecter. You may use it against me.'

'Dave,' I said, 'I'm not Dr. Lecter. I'm not here to hurt you.'

'That's what they all say.' He pushed away from the wall and was about to leave.

'What number are you?' I asked trying to keep him with me.

'I didn't get one,' he responded quietly.

That startled me. 'Why not?'

Like a robot, Dave continued on his way and strode towards the door. It opened automatically and he followed the others into the great beyond, into the unknown. It was only then that I realized he wasn't wearing a coat.

27
Wendy

My previous conversation with Benson did not have the intended effect I had hoped for. It was a bluff, I admit it. I wanted to force Benson to make a decision regarding who his first thoughts would be of, but he called the bluff, and then me a week later. With regards to Benson, I'm weak. I've never met someone who cared about others as much as he does, and when he focuses that care on me, I get all gooey inside. I didn't tell him that, but it was implied by the tone of voice when I answered the phone.

'Hi. I'm glad you called.'

'There's something very wrong with Dave,' Benson blurted out.

This revelation was not exactly Newton discovering gravity. 'What is it now?'

'I can't really put my finger on what *it* is. He doesn't look like he's sleeping and...'

'And what?' I was sitting on the front deck of my house which was positioned near the banks of the Mississippi River – a nice perk for working with the DNR. It was cold, the December kind of cold that should have forced me indoors, but the snow would be coming soon enough, and I wanted to get the last fresh breaths before they became frozen ones.

'Well, we all went in to be typed for our stem cells. All of us except Dave. Don't you think that's weird?'

'Very,' I responded as a wood duck dove beneath the waves flipping downwards for some tasty morsel. 'He's probably already had his done. Maybe twice.'

'Yeah, maybe. I think you should come over and help me talk to him.'

'It's a Thursday night, Benson. I've got work tomorrow. This weekend will be really busy. People are trying to get onto the river before it freezes. Morons galore.'

27 – Wendy

'I would really appreciate it. Could you switch with someone else?'

Why is it that the people you fall in love with can so easily manipulate you with the tones of their voices? Benson and I hadn't spoken the 'love' word yet, but it was in the works (hopefully). We both knew how we felt. We were both adults, both with jobs and places to live. It was a natural progression, yet something held us back. My thought was that Dave was the main restraint for Benson professing his love. While Dave was still in the picture, we were destined to have a platonic friendship with a Dave-shaped hump.

'I'll see what I can do.'

Benson breathed an audible sigh of relief. 'Right after work tomorrow, drive your car as fast as allowable. I think we need to see Ignatius, too.'

'Ignatius? Why him?'

'I think he knows something about Dave's past that will help us get him over whatever he's going through.'

'What makes you say that?'

'Just a hunch.'

I drove over on Friday night. Thankfully, we'd only had a dusting of snow, but the roads were slick, and it was dark by the time I reached Des Moines. When I pulled into the Palms, Benson was standing in the office chatting with Gladys.

I rolled down my window as they came out to greet me. Benson leaned in through the window and gave me a quick kiss.

'Hi Gladys.'

'Hello, Wendy, nice to see you.' She pointed toward the visitor parking spot, pretty much my exclusive place since Benson and I had been seeing each other. Thankfully, Gladys had never been particularly finicky about me spending a weekend. There are some places where the landlords watch like hawks, but not the Palms.

After shutting the car off, Benson grabbed my bag out of the back seat, and we climbed the steps to his apartment. The door was ajar. There were crumbs of pizza, half eaten Doritos, and fingernails caught in the threads of the carpet. On the coffee table were dirty water glasses and three empty cans of Mr. Pibb – no coasters. Unsurprisingly both glasses and cans had left rings on the wood.

The television sat on a low cabinet staring out over the living room like a dead eye. Across the room was the kitchen with a large window-like space where food can be passed over to whomever is sitting in the living room. The kitchen sink was half-full of dirty dishes and two of the cupboards were fully open. How did he live like this? The state of his apartment was one of the primary reasons I'd never stayed over before. I'm not a prude or anything, I simply have standards for how much mess I can put up with.

'Do you mind if I do a little once over on the apartment before I organize my things?'

His face turned red. 'I'm not much of a neat freak.'

'Not even a slightly messy freak.' Hands on hips, I scanned the apartment. Where to start first? Vacuuming? Dishes? 'How about I take care of the kitchen, and you start out here in the living area?' I didn't even want to look in his bedroom.

As if reading my mine, his embarrassment deepened. 'I'll... uh... pick up the bedroom, first.'

It was cathartic cleaning the house together. We were almost like an old married couple. That thought became a warm feeling in my stomach and spread through my body. We'd advanced to the stage in our relationship where we didn't have to be overly conscious of our appearances or idiosyncrasies, although there were a few things I'd be remodeling about him – his neatness being the first order of business.

As I washed the dishes and organized the refrigerator (he had old milk and moldy cheese rotting away in the chiller drawer, along with an alarming amount of overly-caffeinated beverages – no wonder he's always jumpy), Benson finished the bedroom. He was whistling as the hallway closet door creaked open and the vacuum clunked out. His whistling stopped. I poked my head around the corner. 'Everything all right?'

27 – Wendy

'Yeah,' he said as he held the contraption in his hands. 'I just have to remember how…'

'It's been a while?'

He grinned sheepishly. 'Maybe.'

I dried my hands on the towel and helped him extract the cord. He held it up in front of his face as if it was an ancient relic, and bent over to plug it in. On a whim, I patted his backside which made him jump. I'd never touched him like that. He'd probably never been touched like that. He bonked his head against the wall, and I apologized.

'Don't worry about it,' He rubbed his head. 'Just static electricity.'

'Is that what that is?'

It took about two hours for us to finish the apartment, and when we were done, we surveyed the renovation. It looked like a completely different apartment. One that could now be lived in. And I felt like I could stay over.

We settled down onto the sofa, next to each other. He was a little sweaty, but not disgustingly so. At least he didn't stink.

The hairs on our arms comingled and he grabbed my hand interlacing our fingers. He smiled, but it seemed more like a grimace.

'Thanks for coming over. I didn't mean for you to feel like you had to clean my apartment.'

I touched his cheek. 'I'm happy to be here. Really.'

'Now, about Dave.' He must have noticed the flicker of annoyance that we'd passed over the 'us' stuff too quickly. 'I'm sorry, but I'm really worried.'

I sighed. 'All right, lay it on me.'

He explained the hospital episode, and went into great detail about the procedure for stem cell transplanting. His ability to Dr. Google was appalling, and I wasn't sure whether to trust what he was saying or look it up myself. Supposedly, after the marrow typing, if there was a match, it was simply a matter of injecting some other thing (I can't remember what the stuff is) to release the stem cells into the blood stream, which was then transfused to Meg. The hardest part, according to Dr. Benson, was that Meg's body could refuse the very thing that might save her. Also, according to Dr. Benson, the process was much easier than it used to be. He described some real horror stories about bone marrow transplants and enormous needles being shoved into hips and backs. It made me shiver.

'Maybe he's afraid of needles?' I suggested.

Benson swatted the idea away like an orbiting mosquito. 'We're talking about Meg's life here.'

'It was just an idea.'

'Sorry.'

'He must be afraid of something.'

'I know, that's why I want to talk to Ignatius.'

'What is it with him?'

Benson leaned back on the sofa, crossed his arms on his belly, and looked up at the ceiling. 'The few times that Dave talked about Ignatius, he spoke about how the judge had watched over him. Perhaps someone as close as the judge could give us a hint as to what he's going through.'

'Do you actually think Judge Stackworth is going to tell us the private details of that case?'

'What? No!'

I knew that's exactly what he was thinking. 'Supersleuth Benson,' I teased, tapping him on the leg.

'This is no laughing matter.'

'What are we going to ask him then?'

'I don't know, but we're going to meet him in about an hour.'

'Where?'

'There's a Pizza Hut just up the road. It's secluded.'

'You know,' I rubbed his hand with my thumb, 'when I think about solving mysteries, Pizza Hut never really jumps to mind. I think smoky cafés, or deserted mom and pop diners. Pizza Hut? Not so much.'

'What difference does it make where we find it out?'

'It doesn't, but I think it would be cooler if there was a lounge singer standing in the spotlight, while we sit in a corner booth.'

27 – *Wendy*

He rolled his eyes. 'How about we make out for forty-five minutes instead?'

'That sounds like a good idea, Doctor.'

28

Benson

On the way to Pizza Hut, Wendy checked her hair in the sliding mirror affixed to the sun visor. The little light revealed that the hair had been more-than-slightly mussed by our affections. She noticed me watching and she smirked. She called me a *bad boy*.

Awoooooooooh!

By the time we came up for air, an hour had passed. Wendy jumped up from the sofa and yanked me up after her. She had razor burn which kind of looked like a pink goatee. I grinned. I wonder what she'd do if I gave her a hickey?

Why was I thinking about that on the way to Pizza Hut? I had to focus on Dave, and Meg, and Letitia, and... Wendy's got really nice lips, and she knew what to do with them. *Stop it!*

After pulling into the Pizza Hut, where there were less than half a dozen cars scattered around the parking lot, we hopped out of the car. I was glad we wore our jackets. It was definitely getting colder. I could see our breaths in the glow of the streetlights above us. We connected our hands in front of the car. It seemed so natural, as if I couldn't even remember what life was like before her.

I peered through the side windows of the restaurant noticing the interior lights which revealed a dozen people quietly eating at small square tables under green lampshades. Their fingers and faces were greasy shades of rosy-yellow. One family had a stack of plates leaning precipitously to the side. Between the layers of plates, uneaten crusts stuck out like broken pieces of mortar. *It's the leaning tower of Pizza,* I pointed out to Wendy. She rolled her eyes.

I opened the first door which led us into a small cubicle which was like a docking platform on the International Space Station. The inner door swung wide, and we were greeted by a blast of warmth, mozzarella, oregano, and overeating. The smell overwhelmed us, and I was suddenly hungry, even if only for greasy pizza.

Wendy was the first to spot Ignatius. He was in the back, huddled in a corner booth, hunched over a tall red glass full of ice and cola.

We snaked our way through tables and diners. I bypassed one lady's mechanical scooter, and sidestepped another diner making a beeline for the streusel. It wasn't until we were within hearing distance that he spotted us. He didn't get up so we slid into the red, fake-leather seats semi-circling the table.

'Hello Ignatius,' I extended my hand which he shook. Wendy did the same.

'How are you both doing tonight?'

Wendy touched the sides of her hair, an amazingly feminine gesture. I wondered if she thought Ignatius could tell that we had been playing tonsil hockey.

'Good,' I said.

'Have you eaten yet?'

'No,' I responded, 'but we're not hungry.'

'Nonsense, I'm buying.'

'In that case, I'm eating.'

'The salad bar is open already,' Ignatius pointed in the general direction of the buffet where two or three diners were ponderously studying the less-than-healthy options on the opposite side from the green salad.

'Real men don't eat salad,' I stated authoritatively. Unfortunately, I had not noticed the salad sitting in front of Ignatius. The judge's face twisted into a wry grin.

'What he *meant* to say was,' Wendy corrected as she leaned in towards Ignatius, 'that closeted computer programmers don't have time for salad – they must be too busy to be healthy.'

A few minutes later, a waitress approached us with a green pad of paper. She wore a red shirt with the Pizza Hut logo on it and a black visor with greasy fingermarks on the bill. I ordered a large pepperoni pizza. Wendy shook her head and made her way to the salad bar for some aforementioned healthy food. Unfortunately, that was like going to the butcher to buy vegetables. When she returned, it looked like healthy for her was going to be crunchy honeydew melon and rusting lettuce. I smirked that she had peppered her 'salad' with bacon bits.

'What?'

'Nothing.' I sipped my soda unwilling to jeopardize future making out sessions by saying something stupider.

Ignatius placed his forearms on the table. 'What can I do for you two?'

'We want to talk about Dave.'

'Dave?'

'What did you think we wanted to talk about?' I responded as I eyed Wendy's bacon bits.

'I... well... I thought you might be looking for my services for...' he motioned between the two of us.

'Good heavens,' Wendy choked, and the redness reached her cheeks. It just hung there, like red drapes of embarrassment.

'What? What am I missing?' I took the opportunity to grab a few bacon bits from her plate.

'Ignatius thought that we wanted to meet with him about organizing a wedding.'

'A what?'

'A wedding.'

'Whose wedding?'

Ignatius and Wendy stared at me until cognition belted me upside the head. 'Oh, Jeez,'

Taking a deep breath, Ignatius spread his hands. 'Well, let's just pretend none of those false assumptions took place. What do you want to talk about with regards to Dave?'

'We want you to tell us about Dave's parents.'

Ignatius's eyes narrowed. 'What makes you think I know anything about that?'

'We thought since you've kept an eye on him all these years, you would know something about his past. His growing up years. Why was Dave with his aunt and uncle in the first place?'

'Why do you want to know?'

'He's not himself. There is something really wrong with him. Ever since Meg got sick, it's like he's untethered, going crazy – totally weird.' I felt a hitch in my voice. 'I'm getting scared.'

'What does this have to do with his parents?' The suspicion in Ignatius's voice confirmed my own.

'It could be nothing, but it might be everything.'

'Tell me about Meg.' He changed the subject before sipping from his drink again. He was stalling, I could feel it.

We related the last months, the smoking ceremony, Marty, the broken bell, everything.

'Remind me who Marty is again.'

'They met at Alcoholics Anonymous.'

'Ah, yes, we met at Wendy's meet-and-greet.'

'He's a gun dealer. Dave bought a gun from him.'

The judge seemed astounded. 'What? You can't be serious. Why would Dave need a gun?'

'For hunting grasshoppers.'

'Excuse me?'

'I know. It's weird. Dave's got a thing with protecting the flower garden from cabbage moths.' The minute I said it, something fired in my mind. *Moths. The Mothman.* The thought was gone before it really began.

'Sounds like Dave.'

The pizza arrived slightly behind schedule, so we paused the conversation to allow the pizza's presentation in the middle of the table. Judging by the acrid smell of her armpits, it was apparent that the server had not entirely gotten the stench from her shirt, and she had also worked a full shift. I cringed, but thankfully the pizza's aroma overwhelmed the eau-de-eight-hours. I half-heartedly offered a piece to the other two, but they thankfully declined. The first bite was heavenly. It was hot and I almost spit it out. I *lalalalaed* the pizza, but got to my soda just in time. Unfortunately, the roof of my mouth was burned. Blisters were on their way.

When I opened my eyes, they were both waiting impatiently.

'Marty has a gun shop downtown. Back-alley kind of thing. I guess it's pretty popular.'

'So he's shooting grasshoppers?' Wendy asked.

'I know. Kind of strange as there aren't really a lot of grasshoppers this time of year.'

'What does Marty have to do with Dave other than selling guns?' Ignatius' hands worried with the plastic straw rapper in front of him. He had balled it up and was running it around his fingers.

'They're friends. Marty seems kind of dangerous to me, but Dave likes him a lot. He even invited him into Meg's room at the hospital. And, oh, Dave took him to church. Supposedly they asked everyone there to get their stem cells tested, just like at the Palms. Eventually, most of the apartment complex and a few people from the church did it.'

'Any matches?' Ignatius asked.

'Not yet.' I intelligently blew on the pizza this time and took another bite. I held up a finger for the international sign of 'patience while I finish chewing'.

'But the really strange thing is that I don't know if Dave himself ever got tested. He freaked out at the thought of it. Which was why I wondered if it was PTSD from something in his past. Which, mind you, we know nothing about. He's never told us anything. Even me.'

An internal war waged on the judge's face, with weaponry hidden in silos of the past.

'What is it?' Wendy asked.

'I can't tell you,' he whispered. 'Dave would never forgive me.'

Suddenly, we were all ears. I could feel my blood pressure and pulse rate rise. *I was right.* Ignatius knew something.

'Help us help him,' I said.

He shook his head.

'Then tell us what you can. Just give us a clue. Any place to start, and then you won't have to feel guilty.'

Ignatius scanned the room. We all have agreements of confidentiality in life. It's probably a little more pertinent to someone like the judge, but this was Dave we were talking about.

He blew the air out of his lungs and took a quick small breath. 'All I can say is that Dave's case was different than any other I've ever adjudicated, not just because Dave was different, but the circumstances behind why he was in my court were complex. What happened to Dave's parents was tragic, but what was even worse was what it did to Dave.'

'Please,' I pleaded, 'give us something more. A lead. A start. This could be both Dave's and Meg's life at stake.'

The tug-o-war, an emotional struggle between what should have been done and what could be done, played out before our very eyes. Ignatius stalled again by drinking from his Pizza Hut glass. The condensation had made a sticky mess of the white napkin below it. Finally, he reached the bottom of the drink below the ice. It made a sucking sound.

'The only hint I can give you is that if you want to know about his parents, you have to talk to Dave's uncle, his mother's brother.'

'What's his name?'

'I can't tell you that.'

Exasperated, I slapped the table. 'Judge, that doesn't help us at all!'

Ignatius Stackworth frowned and pointed a finger at us. 'Just find Dave's uncle. If he doesn't tell you, there's nothing I can do.'

Without another word, we watched Ignatius unceremoniously extricate himself from the seat and walk out the door. He didn't even say goodbye. We had upset him, but why? Wendy stared out the dark window across from us. Her reflection was both doubled and blurred. She rested her chin in her hand.

My pizza remained neglected in the middle of the table. The oil had pooled in the empty spaces between the pieces I'd already eaten. Neither of us had an appetite anymore, but dutifully, out of guilt, we ate anyway. I was morose – dejected, really – but I felt like something had been triggered, or sparked inside of me. Some little morsel of a clue had been dropped, and now I just had to find out where it led.

We didn't really know how to get the information we needed to begin with, other than to ask Dave who his uncle was, and he was not likely to tell us. No, we were going to have to do some digging.

Half an hour later, doggie box in hand, we parked in front of the Palms. We climbed the stairs. I unlocked the room, and we entered. After flipping the switch, I dropped the box onto the small table that doubled as an eating space and office desk. Wendy grumbled and picked it up.

'We just cleaned your apartment, and you want to drop the pizza box on a clean coffee table?' She tapped the side of her head and offered the box to me. I put it in the fridge and grabbed a beer. 'Do you want one?'

She shook her head.

When I popped the tab, the beer fizzed out. I covered the hole with my mouth and then swigged the first third in one gulp. I belched loudly and Wendy frowned. 'What are we going to do? We can't just Google 'Dave's uncle' and have the answer come up.'

Suddenly, something dawned on Wendy like the blazing shafts of light of the morning sun. 'What's Dave's last name?'

'I…' my mouth was unhinged. 'Honestly, now that you say it, I have no idea. How strange…'

'You mean you guys have been friends – best friends – and you don't know his last name.'

'I've never thought about it. He's always just been *Dave*.'

'That's insane.'

'I know.' Leaving the kitchen, I held the beer against my forehead, then grabbed my laptop. 'There's got to be a way we can figure out who he is.' After logging on, my fingers were a blur on the keyboard.

I leaned back. 'Nothing. No threads, no leads. It's like he's a ghost. And come to think of it, Dave never uses a credit card either. His cell phone is pay as you go. I think he even pays his bills here by cash.'

'Where does he get the money?' Wendy asked.

I shrugged. 'That's the thing – I've never really cared about that either. I just know that he's always taking care of people, their debts, loans, whatever, and he never runs out of money.'

'Curiouser and curiouser.'

Stymied, I added multiple words into the search engine. I checked social media, everything where you'd normally find everyone. Nothing. 'Now what?'

Wendy walked to the window and looked out over the courtyard. It was a Friday night and lights were glowing in various rooms. A few television sets flashed; some of the neighbors were playing cards. An older lady read a book by her window. One gentleman tried to stay warm as he stamped his way through an illegal cigarette outside the front door of his house. By the front gate, Gladys checked something in the…

Gladys.

'I know what we'll do.'

'What?'

'Gladys will have records. Dave would have had to produce some kind of identification – a driver's license, a passport, something.'

'A driver's license! Of course! Benson,' she said approaching me quickly, 'you're a genius!'

I felt a deep sense of happiness about her compliment. 'Thank you, Wendy. I love you too.' Suddenly, before I realized it, the words had blown open my mouth and we were standing on the precipice of another level well beyond the belching/comfort level. 'Uh… what I meant to say was…'

Her face was suffused with exhilaration. 'You do? You do! This is the best night of my life!' She took me in her arms and kissed me in front of the window. As we breathlessly broke apart, I noticed that the older lady who was reading a book stared up at us and smiled. She waved. I turned away.

'Well?' I asked expectantly.

'Let's go talk to Gladys,' she said.

As I turned the handle on the door and pulled inwards, Wendy stopped it with her foot which cracked my head into the side of it. 'What did you do that for?'

'What is wrong with me?'

'I don't understand! We're about to get a break in the case of Dave, and you're slowing us down.'

'You don't know what just happened?'

'Yeah, I told you I loved you and you said it was wonderful. Now let's get downstairs before Gladys heads off to bed.'

She raised her eyebrows.

'Oh! I get it! I get it! You didn't tell me...' My face fell. 'Does that mean you don't?'

'No, dummy, you didn't give me a chance. You were so excited to get downstairs...'

'I'm so sorry. I'm such an idiot. But you do love me, right?'

'Would you let me get this out!' She laughed and smacked my arm.

I made a zipping gesture across my lips.

Taking a deep breath, she looked me squarely in the eyes. 'I love you, Benson Olson.'

'Now that we got that out of the way, can we go talk to Gladys?' *Now that we got that out of the way...* No wonder I've been single so long. I smacked my forehead, which hurt.

'Yes,' Wendy sighed with exasperation.

29
Wendy

We raced to Gladys's office where we found her sitting behind the desk filing her nails and watching television. Her hair was done up in old-fashioned curlers, and she was wearing a quilted dressing gown. Benson rapped loudly on the door which startled her.

'Gladys!' Benson shouted through the glass, 'What's Dave's last name?'

'What?' she yelled back as she pulled herself from her desk chair and opened the flip desk to open the door. She'd been doing her toenails, too, I could see. There were cottonballs between them. She didn't open the door entirely but kept her foot as a jamb at the base.

Benson poked his face into opening. 'His last name? What's Dave's last name?'

'Have you two been smoking marijuana?'

'What? No!'

'Is this a trick question then?' Gladys grabbed a broom from next to the door and held it in front of her like a weapon as she moved back.

We raised our hands in surrender. 'No! Gladys, we just want to know what Dave's last name is.'

She shook her head and lowered the broom slightly. 'Are you serious? You really don't know his last name?'

Benson's eyes widened in exasperation. 'Of course we know what it is, but we want to see if *you* know what it is.'

She pursed her lips. The little wisps of moustache poked a little higher to her nose. 'How stupid do you think I am? It's Stackworth. Dave Stackworth.'

'You mean like the Judge? Ignatius Stackworth?'

'Like, yeah. What are you two up to?'

'Nothing,' I said. 'C'mon, Benson, she passed the test. Let's go.'

As we turned to walk away, Gladys shouted after us. 'What test?'

We retreated quickly back to Benson's apartment. Something wasn't adding up. 'Why is his last name Stackworth?' I mused.

'Is Ignatius his adoptive father?' Benson asks.

Something the judge said. 'No — that can't be right. Why would Ignatius tell us to find his uncle then? They wouldn't have the same last name.'

Benson put his hands to his head and fluffed his hair. 'Mind being blown.'

'Or, what if Ignatius is lying. What if he's trying to hide something from us?'

'That doesn't make sense. We just have to figure out why he is hiding from us.'

Benson paused in front of his apartment door before entering. 'It would explain where Dave gets his money, though.'

'Yes, but judges don't make that much money. Not like Dave spends.'

'Yeah, you're probably right.' Our voices dropped to a whisper now that we were outside Benson's apartment. It was highly unlikely that Dave was listening, but you couldn't put it entirely past him. 'But how are we going to find out? Even if Dave's last name is 'Stackworth', he very well could have found a way to legally change it to someone's he really respected.'

'You're right,' I said. 'We've got to go to the source.'

'We can't ask Dave. He'd never tell us, especially in the state he is right now.'

I peered down the balustrade towards Dave's room. Then, I looked back at Benson. We both had the same thought.

'Breaking and entering?' he gulped.

'We won't be breaking anything. And you already know his room is open. He never locks it. Everybody wanders in and out.'

'But what if he's there?'

'That's easy. We're just checking to see if he's all right.'

'Are you sure?'

29 – Wendy

'No, but we have to do this for Meg's sake.'

'I'm feeling guilty already. What if there is nothing in there? What if he catches us?'

'It will be worth it.'

Trying to appear casual, Benson and I held hands as we sauntered the few steps to Dave's apartment. The fluorescent lights buzzed above us. Spotlights. In the summertime, moths would have been bouncing off the tubes, but it was cold. Quite cold. All the moths were either dead or waiting for spring.

Even as we entered, we were thankful that people were used to Palms residents wandering around at night. Our sneaking would have been no different, especially us going to Dave's.

We paused outside Dave's door. The broken dinner bell was perched on top of Dave's small table outside the room. The clapper had been unhooked and was lying beside the bell. 'What happened to that?'

'Don't ask,' Benson said.

Benson rapped lightly on the door and called out for Dave.

No answer.

'He must be out,' Benson whispered.

'I hope he's not dead.'

Benson's eyes widened.

'Relax. I'm kidding.'

Benson tried the doorknob and, as promised, it was open. We stuck our heads through the opening and called out once again.

'Dave?'

More silence.

Benson flipped the light switch, and a most confusing scene confronted us. In the strictest sense it was clean, but the jumble of decorating assaulted my eyes, and I felt like vomiting. Nothing in the room matched – not furniture, not pictures, not carpet. It was a hodgepodge of colors and fabrics, textiles, and ceramics. There were stripes and solids, squares and triangles, dead branches and fake roses.

Where the television would normally have been was a large dresser with a circular swinging mirror. Hanging on the posts were rosary beads and crosses. Bookending the dresser were matching picture frames with autographed photos of Jodie Foster and Sir Anthony Hopkins. Scattered around the apartment were butterflies, moths, and an extraordinarily frightening sketch of what looked like a man with wings and red eyes.

'This is so weird. I almost feel dirty.'

'Don't.' Benson said. 'Dave is not Buffalo Bill. He just loves the movie.'

'Yeah, but this is creepy. It's like a grotto for...' I shivered, 'a horror film.'

We began to search the room. Noiselessly, we navigated our way through the furniture, past the kitchen island, down the hall to the bedroom. I was a little freaked out about entering the bedroom.

Searching quickly through Dave's belongings, we moved things slightly but tried not to disturb anything greatly. We rifled through drawers. I turned on my phone's flashlight to illuminate the closet and any place where Dave might have hidden something from his past. There were pictures on the wall, but almost all seemed to have been taken by people he'd met along the way – people from the Palms, or on the bus, at the supermarket, maybe on a road trip. Everyone was trying to get a piece of Dave.

'Wendy!' Benson called out from the bedroom. 'Come here!'

I hurried to the closet to find him holding a shoe box in one hand and a picture in the other. 'Look at this.'

I took the picture from his hands. It was old, printed from a negative, not from a smart phone. There were two adults: the man had some strikingly similar characteristics to Dave, but the woman was very different and looked unhappy to be anywhere near a camera. They were standing in front of a Ford Explorer. The car's front fenders had rusted out and the sun glinted against the fire-hydrant red of the Explorer's paint. The young Dave, I presumed, stood apart from the adults. His

29 – Wendy

arms were hanging limply at his sides, and he was unsmiling. His hair was straight and lank, and his clothes appeared three sizes too small for him.

'Do you think that's his aunt and uncle?' I asked Benson.

'It's the best possible lead yet.'

I flipped the picture over and saw that it had been labeled. *Jane and Ted.*

'That's them. Gotta be.'

Suddenly, there was a noise in the outer room. Benson swore and quickly put the shoebox back where he found it in the closet.

'What do we do?' I whispered.

Benson motioned with his head towards the bed. I dove towards it, and we faced each other.

'Take off your shirt,' he whispered.

'What?'

'Dave will think we're getting busy.'

'No, you take off your shirt.'

'He'll never buy that. Nobody wants to see me shirtless.'

My eyes opened wide. 'I do.'

'Hurry!'

From the other room, Dave's voice called out. 'Hello?'

We pretended to scrabble up from the bed. Quickly, Benson put his shirt on backwards and mussed his hair as if somehow we were caught. Dave's head appeared in the doorway.

'Oh, hello Benson and Wendy. What are you doing in here?'

It wasn't hard for us to look guilty. 'We're um... you know...'

Dave sniffed. 'Don't let me interrupt.' He pulled his head back out of the room and went to the kitchen where he rummaged around in the refrigerator.

After a moment, we exited the bedroom. Dave stood in the kitchen with one hand on his hip and the other holding a glass of water. His eyes were glassy, and his sideburns fluffed out. 'Sorry about that, Dave. We got a little carried away.'

Finishing his drink, Dave waved away the suggestion that we did anything wrong.

'Are you okay?' I asked.

He was quiet, but then nodded slowly. 'Just thirsty.'

'Well, we'll get going then,' Benson said.

'Okay, have a good night you two.' Dave turned toward the sink where he rinsed out his cup.

We walked toward the door but paused to look back at Dave's back. The water was running but he had stopped moving. It was as if he had frozen in place. We left the room and quietly shut the door.

'Now what?' I asked Benson.

He held up the picture. 'We've got a lead.'

30

Ignatius

Black holes.

I've seen sci-fi movies that deal with them with always the same result. The spacecraft is drawn inexorably closer, deeper into the intense darkness in search of what it's made of. But any man-made craft begins shaking as it nears the event horizon – the point of no return. Beyond this margin, nothing escapes, not even light. As science continues to investigate these phenomena, they've been stymied by the fact that they're not located by what they see, but by the gravity.

So it was with Dave.

At that time, with everything that was happening with Meg and Letitia, Dave was very much like a black hole, and I don't mean that in a pejorative sense, only that he had a certain gravitational pull that drew all people closer to him. Unfortunately, no one knew what was going on inside him. We tried to approach him, but the darkness was frightening – no light escaped and we feared (perhaps that's too strong a word, but I'll use it) that we would be sucked into that darkness to never return.

Take, for instance, what happened with me, Benson and Wendy, on that evening at the Pizza Hut. Dave's influence over them, his pull and his constant need to draw them close, yet not truly revealing anything, was black hole-ish. I wished I could help them, I really did, but the questions they asked were ethically ambiguous and nigh impossible to answer. Even I didn't know everything.

He spent his high school years in foster care. I kept tabs on him, and he seemed happy. Occasionally, we'd catch a bite to eat, or an Iowa Cubs baseball game. He never truly spoke about his parents, and I didn't bring it up. It seemed best that way. Sometimes when we went for ice cream, he would sit across from me, licking the cone, eyes closed, as if remembering something from long ago, an ancient memory of a different time when ice cream meant more than it did now. Then, without warning, he would stick his nose in it and tell me he wanted to smell it when he went to sleep.

It didn't surprise me that he was a friendless teenager. To be brutally honest, the things he said and did would have made him fair game for his classmates. Like the black hole though, he seemed to absorb everything without revealing anything thus creating a very complex, interwoven relationship. When he took my last name as his, I was honored and deeply moved, but he never told me why he did it. I guess he wanted control over me, also.

On the side table next to my reading chair, I always keep a reading novel and a photo of my wife whose death left me a widower many years ago. To the left of her picture, beyond my reading glasses, is a picture of Dave and I at Adventureland. He is taller than I, and the arm he drapes around my shoulders looks like a rope. He smirks rather than smiles, as if he knew the punchline before the joke was told. That was a good day.

As I picked up that photo again, my thoughts returned to what happened.

As I staggered from the restaurant, smelling of pepperoni and streusel, I wondered what was happening with Dave. Pulling my phone from my pocket, I called his number but he didn't answer. The odds were, instead of answering, he would have looked at the number and been at my house before I got home. Face to face communication was really the only way for Dave Stackworth.

As I ran my hand over my wife's photo and then his, I felt a particular sense of painful nostalgia from those years after the court hearing. We watched from a distance as the Soto family took him in. During the last years of his high school education, they provided housing, food, entertainment, all the things young people needed, but he was still different. Still dark. The nightmare of his parents' deaths surrounded everything he did. It must have been very difficult for the Sotos to try to understand Dave and what made him tick. How they must have been continually unsettled hearing him quote that movie all the time.

30 – *Ignatius*

After driving home from Pizza Hut, I pulled into the driveway of my house and I saw Dave's silhouette underneath the front porch. His shoulders were hunched, and he was motionless. Stooped, hands in pockets, shaggy hair poking out over the collar of his corduroy coat, Dave was a wraith, a figment of my dreams. Sometimes I dream of my wife in that way as she haunts my subconscious with her absence.

I turned the car off and approached him aware that the cold air magnified the silence-breaking noises. The sound of my footsteps on the frosty cement crunched the air between us. The sidewalk to the front of my house is about forty feet, but it seemed like a mile. Each step was further into a deeper darkness.

A black hole.

'Hello Dave.'

'Iggy.'

'How are you?'

Dave shrugged and lifted his head slightly. The dimmest of light illuminated the contours of his face. He looked old, yet child-like.

'You seem exhausted,' I said.

'Not as tired as you.'

'It's been a strange night.' I stopped short of the step and peered up into his shadow.

'You called me,' he said simply.

'Yes. Benson and Wendy met me at the Pizza Hut.'

'Did you bring me some pizza?'

'Not this time, Dave.'

'What did they want? Do they want you to do the wedding?'

'No, they wanted to know about you and your parents.'

Dave's head jerked up. 'Why would they want to know that?'

'They want to know if it has something to do with Meg.'

Even in the dim light, I saw the muscles in his cheeks flex, moving the sideburns. 'I should have guessed.' Dave pulled his head back into his collar like a turtle. His shoulders rebunched.

'What is it like being a father?' he asked quietly.

I wish Charlotte and I would have had children. It was just one of those things I guess, a mishappenstance of life. God's forgetfulness, maybe. I know earthly justice, not cosmic, but what happened to us and Dave seemed thoughtlessly cruel, which is why I think I took him under my arm and guided him in some small way through the meandering path of life. He made it, to a certain extent, by the sheer force of his nature.

'I guess I don't know exactly what it's like…'

'Iggy, what am I to you?'

Nonplussed, I stammered before stopping to collect myself. 'You are the closest thing I have to a son in this here world.'

'Then what is it like to see your child suffering?'

'It's hell – beyond hell, really. As you grew up, I did everything I could to support you and the Soto's, but knowing the things that hurt you and scarred you, I had to wear that every day. I felt helpless most of the time.'

'That's the way I feel, Iggy. I feel helpless. With Meg.'

'I'm sorry.' The apology felt lame, but it was all I had.

'I wish you would have adopted me. Then I could have been normal.'

I stepped up, reached out for his arms, and grabbed them. Every day I have lived a guilty life, and that night was particularly poignant. To have brought Dave into my own home, the house that loomed above us, to share in all the good things I had left – that would have made life different and more beautiful. For him and me. But I was afraid. Having a son, especially a teenage one, and with the struggles Dave had, would have placed a tremendous burden on me as a single parent. Instead, I did the cowardly thing and left him with the Soto's. Even though they were good parents, I'm sure it felt like another betrayal to him. I don't know if his name change was to please me or hurt me.

'Dave, you are the most beautiful human being on the planet. I'm so very proud of you.'

'For what?'

30 – Ignatius

That was the thing. Over the course of the last twenty years, by any social standards, Dave would have been considered a failure. He had never held a long-term job. He did not have expensive things nor expensive tastes. He did not seem to value stability. It was as if he feared that anything and everything might be taken away from him at any moment. He was a human event horizon beyond which no one could see or know or predict what might happen.

'For being you.'

Dave sighed. 'What did you want to tell me tonight?'

'I didn't want to tell you anything, only ask you a question.'

'Okay.'

'Did you have your stem cells typed?'

Silence.

'Did you?'

'Yes.'

'And?'

He pulled away from me and looked out over my ice-encrusted, dried grass. The wind whispered through the trees rustling the few leaves that were left clinging for life. A few flakes of snow were beginning to fall behind us. I hadn't realized it was that cold.

'I'm a match.'

Somehow, I knew he would be. 'What are you going to do?'

For the first time that I could remember, Dave started to cry. The dam cracked one small segment at a time, first a leak here and then a spurt there. Crumbling, his face broke under the weight of who he was and what he had experienced.

'I don't know,' his trembling voice wove its way through the falling snowflakes. 'I don't know.'

'It's different…'

'Of course it's different. It's Meg.'

'Dave, you have to do this. It will be different this time.'

His eyes, streaked with bitter tears of desperation, closed. 'If you were my father, this would be easier to accept.'

'Dave, I *am* like your father.'

He smiled sadly and nodded. 'I know, Dadsworth. I know. But I'm afraid.'

I wished that I could help him withstand the buffeting of his fear, but bravery is most apparent when standing alone.

'I can be there with you, if you'd like.'

Dave squinted, and then blinked, the remaining tears dropped from the corners of his eyes. 'We may yet get lucky. Another match may show up.'

At those words, Dave brushed past me to descend the steps. His feet were heavy and slow. The weight of all worlds was on his shoulders. He was a fragile human being with a dark, horrible past. He took another step down from the porch and onto the glittering cement below. When he turned back, we were roughly the same height. Eye to eye, father to son. A moment passed between us, one of love and despair. Circling. Spinning. Light and dark. Gravity and mystery.

As I took Dave's place on the top step, I wondered how many more times we would be able to meet like this. Would the past finally catch up with us, or would it die? Would Dave choose heroism, or was life-saving-the-common-man much safer.

'Dave,' I spoke to his retreating back.

He didn't stop.

'Dave, where are you going?'

Dave paused and turned around one last time. The streetlamp cast a top light over him leaving his face and much of his body in shadow that I couldn't see.

'Home,' he said with finality. 'I'm just going home.'

'Be at peace, son.' My blessing was caught up in both snowflake and winter air current. Where it landed, I was not sure, but certainly, it did not seem to rest on my son.

31
Gladys

I'm used to residents doing strange things.

12A once ordered a hot tub for the courtyard. 33B strung up Christmas lights in September outside their apartment. There have been domestic disputes and marriage proposals, but nothing compared to how weird Benson and Wendy acted when they left me. How in the world did they not know Dave's last name? Even more curious to me was, what did they need to know for?

I watched them hurry up the stairs to the apartment. Although it was cold and I was not particularly dressed to be outdoors, I couldn't quite tear my eyes from them. When they paused at Benson's door, I thought sweeping my front stoop (even in my robe) would be an appropriate way to keep tabs on them.

Sweep sweep, scan. Sweep sweep, scan. If they would have looked back to see me watching them, they probably would not have entered Dave's apartment. Probably not.

As a good landlord, it's my duty to protect my tenants' assets, even if the intruders are the tenant's best friend and his girlfriend.

After setting the broom back inside the office, I pulled my robe tighter around my shoulders and put on my snow boots. Now, looking very much like a penniless hobo, I stepped back out into the cold night air. The wind was coarse against my face. Snow flaked off the clouds like frozen dandruff. My boots made imprints in the dusting, but I wasn't worried about being tracked.

Climbing the stairs quietly, but not without effort, I noticed a few other residents were up and about. I waved at the Peterson's, a young couple from eastern Iowa, Waverly, who quickly turned away. At the top stair, I turned left. Benson and Wendy had entered Dave's apartment. From this vantage point I would be able to see what they were doing and, if necessary, stop their activities, whatever they might be.

As I waited, a car pulled into the Palms parking lot. My senses were on high alert, especially when I noticed that it was Dave's car. If Wendy and Benson weren't out of his apartment quick, there was going to be a whole lot of splainin' to do.

Dave parked his car, (strange that he was actually driving) and from my peeping-Tom-ish position, I waited for him to approach. Maliciously, I didn't know if I wanted them to get caught or not. I'd never seen Dave angry before. Would this be the kind of thing that pushed him over the edge? Especially with all that was going on with Meg?

My breath and pulse increased as Dave finished his climb and turned right towards his apartment. I hid in the Gustavson's alcove as he passed nearby. Thankfully, he didn't see me in the shadows, so after he turned his back on me, I followed from a distance. Pushing open his door, he stomped on the little welcome mat outside to rid his shoes of loose snow and dirt. Tenderly, he reached out to touch the bell on the little side table.

After he entered the apartment, I hurried down the balustrade and stood just off Dave's window craning my head around the outer windowpane. As I peeked through the lighted room, I saw him stop in the center of the room and call out. I almost laughed out loud when Benson came out with mussed hair and shirt backwards. Why they were going into Dave's room for a romp was beyond me, but Dave didn't seem to care.

Walking to the sink, he began to wash whatever dishes were there. Benson and Wendy came towards the door. When they opened it, I moved back a few paces, arms crossed, hiding myself. I felt like a mother waiting for her children to come home at night. Me in my robe and Uggs.

Wendy was the first out the door. Benson almost ran into her as they exited.

'Oh!' Wendy exclaimed. 'Gladys, I... what are you doing?'

I raised my eyebrows and covered my chest in faux indignation. 'I might ask the same of you.'

31 – Gladys

They looked back and forth between each other, each wanting the other to explain.

'I... uh...' Benson stammered. He was blinking rapidly. Incoming lie. I knew it. 'We... had to get something out of Dave's apartment.'

'Which was?'

Wendy took over. 'Some salt.'

'Salt?' Jeesh, she was worse than he was.

'Mm hmmm.' Wendy's face had turned scarlet. 'Salt.'

'Well, if you needed salt, why didn't you ask me downstairs when you were enquiring about Dave's last name. And why is your shirt on backwards?' I couldn't help it.

Benson's face suffused with blood and Wendy held a hand to her cheek. Benson touched the tag of his shirt just under his chin and his mouth pinched.

'Look,' I said, 'I don't know what you're doing, but I can't have you entering other residents' rooms without their approval. That looks really bad.'

'We're sorry,' Wendy apologized. 'We won't do it again. We promise.' Two competing feelings arose within me: the first, the need to forgive, and the second, to be the landlady.

'I'm going to have to write this up, just in case...'

'Please,' Benson pleaded, 'just let it go. Dave is fine with it. Even ask him.'

We all looked back into the room where Dave stood motionless in his little kitchen.

'How about we go to *your* apartment, and you tell me what's going on?'

'Okay,' Benson said after a few seconds.

On the way to his apartment, I could hear them whispering behind me. I couldn't quite pick up what they were arguing about, but it had something to do with a photograph and what they were going to tell me – or more to the fact, what they *weren't* going to tell me.

Benson brushed past me and unlocked his apartment. Frankly, I was shocked by the state of his apartment. By the amount of pizza delivery and Uber eats that arrived per week, I would have expected trash everywhere and an aroma of bachelor: you know, sweat and dust, and a toilet that hadn't been brushed for weeks. Instead, the interior was clean.

'Now, you two,' I said, my voice carrying the accusations of a mother who had caught her child with his finger in the peanut butter jar. *I wonder if that kind of prying annoyed Eleanor? Was that what drove her away?* 'What in Lorne Greene's name were you doing?'

Benson sighed and plopped down on his sofa. 'We can't tell you.'

'What do you mean you can't tell me? I'm safe.'

Rolling his eyes, Benson stared at the ceiling like a reprimanded schoolboy. Obviously, his assessment of me as *safe* was an actual *safe* with the key left in it.

'Don't you roll your eyes at me, mister.'

'You're not my mother,' Benson sulked.

'No, I'm not, but I'm trying to help. Just talk to me. Maybe I can do some good.'

'Gladys, we're worried about Dave.'

'So you snuck into his apartment...'

'It isn't what it seems,' Wendy interrupted.

'Tell me what it was then.'

'We found some things out – or at least, well, a lead...'

'What, like a clue for a mystery?'

'Yes, but stop interrupting.'

Wendy related the story of their time at Pizza Hut with Ignatius and his connection with Dave when he was little.

A little lightbulb turned on. 'Oh, Lordy, are you thinking what I'm thinking? That the judge is Dave's adoptive father?'

'It's a little more complicated than that,' Benson said. 'While the judge is not his adoptive father, he had more than a passing interest in taking care of Dave.'

'Do judges normally do that?'

31 – Gladys

Wendy shook her head. 'I wouldn't think so. We believe there is some connection between Dave's past, Ignatius's interest, and what is happening with Meg right now.'

'How could that be? Dave is probably in his mid-30's. The trial must have happened twenty years ago.'

'Yes… but… While we were at the restaurant, Ignatius told us to look for Dave's aunt and uncle. Supposedly, they were Dave's guardians for a while.'

'That's some mystery,' I said. 'What are their names?'

'We don't know. He didn't tell us.'

'Aaah, thus your rendezvous into Dave's room to search.' They nodded guiltily. 'That's quite an invasion of privacy.'

'We know,' Wendy whined, 'but we're trying to help him and Meg.'

'What did you find?'

Wendy said 'nothing' but Benson reached for his pocket. 'This,' Benson held up a photo. 'We think this is Dave when he was younger, and he's with his aunt and uncle.' He turned the picture over. 'Jane and Ted.'

'What are their last names?'

'We don't know. Ignatius wouldn't tell us, and it's not written on the back. It's not Stackworth, obviously.'

'Were there any photos of his parents?'

'We didn't have a lot of time to look, but in the short time we were in there, no, we didn't find any.'

'So, what are we going to do?'

I inserted the 'we' word because by then, I felt like I was already implicated. Even though Dave was the most amazing (and bizarre) person in the world, I'd never been part of something like solving a mystery before. I was like Inspector Clouseau or Agatha Christie or…

'There's no 'we' here, Gladys. This is Wendy and me. It's too dangerous.'

I snorted. 'Listen to you, Benson. 'It's too dangerous,'' I mimicked. 'This isn't a movie. It's Dave. People aren't going to come at us with guns and knives.'

'Either way, it's probably best if you stayed out of it. We might be doing some slightly unethical things.'

'Oh, please, Benson. Your idea of unethical is leaving your margarine out of the refrigerator.'

He frowned and looked at Wendy. 'We just broke into his apartment,' Benson said. 'That's pretty unethical.'

'You said it was already open and always was,' I argued.

'Anyway,' he said slowly to me, 'what if we don't need your help? What if you'll be a hindrance to the investigation.'

Wendy put a hand on Benson's arm. 'It's okay, Benson. It might not hurt. Maybe she can rummage through Dave's file for information about Dave's other relatives – maybe parents or siblings. At least a last name. Anything to get us going.'

'No, Wendy,' Benson said, 'Invasion of privacy is a serious crime.'

'But not his apartment? Benson, you've been watching too much TV,' I said. 'Besides, as landlord, it is well within my jurisdiction to check on files and properties if necessary. I'll just have to get prior approval.'

Benson sighed. 'Oh, all right. Just don't get caught. You can't use the 'We got caught up in the heat of the moment' alibi like we did.'

'I won't get caught. Scouts' honor. I promise not to get busted in Dave's apartment with another man.' I raised three fingers, then clapped my hands together and cinched my robe tighter around my waist.

'Not funny,' Benson retorted.

'Don't get testy. I was just kidding. Where do we start?'

It was later in the evening when Benson, searching dozens of websites, made some headway into the 'case'. Wendy paced the apartment working through various scenarios. I went to the office and scanned Dave's documents. Unfortunately, there was very little information available. His file was vacant. No credit cards, no telephone bills – nothing.

31 – Gladys

I felt slightly guilty digging in Dave's past not for the sake of Dave and Meg but just for the excitement of it. If the sock had been on the other foot, I'm not sure how pleased I'd have been if my neighbors were digging through my past for dirty little secrets, but it was what it was. To be fair, I do it on social media all the time. Sometimes I look through renters' accounts before renting the apartment. Let me tell you, there are some real doozies out there.

Benson located multiple Janes and Teds throughout Iowa while Wendy scanned court documents with The Honorable Ignatius Stackworth presiding. Because of Dave's minor status, we weren't able to locate all the details, but there was an interesting tidbit regarding a settlement in a Stackworth's court around the time we believed Dave's case occurred. Dave had received an award for civic responsibility. In the photo, Dave was standing near the stage next to two Asian looking people. I found this online and texted it to them upstairs.

'That's excellent, Gladys!' Wendy congratulated me.

'It was nothing, really.' And yet from that one sentence of appreciation, I redoubled my efforts to come up with even more. Funny how encouragement works. I wrote down a few more things and then wandered back up to Benson's room. It was late and getting colder by the second. This would be my last trip outside.

Eventually, we followed the photo to a news article. Dave was named, and so were Edward and Mai Soto. Wendy wrote their names down. It was getting late, and Benson was beginning to yawn into the back of his hand. Wendy rubbed his shoulders.

'It's almost 11:00. Let's stop for the night,' she said. 'We can continue in the morning.'

Benson nodded. Just as he was about to turn off his computer, I saw something on the screen. On the right were two names with two faces. A Des Moines couple, Ted and Jane Manning, were accused of child neglect and fined $20,000. The news article was dated fifteen years ago. When Benson enlarged the photo, there was something eerily familiar about the man. He was tall and lanky, stooped over. His hair was brown and in disarray, but he had that Dave look – absently amused. The woman seemed apathetic.

'Look at that!' Benson exclaimed as he pointed at the picture. 'That's the older version of Dave, right there!'

We bent over his shoulders, one on each side. 'I'll be danged,' Wendy said. She patted his head.

'If those really are the people the judge wanted us to find, we should be able to locate them relatively quickly.' Benson squinted at the computer screen's time. 'It will have to be tomorrow, though. I've got to get some sleep.'

'Oh, come on, Benson,' Wendy said. 'We're getting close. Can't you feel it? Don't you want to go as far as we can tonight?'

'Uh, yeah, but...' he left the word sentence hanging.

'I'll take that as my cue to move on down the road.' I readjusted my robe and let myself out. By the time I had shut the door behind me, Wendy had already leaned down to kiss him.

32
Marty

There is nothing in life that scares me more than desperate people. The thought of death, I can handle; public speaking – meh; snakes and spiders, not even close. But I get my fill of fear-filled, desperate people all the time. It's part and parcel of doing what I do, and they freak me out.

When Letitia came into the shop, my blood turned ice-cold.

I watched her from a distance as I pretended to find something interesting in the back. Corey was out front polishing stock when Letitia approached him. He cupped his hand in his palm, nodded, then brought her over to the handgun section.

Generally, I'm not one to brush off sales, but I make it a rule not to sell guns to friends and acquaintances. And don't bring up that little peashooter that Dave bought. That doesn't count. If he would have asked for anything else, I would have turned him down. Letitia eyeing a 9mm was definitely concerning.

Why in the world would she need a handgun?

I suspected the reason, or at least could generate one. Dave was not a particularly easy person to be connected to, and with the whole bone marrow fiasco, maybe she was going to force the issue.

Dangit.

I brushed aside the hanging beads in the doorway to the back room and wended my way through the semi-automatics buried underneath glass and locked up tight. The walls were lined and locked with shotguns and rifles, but the handguns were nearest the sales desk in the back of the store. It's much harder to smash and grab that way.

'Letitia.'

Startled, she took a step back at the sound of her name.

The discomfort was palpable. I nodded to Corey. 'You can go. I'll help her.'

Without speaking, Corey readjusted his headphones went back to cleaning and resetting the stock.

'What are you doing here?'

She looked haggard and worn out. Her hands trembled as she pulled the sleeves of her coat down a little farther to hide them. The last time I saw her, she had shaved her head, but this time, her hair was about an inch long. She looked better with it, in my unprofessional opinion.

'I'm just browsing.'

'What are you looking for?'

She turned away from me. 'Why do you want to know?'

'Because it's my shop and I don't want people purchasing products that will harm anyone unnecessarily. Neither the buyer, nor anyone else.'

'Isn't that the purpose of a gun?' She ran her hand across the glass case.

'No. A gun is for protection. Security. It's like insurance. You hope you never need to use it, but it's there just in case.'

'Then that's what I want. Insurance.'

'What kind of insurance are you looking for?'

Voices can lie, gestures can exaggerate, but the eyes can't cope with deceit. Letitia rotated slowly, her hand still on the glass. She pointed beneath where her hand lay. 'What can you tell me about this insurance policy?' She was pointing at a handsome little SIG Sauer 9 mm. Easy to conceal.

I placed my hand on the same cabinet. 'There's going to be a good-sized premium on that. I'm not sure that's the kind of insurance you need.' I let the silence between us speak more about my reticence than anything else.

'You don't know anything about me,' she hissed.

'I know one big part, and I don't think he'd be too happy to see you here.'

'Guess what?' she snarled. 'He's not happy to see me at all. Anywhere.'

'I thought he was with you at the hospital.'

'We're not at the hospital right now,' she said, her eyes moving to Corey who was mouthing the words to a rap song. 'Meg got a reprieve a few days ago. The chemo is stopping the cancer, but not getting rid of it. We need those stem cells.'

'I'm sorry.'

'Now, are you going to sell me some 'insurance' or not?'

'Look, Letitia, do you really need a handgun? I mean, this is Des Moines…'

'You don't think bad things happen here?'

'No, it's not that, I'm just trying to get a read on the purpose. You've got a kid, and they can be inquisitive.'

Her jaw clenched. 'Are you saying I wouldn't be cautious? Is that because I'm a woman?'

I held up my hands. 'No! No! There are just too many stories.'

'Aren't you a big part of the problem?'

That comment always gets under my skin. 'Guns don't kill people. Idiots do. There were more idiot drivers on the road who killed people last year than guns, and you don't see people protesting every time there's a car accident telling the government they need to ban Volkswagens.'

'My question remains. Are you going to sell one to me, or not?'

'Does this purchase have anything to do with Dave?'

The eyes can't lie. 'No,' she said, but her eyes spoke a definite 'yes."

'Then the answer is 'or not'. You're not in the frame of mind to be buying a weapon, even if it is for protection. You're in a highly stressed situation, and those in highly stressed situations should never have an available sidearm.'

'Look, Marty,' her voice dropped to an almost inaudible level, 'there's been some gang activity on my street and the last thing I need is to worry about a break in, especially because of Meg's vulnerability.'

I felt myself taking a step back. There was some truth to what she was saying, yet could I really take the chance?

'I'll take shooting lessons, I promise.'

'Can you get the lessons first?'

Her expression went cold. 'I'm not going to beg, Marty, but by the looks of the store, you could use more sales.'

You need look no further than the threadbare carpet and the chipped ceiling paint to see that her observation was correct. I was lucky to sell half a dozen guns per week. Sooner or later, I'd have to leave the business.

'I still don't know.'

'How about I give you above market value for the gun. Think of it as good faith.' She pulled out her wallet and opened her wallet. Cash. Lots of it. I wouldn't even need to report the excess.

'How much are we talking about?' As soon as I said it, I knew I'd sold my morals. It was just negotiating the price now.

'I'll give you three hundred extra.'

Three hundred. That was some nice cabbage. Corey was messaging on his phone heedless of our discussion.

'All right, it's a deal,' I responded softly, feeling somewhat sleazy for cutting a deal with Dave's girlfriend. What could possibly go wrong with a child-sized adult and a gun?

Letitia removed the bills from the wallet.

'Come to the counter.' I led her to the register where I took up a position behind the glass and in front of a row of shotguns. I punched in the actual cost of the gun before she handed over the price and the tip. 'Wait.' I held up the forms.

'Just show me where to sign.'

'Please be very careful,' I said.

'I know what I'm doing.'

That's what I was worried about.

When she walked out the store that day, I wondered if I had done the right thing. Someday, I was sure that we would all have a laugh about it.

Ha ha.

33

Benson

Even after Gladys left (the old lady finally got the hint), Wendy and I stayed up for another hour and a half discussing the excitement of the day. Her natural intelligence and quick wit, her ability to focus on the present and find pathways across different topics, was incredible to me. All my life I wanted to get a girlfriend just to make out with, but now I had one to actually adore for the other 23.9 hours of the day.

As we lay down together, her hair splayed across the pillow, our faces inches apart, our thoughts turned toward the morning that was coming. 'How do you think we'll find Ted and Jane?' she asked.

I stroked her face. 'I'll keep digging through court records. There might be something more to the article about the $20,000 fine. Or, maybe the Soto couple can help us out.'

She smiled at me. Even in the dim light leaking under my bedroom door from the kitchen, I could see her straight teeth.

'What are you thinking about?' I asked.

'How lucky I am.'

I snorted. 'You? How about me?'

'Tell me how lucky you are,' she said coquettishly.

'The most luckiest guy in the world.'

It was nearly ten o'clock by the time we got out of bed. I was up first. I wanted to make breakfast in bed for her. I'd almost forgotten about Dave, Letitia, and Meg, and was reveling in the business of enjoying life with Wendy.

I busied myself with scrambled eggs, toast, and coffee. As the eggs steamed away in the pan, and the coffee pot gurgled and moaned like an emphysemic smoker, I hummed the theme from *Love Boat*. Today was going to be a great day.

After the toast popped up, I turned to put it on the counter, and I almost dropped the plate when I saw Dave sitting on my sofa.

'Holy crap, Dave! How long have you been sitting there?'

'Long enough to hear the chorus of *Love Boat.*' His smile was tired, but at least it was there.

'What are you doing?'

'Do you have any extra eggs? I'm hungry.'

It had been a long time since we had breakfast together. Before Wendy, we would dine-in at least two or three times per week. When I ate at his apartment, it was (fittingly) something odd like a tossed salad with canned peaches, or banana and carrot smoothie.

'Sure.' I glanced over my shoulder at the bedroom door which was slightly ajar. When I left Wendy, her mouth was open, and a line of drool was rivering down her cheek.

Quickly moving to the bedroom, I shut the door and returned to the eggs which were now starting to char. 'Dangit.' I scraped the carbon from the bottom of the pan. Dave didn't seem to notice. Placing the conglomeration on another plate, I sprinkled some salt and pepper, then dropped a piece of toast on top and handed him the plate. I didn't give him silverware because he liked to eat with his fingers, even if it was hot. He once told me it helped him connect with his ancestors.

Dave ate in silence while I cooked my own breakfast. Wendy's breakfast in bed would have to wait for another day. When I finished cooking, I grabbed silverware and positioned myself in my lazy chair to Dave's left in front of the lounge window which overlooked the courtyard. The cold light spilled lazily into the small narrowness of my living room. If Wendy wouldn't have been cuddled up in my bed, this would have felt just like old times. Just me and Dave. Dave and me.

His eyes were dark, and his cheeks seemed like concave bowls. Either he was not eating, or not eating enough.

'You okay?'

He nodded and grunted. After licking his fingers, he wiped them on his pants. 'No, not really.'

33 – Benson

I waited for him to add more, but he didn't, so we sat in uncomfortable silence until I couldn't handle it anymore. 'Did you need something this morning?'

Shifting his gaze slowly to me, I felt mesmerized by the power he had (or used to have) over me. 'Sometimes you start to think about the past, the way things used to be. Yesterday always seems better.'

Knowing that the love of my life was in the next room, I would have begged to differ.

He swallowed and I watched his Adam's apple bob up and down, a hairy fruit dancing under his chin.

'Everybody kind of floats through life, don't you think? We exist on a smorgasbord of ignorance, disregarding the good things set before us – the scenery, other people, relationships. We treat most of our life like a series of disposable moments, half-eaten, assuming that we'll get another course the next morning. But one of those days, man, you don't get your daily allowance of life – you get three quarters or half or even less than – and we bemoan and bewail the unfairness of it all. Sooner or later, it all starts to rot. Whether you're thirty-five or five…'

I watched as he deliberated over the meaning of life, and I was in awe, continued awe, that he could put into words the things I felt but never thought about. 'So, you get to that three-quarters, half-or-less-than-the-day-before and you turn around and you see all the disposable days, thrown out, casually and purposely, and you think, 'What the heck was I thinking? Why didn't I drain every last drop, eat every last strawberry, savor every last chocolate' – which is code for, 'Why didn't I spend every moment on the people who mean the most to me?" Dave leaned forward and put the plate on the coffee table. 'Don't you wonder if there are people in your life that might be here today and dead the next?'

'Yes, but I don't think about it that way?'

'You *mean*,' Dave said shaking a finger at me, 'you don't think about it at all.'

'Come on, Dave, don't get all judgmental on me.'

'Don't waste it, Benson. Not one minute.' The pitch of his voice raised one notch, pleading.

'I'm not, okay? But I can't be you. I can't figure out how to help everyone like you can. I can't make people like me. I can't *not* care about what people think about me and what they say. I can't afford to invite people off the street for steak and potatoes. That's your gift, not mine. I'm far too selfish to be you.'

On that Saturday morning, I felt the terror of being ripped from him. If something happened to him, if he was here today and absent the next, I would be lost. Though our connection was strong and palpable, it was hemorrhaging. I could see him, I could hear him, but the light was beginning to be sucked inside of him.

Suddenly, I wanted to take it all back, go back to yesterday. I wanted it to be me and Dave, Dave and me. I wanted him to call me Buttmunch or Moronacles – anything to escape this painful separation.

For the first time since he and I had been best friends, I saw a cloud of confusion in his expression, and his face registered fear. In pronouncing the words, 'I can't be you,' what he heard was 'I don't want to be you.' And then, 'I don't want to be with you.' As the house of cards began to crumble around him, my words were sonic torpedoes to his psyche. If his best friend didn't want to be him, or even be like him, or with him, then maybe all the people he had brought into his life as buffers against an ancient ache, didn't want to be him or be like him or with him. He was a human being just like all of us who hurt, and who failed, and who wished for things that could not possibly be accomplished just by wishing for them. Maybe he would have to come to terms with who he was and who others were. In doing so, maybe Dave would have found himself mired in the beauty and pain of humanity rather than floating above it.

'I see,' he said quietly.

'I'm not trying to hurt your feelings, Dave, not at all. You're my best friend, but somehow we have to break you out of this funk.'

33 – Benson

He was about to say something when the bedroom door opened and Wendy, with closed eyes, yawning mouth and nothing but a bra and underwear on, wandered out into the living room. She stretched, her arms high above her head, and I jumped up.

'Wendy!'

Startled, she opened her eyes and saw me – then Dave. Quickly, she attempted to cover her breasts, then her nether region, then back to her breasts and dove straight back into the bedroom. She slammed the door shut.

'Benson!' she shouted through the door. 'Why didn't you tell me he was here?'

I hurried to the door. With my head leaning against the wood, I spoke to the crack. 'I didn't want to wake you up. I didn't know he was going to be here,' I said quietly. 'I'm sorry.'

'I was half-naked!'

'At least you weren't three-quarters naked.'

'Shut up!'

'Look, I'm sorry.'

'You should be.' I heard her moving around the room grabbing her clothes and putting them on.

'When you're ready, come out and I'll make you some breakfast.'

No response.

'I've made some coffee, and we can all welcome the morning with good humor and laugh about this someday.'

The door whooshed open, and I almost fell into her arms. 'It will be funny for *you*,' she said, 'but you weren't flashing *my* friend.'

I lowered my voice. 'But you looked sexy…'

She smacked me on the arm as she exited the bedroom. 'Wrong, wrong, wrong, Benson.'

As she huffed into the living room, the front door was open, and Dave was gone. 'Where…?'

Dave had silently picked up his plate, put it in the sink, and left us to our mutual embarrassment.

By the time Wendy finished her second cup of coffee and downed the eggs that she made for herself, most everything was forgiven. As we talked, we both came to the conclusion that this was a... um... tit for tat... as Wendy's semi-nakedness was traded for Dave's baring of soul.

'Now,' Wendy said rubbing her hands, 'Let's find this Ted and Jane. They kind of sound like serial killer names, don't they?'

'Well, they have been in jail.'

Opening up my computer, I typed in the commands and followed rabbit holes to various places. As the paths to Dave's past wound here and there, I came upon a startling and tragic discovery – Jane Manning died in a car accident years before.

The search continued. Finally, we found a brief newspaper article about a Ted Manning who had been arrested, charged, and convicted of grand theft auto, two years ago. Currently, unless he had been released on good behavior, he was being held at Polk County Correctional.

'Do you think he's still there?' Wendy asked.

'I hope so.' After I said it, I recognized the heartlessness.

Hours later, Wendy and I walked into the Polk County Correctional Facility where we were promptly asked to empty our pockets, walk through a metal detector, and answer a few questions from a wearied correctional officer who had been tasked with manning the front desk. He looked like he'd been sitting in that chair for years. His face had the florid complexion of a person who rarely saw the sun. I wondered if I stared too long, he would morph into something resembling a large albino toad.

After filling out the forms, he notified another area of the facility and told us that Ted Manning would meet us in the interview area shortly. Minutes later, another guard collected us in the entry and took us to a desolate room with rectangular Formica-topped tables and plastic chairs. A few other prisoners were slouching while loved ones or lawyers visited them.

Nervously, we took a seat and waited. Each time a prisoner came in we sat up straighter. We had no idea what Ted looked like.

33 – Benson

'How are you feeling?' I asked Wendy.

Her face was flushed, and her hands fidgeted on the table in front of her. 'Is it wrong to say 'excited?''

'Yes.'

Finally, a tall, rat-faced man, with grizzled cheeks, who looked startlingly like an older version of the photo we had seen, entered. The sleeves on his shirt were rolled up revealing numerous tattoos and slender arms. There were scars on his forearms and he was missing a tooth. He checked the boxes for every stereotype I had about inmates, including the gruffness of his voice.

'Who are you?'

I nodded to the guard who told us we had half an hour. He made Ted sit down and then took up his position by the door.

I leaned forward but didn't shake his hand. We were told not to touch the guest in any way, and certainly we should not give him anything. How very *Silence of the Lambs*. Dave would have eaten this up. That guilty thought hurt slightly.

That thought about the movie triggered something in me – something I should have known, or at least remembered from what Dave had said to me before – but I pushed it back into my subconscious for later retrieval.

'My name is Benson Olson and this is Officer Wendy Larson.' I felt Wendy flinch.

His beady eyes looked her up and down. 'Is she your girlfriend?'

'I'm sorry, sir, that's not really any of your business.'

'Oooh, Mr. Formal.' He waggled his fingers in front of his face towards me. He had a gratingness about him that made me want to punch him. Not that I'd ever hit anyone before.

'Ms. Larson is a government enforcement officer.'

Ted studied her again, her hair, her eyes, her curves. 'Going casual today, Officer?'

'Sometimes it's easier for others to feel comfortable if I'm not wearing my uniform nor carrying my gun.'

'Sexy,' he said and licked his lips.

'Mr. Manning,' Wendy ignored him, 'we'd like to ask you some questions about Dave Stackworth.'

'Dave Stackworth. Huh.'

'Your nephew.'

'I know who he is.'

'Mr. Manning, when was the last time that you saw Dave.'

Ted sniffed and continued to ogle Wendy. To her credit, she did not squirm. He put his leg up towards Wendy and placed a hand over his crotch. His gray hair had not been cut recently, and what was left had been combed across his balding pate. Teeth yellowing, moustache flowing, this man could easily have been a reincarnation of Ted Bundy.

'It was before Jane died. Maybe seven, eight years ago. Why do you want to know about him?'

I ignored the question. I wondered if the police felt like that all the time.

'Why did he come to see you?'

Ted shrugged. 'Maybe he felt guilty about leaving us out to dry. Jane always hated him, even when he lived with us – so superior and... and... dickish.'

I looked at Wendy who, I'm sure, had the same thought as I did. *That's space calling a black hole black.* 'What did you talk about?'

'He came to tell us that he was changing his name to that stupid judge's name.'

'Judge Stackworth?'

'Yeah, that's the one.'

'Why would he care to tell you about that?'

'How the hell would I know? Dave did what he wanted. Even when he was young, he wandered around in his own little world, head in the clouds. He didn't help watch the other kids – his own cousins, for Pete's sake. He avoided all responsibility.'

'What was Dave's name he changed from?' I asked.

Ted's eyes narrowed and he began to laugh. 'You mean you don't know? Some investigators you are.'

'Please answer the question, Mr. Manning.'

'Should I have my lawyers here or something?'

'We're just interested in Dave.'

'And here I thought the attractive officer was part of the Poh-lice.' He scratched himself and leered again at Wendy. 'You want to know about my nephew Dave?' Ted leaned back in his chair and crossed his arms. 'I'll tell you, but it's going to cost you.'

I ground my teeth. 'What do you mean?'

'I'm happy to give a little information, but *quid pro quo*. I give, but you return.'

Shocked beyond imagination, Ted's quote from *Silence of the Lambs* made me physically flinch. 'What did you say?'

'It's from that stupid movie Dave used to watch. He used to quote it all the time. And I mean all the time. Which was weird considering… Never mind. And no wonder he…' He stopped. 'Hey… you're trying to trick me, aren't you. Psychomanipulating me or something.'

That moment felt like we were standing on the edge of a cliff ready to take the picture and just before we clicked, a cloud passed in front.

'No, Mr. Manning, that is not what we're doing. We just want to understand what's going on with Dave.'

'He's messing with you too, isn't he?'

'No, not at all.' I decided to change tack. 'What happened to Jane, your wife?'

Ted couldn't control his reaction regarding his wife's death. Regret, anger, resentment. 'You leave her out of this.'

'We just want to get to the bottom of… who Dave really is, and we believe your wife, would have known some things.'

Ted's gaze shifted uncomfortably back and forth between us. 'Back when our kids were little, we struggled financially. My sister, Rosalind, she married well, and they could have taken care of us – easily, but then… well, Jane and my sister didn't get along so well. Words were spoken. A few barbs at Christmas, if we saw them at all. Gradually, we grew apart.' He stopped, and his mouth twisted into an evil grin. 'But then things went bad for them. When they died, we took on the little brat. He was hard work, and we didn't really want to do it, but we hoped that his inheritance would help us along.' He motioned with his hands. 'You know, repaid for taking on their retard.'

Wendy's jaw was clenched like mine. 'You haven't told us what happened to Jane.'

'One day, out of the blue, Dave came to visit us at our home. Jane went off the rails. And after he left, she started drinking and doing drugs. Two of our kids had moved out at that time, but when Jane started sliding further, they stayed away. Dave ruined our family and my life.'

'What did Dave say to Jane that was so disagreeable?'

'He said, bad things happen when...' Like a lawnmower hitting a rock, he stopped and stared at us. Then, after a deliberate second or two, he peered over our shoulders at the security guard and leaned forward. 'If Dave would have shared some of his unearned cash, none of this would have happened. Jane would still be alive, I wouldn't be in jail, our kids would be happy.'

'I'm sorry for what has happened to you,' I said lamely.

'That's total crap, Backgammon or whatever your stupid name is.'

Suddenly, it became very clear to me where Dave might have inherited his predilection for name calling. 'Mr. Manning, Ted, what happened to Dave's parents?'

Ted sat forward quickly. 'I tell you what. You send me some care packages, some goodies I can trade in here, maybe some cigarettes and cookies, and I'll let you know what happened with Dave's parents.'

'*Quid pro quo*, Buffalo Bill,' Wendy said.

Ted smirked and leaned even further back in his chair. His chin rested on his chest.

'Either you give us something or we'll walk out of here right now. We have other ways to find out.'

'Yeah, right.'

We waited until finally Wendy stood up. 'Time's up.'

'Wait,' Ted hesitated and motioned for us to sit back down. 'At the very least, I'll tell you the name he changed it from, but you have to send me the package. Anything, just a few things to make life in here a little bit more bearable.' His pleading voice was irritating, and I wanted to refuse, but we needed a lead.

'Okay,' I said.

He sighed. 'Dave changed it from Soto. He was Dave Soto.'

I looked into his eyes. I wished I was a real investigator so I could have told if he was lying. Wendy was looking at me because we both recognized the name – Dave's foster family. That would make sense. But that didn't really help us. We already knew their name. What was his original name?

'Are you sure you don't want to tell us anything else?' I asked. 'What was his original name? Maybe for a larger care package?'

He shook his head. 'Come back again. I'll wait…' He stood, joining us. 'And wear something skimpier next time.' Ted reverted to the lascivious little lecher we first encountered twenty minutes before. He puckered his lips and blew Wendy a kiss. As we turned, I noticed he was staring at Wendy's backside.

He was laughing when we left.

34

Mrs. Soto

It is dark now, darker than it's ever been before. I have everything I need – a warm house, plenty of food, a faithful pet – except light. It would not be a stretch for me to point to the exact moment when the light in my life was extinguished, but it had been dimming for some time before that. I just didn't perceive it as such. We live, we love, we marry, and the flame flickers. And it's not just one love, but multiple. Spouse, parents, friends... homes... whatever. We love and we lose, and then we love some more, and we lose some more. With each successive loss, a little piece is torn from our hearts. That's the way I've felt for some time now. My name is Mai Soto. Because of tragic and avoidable circumstances, I'm the widowed mother of Dave.

Dave has been my son for twenty years.

From what I understand, you've only heard rumors of me so far – about us and... them. Or, maybe Dave had said something to you about us. That would surprise me, though. He's not generally one to talk about the past. But I do, because it feels like I have no future. The past is the only place I find meaning. If you'll indulge me for a few moments, I'd like to tell you a little bit about my story.

Edward and I were married in the 90's. Our parents were Japanese immigrants who moved to California in the 70's. Eddie and I met at Iowa State University, and settled in Des Moines. We had a modest income and nice little house, but it was empty without children. Thus, when Dave entered our lives, the house became a home, and we grew into a family.

We knew Judge Stackworth from his volunteer work with the foster care system. When the opportunity arose for someone to take Dave on, we leapt at it. He was young and precocious, a little strange, but not overwhelmingly so.

We had our quarrels, little fights over little things. Eddie didn't always appreciate the way Dave saw the world, and especially the way he quoted that awful movie. Unlike other children, Dave didn't socialize. He was out a lot, just by himself – in the park, or at the river. He liked green things. And animals, of course. What child doesn't like animals? He had a specific affinity for moths and butterflies and kept a collection pinned in his room. Sometimes it frightened me to see all those creatures pinned and hanging on the wall, especially those luna moths with those gigantic eyes on their wings. Made me shiver. But everyone collects something, I suppose.

We knew that Dave was being picked on in high school. We tried our best to support him and the teachers, but those terrible children and their social media. This was just the beginning when all those companies started ruining our children. Video games and all that brain rot. Dave, though, was not into games and social media. Amazingly, he never wanted a phone. His lack of phone was one of the primary reasons they would bully him to his face. Called him 'giraffe' or 'Fortune Cookie'. Kids can be cruel, but their parents should be punished for what they allow their children to do.

Even though Dave and Eddie weren't that close, they would have done anything for each other. It was in both of their natures, I guess, though Eddie's was a little more subtle because of his Japanese background.

It wasn't until Eddie's death that Dave truly started to change. After the accident, Dave came around a little more often. Brought me gifts. Stayed for a few minutes, but he never could quite erase the shame he felt for Eddie's death. I suppose I didn't purposely blame him, but if not for Dave, and Dave's family, Eddie would still be alive. And I might be happier. I deserve to be happier.

Maybe.

That sounds terrible. If I were you, I might think, 'She's quite a piece of work wanting to rewind her time with her adopted son.' Be gentle with your judgment. You may yet find grace for me.

When Eddie died, Dave retreated further and further into the strange shell of himself, and he kept telling me how guilty he felt. Which, of course, was silly. His part in Eddie's death was circumstantial. It was only her. Just her.

Ironically, after Eddie's death, Dave's conscience was eased only by purchasing a house for me. A guilt offering, I suppose. And this drove Ted – Dave's uncle, if you haven't heard – insane. Got himself arrested, he did. They always wanted Dave's money. Dave gave me the money they thought was rightfully theirs, and I feel worse than when I didn't have it. Now I have this house, and objects to fill it, but it is lonely. So lonely. Quiet. I wish I could fill it with noise and with grandchildren, but that's for the next life.

Oh, listen to me. I'm prattling on like an old woman. Maybe I am getting old – and sentimental. You will too when you lose love.

I suppose I should tell you about the beginning of the rest of the story and then you can make your judgments about us all.

It was mid-December, not long before Christmas, when I decided to sit in the front room by the bay window. The snow had been glistening all day and the temperature hadn't risen above freezing for almost a week. I always thought there was something magical about the Christmas holiday, with the music and the trees and the lights, the gifts and colors. It's the one time of year when I feel somewhat hopeful, like the last minutes before dawn and the glow turns the sky a majestic purple. Are you like that, too?

My watch said it was almost 5:00 p.m. It was before dinner and I was hungry, but the energy required for cooking seemed beyond me, so Kaze, my dog, and I sat near that front window, me stroking her fur, imagining what hope might feel like again, when lights appeared in the driveway. I remember thinking to myself, 'Now, who could that be?'

35

Benson

The meeting with Ted felt like a trip to the dentist. Uncomfortable, painful, necessary, and never wanting to go back. Instead of free floss and toothbrush, our guard returned our belongings, wishing us a nice day – not sure that he meant it, but whatever – and ushered us back into the cold, pre-dusk outdoors.

As we strolled to the car, Wendy reached out to hold my hand. Ted had unnerved her. He had been like a botfly, burrowing under the skin. You couldn't quite get at him, and you were patently disgusted, but you just had to wait for the time to finish. When she held out to reach my hand, it was a natural projection of where we were moving as a couple. Standing together against all the horrors of life.

While we walked, my mind couldn't rid itself of questions: Why had he never told us these things about himself? Why had I never asked? What else had he been hiding? What happened to Dave's parents? What happened to the Sotos? What about Ted and Jane?

Wendy's pickup was parked in the middle of the parking lot underneath a light post. The yellowish light illuminated the snow crystals as they fell silently to the ground. There was a dusting of ice and salt on the windows. The doors rustily screeched as we pulled them open and we crawled into the front seats. While I positioned myself in the driver's seat, Wendy retrieved her phone and began to search for any Sotos living nearby. Within moments, she had found them.

Edward and Mai Soto.

The couple had remained in the Des Moines area residing just north of us near Ankeny.

'Oh,' Wendy's voice cracked as she stared at the screen, 'that's not great.'

'What is it?'

'Mr. Soto died in a car accident about six years ago.'

'It happens.'

'Don't be so callous. What do you think that did to Dave?'

'I didn't think about that. Maybe that's what has pushed Dave over the edge?'

'From what Ignatius and Ted both said, Dave has always been a little different. It *has* to do with his parents' deaths. I can feel it.'

'I'm sure you're right.

I pulled out of the parking lot checking both directions before making our trip northwards out of the city. Traffic was sparce, mostly semis with their lonely drivers trucking goods along the arterial interstate roads in every direction.

The silence in the cab of Wendy's pickup was not uncomfortable. We were both lost in our own thoughts. Maybe silence comes naturally when people leave the combustion of the metropolitan machine. The noise and traffic, the aggravation of squealing brakes, transit systems, dirty buildings decorated with spray painted gang symbols. I'm so glad that Wendy wasn't from Des Moines. Someday I wouldn't mind living somewhere else, even if that meant leaving Dave. I smiled realizing that I was thinking about a future with her.

'How are we going to do this?' I asked.

Wendy chewed her bottom lip and tapped the door as she thought. 'First, we need to know Dave's parents' names. Without them, we can't dig any further.'

'Did you know that Ted accidentally slipped with his mom's name. Rosalind.'

'No, I missed that.'

'You must have been checking him out.'

'That's not something to joke about, Benson. I felt really uncomfortable. He was a dirty old man.'

'I could have taken him,' I said.

'I don't need you to *take* him. I need you to understand what that's like for me. I'm a woman in a man's world, doing a man's job, and every man I encounter on the river looks at me like that. I'm sick of it.'

'Sorry,' I pouted.

35 – Benson

'Apology accepted. You're the only one who gets to look at me like that.'

So I did.

'Not while you're driving, mister.'

'Yes ma'am,' I said as I saluted her without taking my eyes from the road. 'What was the address again?'

Wendy checked her phone and the blue line leading us to the house. 'Ankeny. 1115 Arden.'

We approached the exit from the interstate and turned west. The houses grew bigger. Suburban houses. Places where rich people lived, people with salaries, not incomes; people who distribute funds and find tax loopholes, not people like me who live paycheck to paycheck and get tax refunds. In the suburbs, long gravel lanes covered with snow led up to mansion-sized houses. Some were hidden behind trees. Others looked like golf course fairways, with 19th-hole monstrosities at the end.

It was dark now. Almost 5:00. The time from daylight to night was so quick during a Midwest winter. Now with the darkness, timers for Christmas lights created a glittering wonderland of Santas, reindeer, mangers, and blue snowflakes. Some houses had strung thousands of lights around gigantic trees making them shine. For just a little while, we set aside our mission, and I slowed down as Wendy oohed and aahed over the decorations. She looked like a little girl with her face pressed against the side window. Our first Christmas together.

Eventually, Wendy ducked forward under the windshield to look for address numbers on the sides of mailboxes. The farther we went, the bigger the houses got, until we finally reached 1115 Arden where we marveled at the immensity of the house at the end of a long lane. Two stories, at least 4,000 square feet, the home sat on three or four acres perched squarely behind mammoth oak trees, now leafless, and a beautifully tended front yard with boulders. In front of it all was shrubbery and a little ceramic boy fishing in a small pond.

'That's it! Look at that. Wow!'

I stopped the car at the end of the driveway. 'Holy Moses! I wonder if she's a celebrity?'

'I hope she's home.'

We pulled into the driveway, an asphalt covered lane as long as a football field and lined with miniature fir trees, and I parked in front of the four-car garage. The place felt like an insulated, alternate reality, like Narnia. For a few moments we simply stared through the windows at the cultured, sterile appearance of the place. If it would have been a country house, there would have been outbuildings and sheds, a few grain silos and a barn, but the only extraneous building was the garage. The rest of the acreage was just shivering trees and snow-covered grass.

As we stared, I wondered aloud what they could have done for a living to purchase a monstrosity like that. I felt a twinge of jealousy. Why couldn't normal people live in mansions? How could Wendy and I ever afford something like this? We'd struggle to pay for a modest home, much less a dream house.

After pulling ourselves from the car and wrapping our coats tighter around us, we followed the path up to the front door. It was festooned with Christmas lights and a wreath with two fake cardinals peeking out. The dark gray siding perfectly camouflaged the house in the early darkness. Everything about this home seemed carefully cultured – the perfect exterior.

Wendy pushed the intercom button, and after ten seconds or so, a voice spoke. 'Hello, who is it?'

'Hello, Mrs. Soto, my name is Benson Olson and I'm with Wendy Larson. We're friends of Dave.'

Silence. Then, a scritching sound as the intercom was reactivated. 'Is he in trouble?'

'No, ma'am, he's not in trouble, but we are worried about him. We were hoping you would speak with us.'

There was another pause and then her tired voice responded, 'Yes, okay.' The door buzzed and clicked open. We entered the foyer which was a stunning, architectural wonder, with marble floors and a twenty-

35 – Benson

foot vaulted ceiling. A chandelier hung to the left of a grand oak staircase strung with tinsel and pine wreathing. In the background, Christmas music played – oldies, jazz. I could smell coffee brewing.

As we stared upwards at the chandelier, a small, hairy dog, looking very much like an over-sized rat, raced around the corner and skidded to a halt near our feet. It began yapping with great intensity which, in the echoey space, was shrill and painful. Wendy bent down to touch it, but it grizzled and kept a wary distance while continuing to noisily alert its owner of stranger danger.

Mrs. Soto reached down to the dog and picked it up. She remonstrated the little mutt before it ceased yapping and settled for a low growl behind sharp, pointy teeth.

Mrs. Soto wore white pants, a pink cashmere sweater, and white soft shoes. Her fingernails were painted white, and when she extended her hand limply for me to shake, I noticed little red Santas on the tips. Her eyes, decorated with blue eye shadow, were curious. The red lipstick and generous amounts of rouge made her features look warm. Her hair had been pure black at one time, but it was streaked with gray and coiffed with great care. In my opinion, she looked like a Christmas geisha.

'Kaze!' Mrs. Soto chided the dog as it yapped once more. 'Be quiet.' Even though it was secure, it began to tremble with excitement or rage. At least it shut up. 'Don't mind Kaze. She's all talk, aren't you?' The woman nosed in the dog, and it licked her lips and cheeks.

I felt kind of ill. I imagined that the little mutt had just finished licking the floor (or worse) with that tongue.

'Hello, Benson. Dave has mentioned your name a few times in his letters.' Her eyes fastened on me, then Wendy.

'I'm Wendy.'

'Wendy. How nice.'

Why had Dave never talked about her? Writing letters? We only live twenty-five minutes from her house. She was so close, and yet how could he have hid her from me?

'Won't you come in?' She motioned towards the front sitting area, and we followed her into a large room with hearth and fireplace, generous furniture and a gigantic Christmas tree, fifteen feet tall and topped with an immense silver star. It took up an entire corner of the room. There were only a few presents under the tree, and the branches were sparsely ornamented. This was definitely not a traditional family Christmas tree. This one looked like she'd bought it from a designer magazine.

'Would you like some coffee?'

I declined, but Wendy took her up on the offer. Mrs. Soto invited us to sit down in the upholstered chairs in the bay window while she went to prepare the coffee. As we stared out the dimly lit window into the winter wonderland beyond, I marveled at the location. The perspective in the front yard, one of oak trees, a small bridge, the perfectly manicured surroundings, and various matching objects was one of comfort. It could have been a Norman Rockwell painting for the Saturday Evening Post.

Mrs. Soto asked, as she took a seat opposite of us. 'You would like to talk about Dave?'

'Yes.'

She spread her hands. 'How well do you know him?'

'We've lived next to each other for a few years. He's been a wonderful friend, sometimes a little…' I didn't want to offend her, but she filled in the blank correctly.

'Odd?'

'Yes, that's a good way to put it. Until recently, Dave has been doing really well.'

'Does he have a job?'

'Not that I know of, but he takes care of a lot of people.'

Mrs. Soto's jaw hardened, but she didn't respond.

'A few months ago, Dave began to change. It coincided with when his girlfriend's daughter fell sick.'

35 – Benson

She raised her eyebrows at the word 'girlfriend'. 'Dave has a girlfriend? What is she like? The girlfriend.'

'Letitia is very kind, strong, and gives Dave space to be Dave, if you know what I mean.'

'What does she look like?'

'She's tiny, only about five feet tall, dark skin. She shaves her head.'

'She's black?'

'Yes,' I answered as Mrs. Soto's mouth pursed. I heard her mumble, *That figures*, under her breath. Wendy stiffened.

'Do you mean that Dave hasn't told you about Letitia.'

'Obviously. Would I have asked you about her appearance if we'd met?'

I felt the blood rush to my cheeks. 'My apologies.'

Mrs. Soto straightened in her seat as she pondered us over the coffee cup. 'You said that he's been struggling…'

We nodded. 'Once Meg got sick it's like… he's a rat in a trap. When we try to talk to him about it, he retreats.'

'This Meg… Is it Dave's child?'

'No,' Wendy replied. 'Letitia is a divorced, single mother. A professor at Drake University.'

Once again Mrs. Soto muttered something unintelligible. 'What does that have to do with me? Does the woman need… support?'

'Mrs. Soto, we aren't here to speak with you about Letitia and Meg, but Dave, and his past. The way he's been behaving, we thought it was a response to his early years. Before you. With his parents.'

Mrs. Soto stiffened, and her eyes narrowed.

'We spoke with a few people, Judge Stackworth and… others. The judge didn't give us any information at all except what we would find in public documents. You and your husband's names came up.'

'So you thought you'd drive out here and motivate me to share more about Dave's upbringing.'

'Yes, something like that.'

At that moment, seeing Mrs. Soto and her surroundings, I felt a profound sense of disorientation. Everything I knew about Dave, and the people he was normally connected with, was out of sorts with Mrs. Soto and this house. Dave lived in a shabby, one bedroom apartment; Dave hung out with the poor, the wretched, the outcast; Dave drove a pre-loved vehicle and owned a flip phone. Dave's Christmas decorations were second-hand, scavenged from Goodwill stores and garage sales. Though he always seemed to have money, I couldn't even begin to imagine Dave growing up in a place like this. Instead, being who he was, he would have needed a dog and a tricycle, a dirt pit, and lots of used toys.

As we listened to Mrs. Soto, I wondered what kind of mother she had been? Was she as stiff as she presented herself to be? How would Dave have reacted to that?

'Mrs. Soto, why doesn't... er... he have... um...' I waved my hand around the house, trying to find a polite way to say that Dave didn't live ostentatiously as she did.

'Why doesn't he have all the things that I do, is that what you're implying?'

I nodded.

'Dave never really cared about toys or games or *things*. He was only interested in people, right from the very beginning. When other kids wanted cell phones and video game consoles or radio-controlled cars, Dave wanted to spend time with the poor kids in the neighborhood.'

'There are poor kids in this neighborhood?' I asked, but winced when I heard my judgmental voice ring through.

Studying us, Mrs. Soto leaned forward in her chair while placing her forearms on her thighs. The coffee mug was cupped in her hands. 'We never lived here when Eddie was alive. In fact, it was not my choice...'

'What do you mean?'

Her eyes narrowed as if sensing we were about to open the door to a long passageway. 'Do you mind if I get something stronger?' She pointed at her cup of coffee.

'It's your house, your rules.'

35 – Benson

Nodding, she stood up and we moved into the kitchen. She opened a long skinny cupboard and took out a bottle. She withdrew three small snifters and brought them to the table which sat perfectly in a small alcove. On the windowsills, ceramic snowmen and reindeer were motionless performing their wintery duties, watching us prepare to have a drink.

'Oh, no thank you, Mrs. Soto,' Wendy protested, but Mrs. Soto ignored her and continued putting one in front of each of us. Pulling the cork from the bottle, she poured a finger of liquid for each of us.

'These are things I haven't spoken of for a very long time. Not since Eddie died.' She recorked the bottle and set it off to the side. 'Eddie was a wonderful, kind man – a gentle man, one of principles and accomplishment. Perhaps it was the culture we were brought up in, but as Japanese Americans, we believed in these things, respect, honor, and above all, hard work. Though Dave was honorable and respectful to a point, he was somewhat averse to work, and as such, Dave and Eddie clashed. Not because Dave was rebellious, but because Eddie was too much like Dave's own father.'

My heart began to race. 'You knew Dave's parents?'

'No, we never met. That was part of the deal with foster parents. We don't generally meet.'

Duh, I thought, *Dave was fostered. He wouldn't have been if they lived.* 'Do you know what happened to them?'

Mrs. Soto saluted the glass in front of her to us. *'Kanpai.'* I checked Wendy who grabbed her snifter. I smelled it. It was very strong. Beer is one thing, but scotch? You might as well roll me in turpentine and set me on fire.

Mrs. Soto tilted the glass back quickly and drank. When I swallowed mine, the world was constricted to a pinpoint, and I began to cough. So did Wendy.

When I finally could speak, my voice sounded like a wheezy old man. 'That was not pretty.'

She smiled sadly and peered out the window. Kaze begged at her feet until she lifted the animal onto her lap. Before she spoke again, the dog curled itself into a ball, and she began stroking it.

'We signed court documents that disallow us from speaking about the proceedings. I cannot explicitly tell you anything.'

'Explicitly?' Wendy asked. 'Does that mean *implicitly* is allowed?'

'Read of it what you will. I will answer your questions to the extent I can.'

'Where were Dave's parents from?'

'Pennsylvania.'

'How did they die?'

'Next question, please.'

'We know that Dave has discretionary funds. He spends it lavishly on friends, and even strangers.' Mrs. Soto's cheek muscles flexed. 'Where did his money come from?'

'Inheritance.'

'What did his parents do for a living? How did they get their money?'

'I cannot answer that.'

Frustrated, I glanced at Wendy. 'Where did you get your money?'

It was a question I wouldn't have asked. It was like asking a woman how much she weighed. 'Clever girl, even though that's a very personal question.' Mrs. Soto dabbed at her lips with a napkin. Some lipstick remained on both the napkin and the glass.

'When Eddie was killed, Dave bought me this house and everything in it. It was his, how shall we say, guilt offering.'

'Guilt offering? I don't understand,' Wendy pushed.

'My Eddie was murdered in a car accident. A head on collision.'

Suddenly, a few puzzled pieces fit into place. *Oh, wow.* 'It was about six years ago, wasn't it?'

Mrs. Soto sniffed. 'The other driver was a woman that Eddie, Dave and I knew well enough. She was suffering from a despicable case of vengeance. She was drunk.'

'Jane Manning,' Wendy responded as the last coin dropped.

The glass in my hand took on ironic symbolism. Her husband had been killed by a drunk.

'Yes,' Mrs. Soto answered.

'Can you tell us a little bit more, please?' Wendy asked.

She continued to stroke Kaze who, feeling its owner's emotion, peered up into her face, then sighed and reburied its head in her paws. 'We lived on the southwest side of Des Moines in a lovely little neighborhood. We had a house with a small front yard, a tire swing, and a little creek in the back. The maple trees were gorgeous and filled our world with color. They were red turning gold the day he died. Eddie was on his way home from work. As the police report stated, Eddie was traveling west, minding his own business, when Jane Manning came out of nowhere from the cross street and rammed him at fifty miles per hour directly into his driver's door. He had no chance.'

'I'm so sorry,' Wendy said.

'Somehow, Jane survived, but she spent a long time in the hospital and then recovered in prison.'

'She died,' I said.

'I know.' Mrs. Soto's face hardened. 'I hope she rots in hell.'

'What happened after the accident?' I asked.

'Nothing, until Dave showed up later. He pulled me aside, tears streaming down his face, and he apologized. Said it was all his fault. He said he'd make things right with me. Keep me safe from anything else. Stay away from me.'

'Stay away from you? Did Dave say why he believed the fault was his?' I asked. 'I mean, it's one thing to be driving, and another thing to be related to the person who actually did it.'

'The family of murderers all feel a sense of guilt, don't they? Was there something they could have done? Were there signs they missed? Why hadn't they stopped them?'

'I suppose. But Dave didn't even like the Mannings, right?' Wendy asked.

'Dave believed that he was lethal to the people he was closest to. His parents died; Eddie died; Jane died. Even the judge's wife died. When his aunt died, this, too, was difficult for him. Blaming himself was easier than blaming the fickleness of fate. When I saw him a few weeks after Eddie's funeral, it looked like he hadn't slept in weeks. As we stood on the porch of the house he was raised in, Dave gave me a wrapped present and told me not to open it until after he had left. When I did, there was an account number and a password with my name on it. There was one million dollars in the account.'

'Holy crap!' I covered my mouth. 'Sorry,' I apologized.

'Inside the present was a note which read, 'I realize at a time like this, you won't want to think about money, but you never should have needed to. I should have given this to you a long time ago, but you know me and money – it's here one day and gone the next. If you don't want it, leave it, and I will give it to charity.'

'What I don't understand is where did Dave's inheritance come from?'

Mrs. Soto's jaw hardened again. 'I cannot fill in any more of your blanks. By court order, I must remain silent. You might think, 'No one is here. No one is listening. It's for Dave's sake.' but once again, honor and respect are built into our genetics. Only Dave's parents can help you with what you're looking for.'

'What?' *How could they possibly tell us anything? They'd been dead for decades.*

Her eyes shifted above our heads and fixed to the wall behind us. 'Only Dave's parents can help you,' she repeated.

Our eyes followed hers. Behind us, there were picture frames of smiling family faces, adventure scenes, idyllic days of lying on a picnic blanket and blowing dandelion heads from their stalks. I pushed back my seat and got up. Walking over to the photos, I scanned them and looked to Mrs. Soto for confirmation. She shifted slightly and returned her gaze to the reflecting window in the kitchen nook. Kaze jumped down from her lap panting happily as she ambled over to us at the wall.

35 – Benson

We inspected photos of young versions of Dave. In the midst, there was one photo that stuck out like a sore thumb. It must have been from mid-90's, a grainy, faded image of a tall, gangly man and his tall, gangly wife. They stood in front of a white, two-story house, surrounded by a picket fence. A cat, with its tail standing straight up, rubbed itself against the man's legs. The picture seemed overexposed and out of place with the other beautiful photos surrounding it.

'It's this one,' I whispered. I peered closely at it for any significance that could tell us exactly what she meant by Dave's parents giving us some information. Apart from the fact that they were together, somewhere – must have been in Pennsylvania which I inferred from Mrs. Soto's information. But there was nothing that would indicate special significance.

'What is it? What are we missing?' Wendy asked.

Mrs. Soto spoke again. She appeared despondent with her empty glass on the table in front of her and a happily panting dog beneath her. 'You can take it off the wall, if you like.'

We did. And as we plucked it from its place, a sheet of paper fell from the back. A newspaper article.

'Is this what we were supposed to find?' I asked.

Mrs. Soto's eyes were filled with tears. 'I can't tell you that,' her voice trembled.

Wendy opened the newspaper and gasped.

Suddenly, everything became very, very clear.

35.5
Mai

The snow reminds me that I'm in the winter of my life. I'm not that old, but I can feel the change of seasons in my bones; they are chilled and grate together. There is pain in the coldness, especially in suffering it alone.

It was incredibly conflicting to have the young couple with me that day as their questions resurrected buried emotions. It surprised me greatly that Dave had not told me about his girlfriend or his daughter. When he was younger, he revealed most things to me, even though some were cryptically buried in those dreadful movie quotes which Eddie and I found so disturbing.

When I heard the voices on the intercom and the request to come in to chat about Dave, I felt a swirling sense of vertigo. The day had come. The day I had both dreaded and prayed for. How long have I been holding on to these secrets?

My life is full of if-onlys: if only Dave would have been normal. If only the Mannings would have been kind. If only Eddie would have driven a different route home that day. Unfortunately, I cannot change any of those events now.

I'm still filled with rage at Eddie's death. At the trial, Jane was charged with vehicular manslaughter. I sat in the second row, hands in my lap, trying desperately not to rush her chair and beat her with anything I could find. Dave, sensing the inner battle, reached out to my arm. His touch was firm but trembling.

Jane suffered terribly from the accident, and for that, I believed there was some sense of cosmic payback. She deserved the perpetual limp and rearranged face. She deserved the amputated fingers and glass eye. She deserved every single agony because her act of vengeful stupidity wasted so many different lives. During the trial, she kept turning around to look at Dave. The smirk was another dagger, and her apathy to his misery bordered on psychopathic. Ted was much more invested in the trial, and his lawyer's attempts to get the judge to reduce the charges on psychological trauma were unfruitful. It was an open and shut case. She was guilty.

And yet we're all guilty of something, aren't we?

Jane Manning, driven insane by Dave's inheritance, took matters into her own hands to hurt him, and, by taking my husband from me, ruined my future. I had no family, no husband, no son – nothing but memories and a mansion.

I did not feel anything when Jane died in prison. There may have been some who mourned, perhaps Ted and the children. Jane had no life insurance policy, so Ted and the children would have to keep scrounging.

On that night Benson and Wendy visited me, I brought out the bottle of scotch that Eddie bought for us years ago on our 15th anniversary. I don't drink at all, generally, because of how he died. Only on important occasions, and I guess this was one of them.

I know how Dave's parents died. I know what he went through. It wouldn't get any easier for the couple. They would have to be very careful or we would all lose him forever.

36
Meg

Some days, I don't feel so bad. But most of them I feel godawful – that's mommy's word. Godawful – like I puke and then they wipe my mouth and then by the time I sit up again, I want to puke again. The first time they gave me the medicine, they said it was supposed to help me get better. I was scared because the medicine made me feel sick all the time. They put needles into my arms. I hate needles. I hate them really bad. They stuck out of me and they hurt and they were connected to all sorts of machines. Doctor Booji said that they put medicine into my body, but if the medicine made me sick, what difference did it make. I'm sick no matter what.

I had to stay in the hospital most all the time. Even though I wanted to go home and be with my friends and my toys and go to church, I couldn't. I heard the doctor say something about finfekshun risk. Mommy nodded when the doctor said it, but her arms were crossed. That's her way of looking bigger. She's always looking up at people, or as she tells me sometimes, she hates that people are always looking down on her.

We had been marking off the calendar until Christmas – each day I got to put a star next to the number and then color in the box with whatever I wanted. Sometimes I drew animals or rainbows, but mostly I drew my family: Me and Mommy and Dave.

But Dave didn't come to see me very much. That made me very sad. The last time he came, Mommy was really angry, and she talked very softly so I wouldn't hear her, but I could. She told Dave he'd better put his big boy pants on and help out or he could… well, we don't say those words much. Dave looked scared. When he looked at me at all, he kind of stayed in the corner and tried – yeah, he tried to make me happy, but I wanted him to hold my hand. I wanted him to tell me that it was all going to be okay. Mommy wanted that too, but he was scared.

That made me scared.

36 – Meg

They didn't tell me much about my sickness only that it had a funny name, like two people's names: Luke and Mia. I wonder if it was named after them? I wonder if they both got sick and somebody said, we should name that Luke and Mia disease.

I would feel sorry for Luke and Mia and I hope they didn't puke as much as I did from the medicine.

I looked at the calendar a little while ago, and I filled in the date with a snowman. I'd really like to build a snowman with Anna and Elsa, but the doctor said maybe next year. When they were talking, he told Mommy that I don't have enough white blood cells and I told him I didn't need any because I was a black person. My mom started to laugh and laugh and laugh. She never does that anymore. That made me happy.

And then I puked.

The doctor came back this afternoon and as they talked, he said he was happy because I was a merission, which made Mommy's face light up a lot. She told me that meant that Luke and Mia's disease was going away. But then the doctor held up his hands (he had a pen between his fingers) and said that most kids go into a merission after the first few months. I guess I'd have to have more medicine.

I hoped it wouldn't make me puke. It's okay, I was getting used to it. Mommy said I'd have good abs.

Instead, I waited and watched more movies. I liked watching movies, but when I looked outside, I thought I'd rather be there. I like the snow and the feel of the wind on my face. I love the sound of the sky as it swirls overhead and the sound of other kids shouting in the park. I love to smell the hot apple cider when I come in from outside. It all means Christmas is coming and that means presents. Presents and people and music and, oh, I just wanted to clap my hands but I couldn't because there were needles in them and that hurt.

Dave came and visited. He was only there a couple of minutes, but for the first time in a long time he touched me. Held my hand. When he left, he kissed the top of my head. I was so happy.

'Love you, Megsy.'

'Love you, too, Davetronica.'

Mom didn't say anything. She just rubbed her hands like there was a spot on there or something.

37
Gladys

Initially, I was disappointed that I wasn't asked to go with Benson and Wendy to visit whoever it was they were going to visit. Fortunately, I had plenty to do to pass the time. Some laundry, an apartment had opened up, so I needed to advertise that; the Kelso's in 42 needed an oven fixed so I had to get a hold of Bill, the maintenance man. Rouse him, more like it. The old man sleeps most of the day and the other part he's watching TV. I swear I pay him to pretend to work.

When they got back, Wendy looked in my direction and waved. She spoke and Benson nodded and then they began walking towards me from the stairs. The bell above the door tinkled as they let themselves in. I saw that they were carrying something in their hands.

'What is that?'

'An important piece of the puzzle.'

'You found out who Jane and Ted were? The Sotos?'

'Can we talk somewhere more private?' Benson asked.

'Do you want to come back into my apartment?'

I felt a glow of happiness as Benson and Wendy took seats at my small kitchen table. I offered them some coffee which they gladly accepted. As I was making it, Benson flattened out a newspaper article on the table.

'Is that it?' I asked as I poured the grounds into an off-white filter, filling the pot with water.

'This is the piece that we've been searching for.'

'Is it about Dave?'

'It is.'

'Read it to me while I get this ready.'

Clearing his throat, Benson began. 'This is from the Allegheny Daily Herald.'

'Where's that?'

'Somewhere in Pennsylvania.' Wendy had already begun mapping its location on her phone and pointed it out to us on the small screen. Even though I couldn't see it, I nodded anyway. Taking three mugs from the cupboard, I lined them up on the counter and waited for my coffee pot to start gurgling.

In what could be considered a Shakespearean tragedy like Henry VIII, *which began, 'I come no more to make you laugh,' a story took place in the lonely hills outside Alleghany, one which causes the bones to ache and the soul to shiver.*

On the eve of September 27th, 1999, Anthony Scholl complained of a deep, piercing ache in his thigh bone. Before he fainted from pain, Rosalind Scholl grabbed her eight-year-old son, David, and rushed her husband to the hospital.

Scholl was well known and well-regarded in the Alleghany community and region. It was his coal mine that employed most of the county. Unlike many mine owners, Scholl was almost universally beloved for his treatment and care of employees, often taking time to understand their needs and struggles. After employees were injured in mine accidents, it was not uncommon for both Anthony and Rosalind to visit the injured in the hospital. Like Prince Charles and Princess Diana, at least before their breakup, they were as royalty to the people.

When the Scholls arrived at the hospital, Anthony was diagnosed with stage III lymphoma. To make matters horrifically worse, only days later, Rosalind found out she had the exact same kind of cancer as her husband, but stage II.

The odds were astronomically against this.

As treatments began over the next months, it became apparent that the only cure would be stem cell treatment. News spread. Everyone in the mine volunteered to be tested for the painful procedure, but out of the hundreds of people, only one person was found to be a match.

David.

37 – Gladys

Their eight-year-old son, confused and frightened, but desperate to help his parents, accepted the responsibility and endured the painful needles into the deep marrow of his hipbones. Extracting the precious, life-giving marrow was extraordinarily difficult for David, but the hope of healing for both his mother and his father was paramount.

Unfortunately, despite the stem cell treatment, Anthony Scholl died of complications from lymphoma four months after the transplant, and Rosalind followed her husband in death less than a month later.

The mining community grieved. Not only had their benevolent owner and his wife passed away, but so did their future. Due to financial pressures, bad management, and a series of accidents, the Scholl mine closed two years after their deaths. What was once a happy, hopeful community and family, was now an empty pit.

As I stood in front of the counter, the last of the coffee dripped into the carafe. Silently, I filled the mugs and turned back to where Benson and Wendy were sitting. Wendy's eyes were filled with tears.

'Poor Dave,' she said.

'What a nightmare,' Benson added as he reached for the mug. 'I can't even imagine what his life has been like for him.'

'But why,' I asked as I sat down, 'does it seem like Dave has everything together? You know, whenever we're doing something, nothing gets him down?'

Benson's frowning face peered over the edge of his mug. 'Until Meg's diagnosis.'

Wendy covered her mouth with a hand. 'She needs a stem cell transplant. Oh my! I bet Dave is a match.'

'And he thinks he's going to 'kill' her too. That would explain everything,' Benson said.

'Explain what?'

'The way he has been acting. He's been trying to see if there is anyone else whose stem cells match so it doesn't come down to him. He and Meg are so close. Her death would destroy him.'

Wendy tapped the newspaper article. 'That would make sense of so many things, like why he never really settles into long-term relationships. I mean, you're his best friend. But notice how he insults you, or confuses you, or even leaves you for new people all the time. He can't contend with the thought of losing people he loves so he keeps them at a distance. But Meg, she's pure love to him. He couldn't keep her at a distance even if he wanted to.'

'And yet,' Benson interjected, 'while he stays away from the hospital, he's ripping all of them apart at the seams.'

I watched the back-and-forth between Wendy and Benson. They seem so perfectly matched. They thought the same, they spoke the same, they even seemed to be dressing alike. Unconsciously, they reached across towards each other and touched. Strangely, I wanted to back out of the room, to leave them in their own space.

'Okay,' Wendy held Benson's forearm. 'Let's unravel this ball of thread through to the beginning so that we can figure out what to do next.' She took out her phone and began to input notes. 'Dave was raised in Pennsylvania; his parents are wealthy mine owners. Scholl mine.'

Something about this statement tripped something for me. What was it?

'At age seven, his parents horrifically and simultaneously contracted cancer.'

'He was eight,' Benson corrected. Wendy changed the note on her phone.

'Dave was miraculously a match for both of his parents.'

'Then,' Benson pointed to the phone, 'after the stem cell transplant, neither parent was cured. Both of them died, leaving Dave an orphaned, only child.'

'So he inherits the mine?'

Benson shrugs. 'From the article, it sounded like he inherited it, but it was shut down. Probably sold. As sole heir, he would have received an enormous fortune, even with the sale price going down.'

'Which explains his ability to purchase anything at will,' I said.

37 – Gladys

Wendy nodded. 'Then, Rosalind's brother, Ted, in Des Moines, takes Dave in, possibly thinking that he and Jane will be trustees for Dave's estate while he grows up.'

'But,' Benson put up a finger, 'there must have been something in the will forbidding it.'

'We'll have to talk to Ignatius again,' Wendy said.

'Dave's aunt and uncle proved incapable, or at least insufficient, in providing for Dave's needs. He's withdrawn – strange – as people seem to always put it.'

'And no wonder, considering what we know about Ted and what happened with his parents…' Wendy sipped her mug with both hands. 'After the court case, Dave was shipped to the Soto's for high school where he finally found true care. At some point, the Mannings, resentful that the Soto's had stolen 'their' inheritance, or at least a significant chunk of it, couldn't handle it anymore. Both Jane and Ted are perpetually angered, but Jane lost it. After following Edward Soto with her car, she crashed into him. Whether wanting to kill him or not, she succeeded and ended up in jail.'

'This,' Benson butted in, 'was the ultimate slap in the face. Dave had already taken their name, Soto, but he was unable to deal with his adopted father's death. He gave Mai a 'stem cell transplant' of his money, but when we saw her, it was easy to see that she was slowly dying from the cancer of despair and loneliness. She doesn't want his money. She only wants Dave.'

'That's amazing, Benson!'

Benson grinned. 'Thinking that he was killing everyone he loves, Dave backed away from Mai and took on the name of his mysterious benefactor, Judge Ignatius Stackworth, whose wife had already passed away.'

'And, and, and,' Wendy stammered excitedly, 'because Ignatius watched from a distance, Dave felt the relationship was safe.'

Suddenly, the clouded crystal ball became very, very, very clear to me. I was not as close to Dave as Benson was, but maybe my distance brought a different perspective. One that allowed me to back up and find the one significant detail that all of us had been missing the whole time.

Oh crap.

'*The Silence of the Lambs,*' I said with a whisper.

Benson and Wendy looked at me as if I'd gone crazy. 'What?'

'*The Silence of the Lambs.* I get it. Why he keeps quoting from it.'

'What are you talking about, Gladys?' Benson asked.

'Dave thinks he is every character in the movie. Somewhere in his mind, he is killing people and taking pieces of their lives with him. And, as much as he tries to help, like Clarice Starling, he ends up hurting people.'

Benson's eyes widened. 'Holy smokes, Gladys, that's brilliant!'

'How well do you know the book, or even the movie?' I asked.

Benson shook his head. 'Only the strange quotes that Dave speaks. Frankly, I've never taken the time to know it well. I mean, I've watched it before, but I can't say it's one I fall asleep to.'

'I watched it with him,' I said. 'Because it was so important to Dave, we saw it multiple times, actually. Frankly, I was creeped out every time we did, but it really sticks with you. Now, think about what he quotes to us: it's not just Hannibal, but Buffalo Bill, Starling, Crawford… Dave's parents were miners. Remember what Lecter says to Starling, 'You're not one generation removed from white hillbilly trash,' or something like that.'

'Wow,' Wendy said. 'You've got a great memory.'

I leaned forward on the table. 'Buffalo Bill takes what he needs from his victims. Dave doesn't purposely take from people, but he can't really help absorbing our stories and making us more like him, you know? And Crawford? He's always trying to control every step of the way while Lecter psychologically manipulates everything because he doesn't, or can't, feel anything.'

'Dave struggles to feel things, doesn't he?' Wendy added.

'Yes,' Benson leaned back in his chair and the air whooshed from his lungs. His cheeks were rosy with excitement, and his eyes had a wild

37 – Gladys

look in them, as if he was about to ride a bucking bronco. 'For all the time I've known him, he only has passive emotions. Unless, that is, he's touched by something incredibly beautiful.'

'Like the Mississippi River.'

'Like different cultures.'

'Like Meg.'

The air in the room had become electrified, and suddenly we felt exhilarated and exhausted. 'What do we do now?' I asked.

'We've got to confront Dave,' Wendy said.

'And Judge Stackworth,' Benson insisted.

'Well,' I said, 'I suppose we'd better get started.'

'I just hope we're not too late.'

'Too late for what?' I asked.

'For Meg's sake.'

38
Marty

I wasn't expecting Dave to show up at the shop because he had made his purchase months before. The day he bought the *second* Daisy air rifle, he brandished it against my taxidermied animals, 'shooting' the already-dead-heads on the walls while making Star Warsian blaster sounds (pew pew pew).

'How about we wrap this up, Dave?'

He studied the new BB gun in his hands. The matte finish did not gleam but seemed to absorb the fluorescent light from above. Its natural malevolence shone out. Yet in Dave's hands, it was just a toy. And that's a dangerous thing, no matter what kind of gun it is. People who believe that guns are toys should not have guns.

'Yeah, sure, Mount Marte.'

'I can't let you take that home with you today, Bud.'

'Why forever not? It is precious to me.' His simple response chilled me, it was slow, almost a whisper. *My Precious.*

'Because I don't sell guns – even BB guns – to people who are having bad days – or months. That's just the way it is. And why do you need a second BB gun? What's wrong with the first one? Did you break it?'

'Nope. Just an insurance policy for the other one.' He eyed me strangely out of the corner of his eye. 'Oh well, it's just a BB gun. *Se la vis.* As you wish.'

'How are you getting home?'

'You're going to drive me, right?' He didn't take his eyes off the BB gun as he spoke, so I gently took it from his hands and placed it back on the rack in front of us.

'It's only 3:30. The store is open until 6:00 – Christmas hours, you know?' I really didn't want to drive him home.

'I'll wait.'

As I turned to leave him, he picked up the gun again and went to stand in the corner by the door. The gun was not loaded, and it was probably more effort than it was worth to take it off him again, so I let him have it. It did make me nervous to have him so close to the exit, but even if he tried to thieve the gun, he did not have ammunition. And better yet, I knew where he lived.

And wait he did. As customers straggled in, some lonely, some excited, some middle-aged hunters hauling their sons through the door, bored teenagers who were far more fixated on their phones than my products, Dave hunched in the corner holding his rifle monitoring the store like one of the taxidermal specimens. As the excited fathers pointed out various hunting gear, rifles, shotguns, camouflaged and orange vests alike, Dave just stayed there. Motionless.

To be quite honest, I truly wished he would get tired of waiting and drop the air rifle at the desk to melt into the night. But he didn't. For better or for worse, he remained Dave. On that day he was worse.

We had only briefly discussed Meg and Letitia and how they were doing. He mentioned that Meg hadn't returned to the hospital, but he was sure that any day now a stem cell donor would miraculously appear in Santa's big red sack. I wasn't so sure that donors were that easy to come by.

Around 5:40, I told Corey he could go home. There was only one other customer in the store – a grizzled gentleman with white-stubbled cheeks and thinning hair. He was wearing a threadbare flannel jacket, sweatpants, and waterproof boots. He had the misty look of a man whose mind was living in the past while his body was decaying in the present. He wandered between the glass cases touching them gently, almost intimately, as if the guns were photographs of long-lost friends. I didn't want to interrupt him, so when Corey left, I went behind the front desk to start closing up the shop. Before I knew it, though, Dave, with his weapon in hand, approached the older gentleman.

'Howdy, partner.'

The older man was startled from his reverie, and he stumbled backwards tripping into one of the clothes racks containing Carhartt overalls. He mumbled something unintelligible as he steadied himself.

'I got me a gun.' Dave held the pseudo-firearm out in front of him so the man could see it.

When the man recognized what kind of weapon it was, he frowned. 'That's a BB gun.'

'Yup. My second one. Never know when you'll need a spare.'

'Why do you need a BB gun?'

'I'm going to shoot me some grasshoppers.'

'It's winter.'

'Ya never know.'

The old man snickered. 'I used to have a BB gun when I was young. I lived out to the west, kinda near Adair. My parents had a farm there. We raised cattle and grew corn and soybeans.' Dave followed with his face, nodding where necessary, intent, but distracted. 'Every summer, the moths would come fluttering in all flippity floppity, hopping from flower to flower, cabbage to cabbage, destroying them, you know?'

At the word 'moths,' Dave froze.

'And they had them little dots on their dusty wings, like eyes, and sometimes it would seem like they were staring at you, teasing you. So me and my brother would sneak up on 'em, crawlin' in the grass, arms itchy, but knowing we were rescuing the cabbages. That's what we told our mom. Cabbage protectors.'

'Real Cabbage Patch Kids,' I said, drawing nearer to them. I glanced at Dave. There was something frightening about his frozenness. I nudged him, but he didn't move. His gaze was glued to the old man and the story of the moths.

The old man didn't seem to know what I was talking about regarding Cabbage Patch Kids, so he continued his story as if I hadn't spoken. 'After we'd picked off a few, and they'd be flopping around on the ground, holes in their wings, we sat back leaning against an oak tree by the garden. But outta nowhere, another moth showed up, real sneaky-

38 – Marty

like. And it'd land right on you without even you knowing it. One time a moth landed on top of my brother's head and I shot at it. I missed.' He giggled.

'Are you the Mothman?' Dave whispered.

'What?'

'Did you keep the moths once you'd pierced their skins? Got into their blood?'

The old man was startled by Dave's line of questioning, and he took a step back.

'They say that serial killers keep trophies. Did you keep any trophies? Any wings? With eyes?'

The old man's eyes darted back and forth between Dave and me and back to Dave. 'You're a freak,' he said and retreated slowly towards the front door where he stopped and turned around. 'He shouldn't be in here. He's the reason people get killed out there.'

The door closed behind the old man with a Christmasy jingled bell. Nonplussed, I remained silent, wondering what in the world just happened with Dave.

'What was that all about?'

As if woken from a dream, Dave shook his head. 'I… he was… Mothman. The Mothman cometh.'

Without taking my eyes from him, I went to the front entrance to turn the sign from OPEN to CLOSED. After locking the door, I returned to Dave and relieved him of his weapon and set it on the nearest glass shelf. 'I think we need to take you home.'

'Home?'

'I think you're having a breakdown.'

'Home?' he asked again.

I gently grabbed him. My touch cleared the fog. 'Marty?'

'Come on, Dave. I need to get you back to your apartment.'

'No,' he rooted himself in the spot, legs spread, and pulled his arm out of my grasp. 'I need to see Ignatius.'

'Ignatius?'

'My father.'
'Where is he?'
'Altoona.'
'I'll drive you there.'

Dave was three steps behind me when I opened the rear door of the shop. I allowed him out first, then I set the alarm and walked him to my car. It was quite dark. Only the streetlights glowed dimly through the gently falling snow. There was a gentle breeze tossing the large snowflakes upwards and sideways, twisting and turning, sending them here and there, floating like winter moths, hitting the ground softly only to disappear quickly on the warmer ground.

We drove mostly in silence, although Dave would occasionally mumble and chew on his mittens. We drove eastward out of Des Moines and then exited south. The snow created a mesmerizing pattern in the headlights. Twice I had to shake my head to refocus on the road lines. Thankfully the heater in my pickup was working so we weren't too cold, but once we stepped outside again, it would be rough.

'Is this the road?' I asked Dave.

He mumbled an affirmative while munching his mittens.

Finally, my GPS found the correct lane, and I turned down it. At the end of the road was a looming brick mansion with evergreen trees in front. There was another car parked in the driveway, and I pulled in behind it. Dave's eyes focused on the car, and once again his words were unclear, although Letitia's name was one of them. Was that her car?

After killing the engine, both doors of the pickup creaked open and we stepped down onto the white gravel. As we passed the other car, fresh footsteps led from the driver's door, up the sidewalk, and towards the house. They were tiny, childish footsteps.

I had a bad feeling about what was about to happen.

A very bad feeling indeed.

39

Benson

I felt terrible leaving Gladys behind, but we needed someone to remain at the Palms in case Dave returned. If he did, we would turn around and come back, but first, we needed to see Ignatius. We could have called him, but both Wendy and I thought it would be better if we asked him the questions in person.

The problem was, I didn't know where the judge lived. Dave had once told me that his address was unlisted. Being a judge left him exposed to the wackos out there, supposedly.

Instead, I re-broke into his unlocked apartment (without telling Gladys, of course) and used the light on my phone to search. As I made my way around the room, I suddenly screamed. Wendy, who had been surreptitiously standing watch outside the apartment, ran in.

'What is it?'

I held the phone up and pointed at the wall.

'Oh, my…'

In black marker, Dave had decorated the wall of his apartment with the outline of a man with wings. Most frightening were the glowing red eyes which seemed to be dripping blood. There were no whites or pupils, just red where the eyes should have been.

'Okay, now I'm getting very scared.' The hair on my arms and neck was standing straight up.

'We need to find that address now,' Wendy said.

It took ten minutes to find Dave's phone. He had left it on his bedside stand next to a glass diorama of various kinds of moths. I couldn't for the life of me understand why, if Dave was so afraid of the Mothman, he would have these representations around him. Was it some kind of therapy?

I turned his phone on and scrolled through his address book until I found Ignatius Stackworth and his residence in Altoona.

'I found it.'

'Let's go,' Wendy said.

In the darkness, I made the dreadful mistake of uttering one of the worst Hollywood tropes of all time. 'I think you should stay here, Wendy. It's not safe.'

Oh, boy, did she go off on me. First, *she* brought up the fact that *she* was the one used to criminals, and *she* had the ability to defend herself, and *she* was stronger than I was, and *she* would 'MOST CERTAINLY NOT BE LEFT BEHIND, YOU IDIOT!'

Duly chastised, I submitted meekly to her diatribe and slunk to the car. It was frigid outside and even colder inside the car. I know that I'm not a particularly experienced guy when it comes to dating, but even I know that there are warning indicators on the engine light of relationships, and mine was flashing wildly.

'Look, I'm sorry.'

'You should be.'

'I am.'

My pouting was enough of an apology for her to implicitly forgive me. 'What do we need to ask the judge when we get there?' she asked.

'Does he know anything about Dave's history, his parents' deaths? Does he know that Dave was a stem cell donor for them? Does this mean that Dave is a donor again? And if he is a match, then why can't he get over his fear and save her?' I could feel my hands gripping the steering wheel harder, so I took a few slow breaths to relax.

'Imagine if he is,' she whispered, 'and he is holding out.'

I had a deep sinking feeling in my stomach that *that* was exactly what was happening.

Wendy reached her hand across the front seat to me, and despite the bad weather, I grasped at it. Her touch felt good, calming.

The last miles of winter night driving passed swiftly, and before we knew it, we were turning down a long, dark driveway. My headlights revealed two other cars in front of me.

One of them was…

40
Letitia

'Letitia.'

Judge Stackworth was a big man. His persona could have been even larger than his stature, but as he stood in the doorway pondering me in my winter coat, the top of my head barely reaching his collarbone, he seemed gigantic. At that moment, I bottled the impulse to flee. It would have been easy to run – self-preservative – but I desperately needed to know, once and for all, what was going on with the man I loved.

As I stood in front of Ignatius, I felt like one of those stuffed animals on the wall of Marty's gunshop, beady-eyed and staring passively out over the instruments of their deaths, surprised that they hadn't understood sooner that their lives were about to be cut short.

'Ignatius.'

'What can I do for you?'

He leaned over the top of me peering both directions. Either he was trying to spot who I was with or at least hope for an eyewitness. Someone who would corroborate the fact that it was I who had shown up at his house unannounced, not he who had summoned me.

'Do you mind if I come inside? It's cold out here on the porch.'

The dim light illuminated the slope of his forehead and the long nose bisecting his face, but his eyes were in shadow.

He hesitated. Then he stepped to the side.

After stamping my feet on his bristly carpet, I asked him if I should take off my shoes. 'Do what you like,' he said softly.

Seeing that he had slippered feet, I took off my shoes, instantly regretting the fact that there was a hole in the big toe of my right sock. I kept my coat on, though.

'Has Dave been by?'

The judge went to his chair but did not sit down. Lights from the television behind my head flickered across his face distorting his features. There would be no pinning him down. He reached for the remote control beside his chair and lowered the volume of the Christmas music playing through the television speakers.

'No.'

'That's disappointing.'

'Yes, I suppose so.' He paused. 'How is Meg doing?'

'Pastor Jonathan is at home with her. She's holding in there. She's strong.' *Unlike me,* I thought.

'You must be suffering greatly.'

'I am.'

In the background, Bing Crosby wistfully reminded us that he wanted to be home for Christmas.

Sometimes we can't go home.

'Can I get you something to drink? Coffee? Apple cider?'

'No, thank you.'

He cleared his throat as the awkwardness between us grew. No doubt neither of us knew entirely why I was there, yet he was kind enough to be patient.

'Would you like to sit?'

I nodded and sank into a plush chair in front of the bay window. The judge's chair was situated to the right and at the foot of the oak staircase. Behind the chair and tucked into the spandrel were dozens of books by popular authors, some of whom I'd used in my class. A lampstand dimly lit the cosy reading nook.

While I sat in the chair, I was aware that my feet did not touch the floor. Most chairs are built for normal-sized adults. I felt like a naughty child about to be punished by a parent. I wriggled forward slightly to at least graze the floor with my toes.

'I need to see Dave.' I tucked my chin and mouth inside the buttons of my coat aware that the gesture seemed childish.

'As I said before, I haven't seen him.'

His eyes shifted. He was lying. 'But you know where he is.'

'Perhaps.'

'When was the last time you saw him?'

40 – Letitia

The judge crossed his legs and turned his head to the bay window momentarily. Without looking at me, he spoke again. 'Last week.'

'Where were you?'

'Here.'

'What did you talk about?'

His hands shifted from his lap and adjusted the cardigan sweater. The discomfort was obvious. He looked like a man wearing a tuxedo at the gym.

'This and that.'

'Did you talk about Meg? Does he at least talk about her?'

'Yes,' he responded carefully, 'he loves her very much.'

'He's very good at hiding it.'

Ignatius did not respond.

'He hasn't been to see us in over a week. Hasn't called. Hasn't done anything. I've been… worried out of my mind… Meg… him. Our relationship.' The words and frustrations poured out and I could feel the tears puddle in my eyes. 'Life is not supposed to be like this. We're not supposed to feel powerless and rudderless and hopeless and…' My voice faltered. 'We need people who will not jump ship at the first sight of rocks. I don't feel like Dave has jumped ship, per se, but it sure feels like he has purposely decided to walk the plank, to sacrifice himself, and us, for some mysterious and unknown reason, and at the worst possible time.'

'It must be very difficult for you.'

'Difficult?' I scoffed. 'Dave has always been difficult, but this is something on a completely different level.'

'I'm sorry.'

'I don't need your apologies.'

He spread his hands.

'You say you talked about this and that. Did he tell you about the stem cell transplant?'

Ignatius again cleared his throat uncomfortably. 'He mentioned it.'

'Did he say if he had taken the test?'

'Why would he not take the test?'
'Because he's afraid of something.'
'What do you think he's afraid of?'
'Commitment.'
'To what?'
'To anything.'
'What do you mean?'
'He can't commit to a job. He can't commit to friendships. He can't commit to me, or to Meg. He even pushes Benson away.'

Studying me, the judge uncrossed his legs and leaned forward. 'Why do you think that is?'

'I don't know!' I felt myself shouting as if from a long distance away. My voice was swallowed up by the room and Ignatius Stackworth was a mile away on a lonely shore while I was in a sinking boat with no paddle.

'Did Dave ever tell you about his family?'
'No,' I replied sullenly.
'He never told you about them?'
'I just said that.'
'I'm sorry. I just needed to make sure.'
'Why? What's he hiding?'

The judge rubbed his cheek and pondered me. 'Would you like anything to drink?'

'Do I look like I need something to drink?' I responded with irritation. The conversation was going nowhere.

'If I'm going to reveal anything about Dave, I'm going to need something warm in my hands.'

'You're finally going to tell me what's wrong with Dave?'

He struggled from the chair grunting, and then seesawed his hand as he stood. 'Some things.'

I dropped my feet to the floor and began to follow him to the kitchen. As I did, I reached inside the right pocket of my coat.

It had never been my intention to bring the gun, and yet I bought it for a purpose, right? That's what guns are for – unintentional purposes. Insurance. Back up. If pressed, for extreme forms of coercion. The judge's dance around the subject of Dave's abandonment was forcing my hand. I didn't want to wield this kind of power, but when a lioness is pressed into a corner, she will do whatever it takes to protect her cub. Including unleashing her claws. The claw in my pocket felt sleek and sharp. The barrel was smooth, somewhat ironic for an instrument of death. As we passed through the kitchen arch, it felt as if we were entering the point-of-no-return. It was now or never.

And I was going to make sure it was *now*.

The old-fashioned kitchen was painted pistachio green. Lining the walls were cupboards from a different decade, maybe the 70's or 80's, with white trim and round brass handles. An island squatted like a flat-backed troll in the middle of the room. Pots, pans, ladles, and spoons hung from hooks above it. Above the kitchen sink, the cupboard doors had frosted glass panes, and inside the panes was a collection of spices. A refrigerator hummed on the far side of the island, content to be doing what it does. On its face were a few pictures, not many. He had no children of his own; just a few nieces and nephews, and then one of Dave when he was in his teens. I could see it from where I stood. He and Ignatius stood side by side. Dave's arm was curled around the judge's neck. The judge appeared uncomfortable in his robe with the youngster gripping him thus, but there was a smirk on both their faces.

As Ignatius busied himself making hot chocolate, he began to narrate a tale. 'Dave was born in Pennsylvania. His parents were Rosalind and Anthony Scholl. They owned a coal mine.'

'Dave's last name is Scholl?'

'Yes. No. No. He's never told you?'

'What do you mean, 'yes, no, no'?'

'The name on his birth certificate is David Scholl, but he has changed his name twice since then. In high school, his name was Dave

Soto, and lastly...' The judge scooped a heaping spoonful of cocoa into a mug and poured hot water from a kettle into it. 'Stackworth.'

'He took your name? Why?'

'That, Letitia, is a story in and of itself.' He leaned backward against the kitchen sink, the island between us, and blew on the cup. 'When his foster and adoptive father, Ed Soto, was killed in a car accident, he changed his last name to mine in hopes of saving Mai, his mother.'

'That doesn't make any sense. Was Dave involved in the accident?'

'He thinks he was.'

I reached into my pocket. *Not yet.*

'After his parents died, he chose foster care over familial guardianship.'

'Who was watching him before that?'

'His mother's brother. Uncle Ted and Aunt Jane.'

'Did they abuse him?'

Judge Stackworth shook his head slowly. 'Not physically. They wanted to abuse Dave's inheritance.'

'What was the inheritance?'

'The Scholl coal mine.' He held up a finger. 'I'll amend that. The proceeds from the coal mine's sale. When his parents died, the corporation was sold.'

'For how much?'

'9.2 million dollars.'

I was flabbergasted. *Dave? Rich?* I knew he had money to burn, but millions? Why didn't he buy himself a new car, a better place? Selfishly, I wondered why he didn't do that for me and Meg. The thought of my daughter spurred me to urgency.

'Dave is worth 9.2 million dollars?'

'No,' Ignatius responded cautiously. 'He's worth fifty-two million. The money he would have inherited was put into a trust and has been invested wisely by people not named Dave. As you know, Dave is much more willing to give it away than spend it on himself.'

'Why?'

40 – Letitia

'Because he thinks it's cursed.'

'Because his parents died?'

Silence reigned though the refrigerator kept on ticking. The furnace kicked in with a whirr.

'Dave believes that everyone he loves dies too soon.'

The lightbulb went on. *His parents. His foster father. And now he thinks Meg is going to die.*

'So why doesn't he just give the money away?'

The judge shifted uncomfortably. 'I won't let him.'

'Why not?'

'When you've seen as much greed as I do, you tend to be much more careful with people you care about. Dave wouldn't survive a year without me watching out for him.'

'You don't trust him?'

The question surprised him. 'It's not a lack of trust, really. It's that I worry whether he can make the correct decisions under pressure. Take Meg, for instance…' His eyes widened. 'I'm sorry, I shouldn't have said that.'

He knew something.

'What do you know about Dave? Did he take the test?'

'Letitia, please. I've said too much.'

'No, Judge. Tell me. I need to know. There's too much at stake. Meg's life is on the line.'

The inner battle returned. He desperately wanted to tell me something, but I could tell he was far too invested in Dave's life protecting him. Why, I was just a thirty-something single mother, a black woman, who had latched onto his precious Dave. He probably thought I was a gold digger.

'You'll have to ask Dave. I…'

'You're protecting him.'

He stammered. 'Yes, but not from you.'

'From whom?'

'Himself.'

'Come on, Judge. That's a cop out. Tell me.'
'I can't.'
'You won't.'
'I will not.'

My hand slowly slid into my pocket. The gun would pry out the truth. But did I have the guts to do it?

Suddenly, there was a sound from the living room.

'Iggy Pop?'

41
Marty

I don't begin to presume that I understand everything regarding life or why certain things come about while others stay safely ensconced on the shelf of non-history. As for what happened that night, I can only say it still plays out in my nightmares. After that night, I began to drink again. Just enough to be forgetful but not enough to forget myself entirely. No one would have wanted that, not the least of which, Dave.

It was pure Dave as we entered the Judge's house. He had the determined look of Julius Caesar crossing the Rubicon, or Jesus Christ himself overlooking Jerusalem on his way down the mountain. The set of his jaw and the steel of his gaze was out of place, so un-Dave-like, that I was shocked, and it took me a moment to free myself from the car seat and follow him to the house.

By the time I reached the door, he had already pulled it open and was scuffing his feet on the inner door mat. Within seconds, his shoes were off. I should have held up a finger and shouted, 'Wait, Dave.'

It was only then, after hustling into the house myself, that I caught a glimpse of Dave in profile in the wide arched opening joining the Judge's kitchen to the living room. He called out 'Iggy Pop,' and then froze, his mouth and eyes agape, startled, but not surprised.

It happened so fast, and yet each piece of that night remains frozen in my mind: the wall size television projecting yule logs and Christmas music; the wet smears of Dave's feet on the floor; the eerie, bright glow of the kitchen lights as they illuminated half the living room. The half that contained the Judge's sitting chair and lampstand, with his reading glasses and a book, in front of the oak stairs leading to the bedrooms above. I can still see them in my mind, even while I pour numbing drinks into the glass tumblers lined up before me. Yes, these things I still see as I rounded that corner to stand next to Dave.

She was there already.

Letitia.

You already know what happened, don't you? You can feel it inside you welling up – you desperately want everything to turn out all right – like that trip to the doctor who you've been praying will tell you it's nothing but your imagination; a little bit of indigestion, but deep down inside you know. It's dark and greasy billowing up in your guts just within reach of your emotions, taloned and sharp, scratching softly at first, but always in the same place. You want the happy ending, the white wedding with the flowers and streamers, the joyful walk through the celebrators. But you know, don't you? It's the opposite. It's not benign, but cancerous, and it's eating away at your insides. And you can't stop it.

I knew she would have it.

That stupid little insurance policy I sold her. SIG Sauer P226, a delicate and deadly thing shaking in her hand. When I entered the picture, she swung it briefly from the Judge, to Dave, to me and back again to Dave. Her face, contorted by emotion, love and hatred and fear and loathing and back to love. It burned with a furious fire.

'Stay there, Marty.'

I held up my hands.

'Letitia,' I said calmly, or as calmly as I could under those circumstances, 'please put the gun down. We can talk this out. Whatever it is, we can help.'

'Nobody is trying to help *me*.' Her clenched teeth made her words hard to understand. 'Everyone is trying to 'protect' *him*.' She motioned with the gun to Dave. 'They're worried about his mental health or his instability. I get it. I understand. I'm *supposed* to be his fiancée.'

'Letitia, please.' The Judge set down his cup and stood erectly, arms by his side. He seemed larger, a presence that filled the room rather than overshadowed it.

Letitia turned the gun on Ignatius as her voice shook and her lip quivered. 'Don't make me do it, Judge. Don't.'

'What do you want?' he asked softly.

'I want the truth.'

41 – Marty

'He's here now. Ask him. Anything. Dave, this is your time. Your chance.'

So intent were we on the scene in front of us that no one heard the car doors slam outside the house, nor did we hear the front door open, nor the footsteps behind me. When Benson spoke, I nearly jumped out of my skin.

'Hello? What's going on?'

I spun to see him and Wendy walking across the living room towards us.

'Stop.' I held up a hand.

Undaunted, Benson frowned and shook his head. 'What are you guys d…?'

I tried to shield him, truly, I did, but he was adamant. 'Get out of my way. I need to talk to the Judge and Dave.'

The gunshot was immense and my ears began to ring. Ducking (it seems so unnatural now as my scotch swirls in the glass), I turned to Letitia whose eyes were about to pop out of her head. The gun, pointed at us, had missed me and Dave but hit Benson. He cried out in pain and fell to the floor where Wendy rushed to him.

'What have you done?' I asked Letitia.

With trembling hand, she covered her mouth but did not lower the weapon. It was trained back on Dave.

Benson was lying between Dave and I. Wendy pulled Benson's hands from the wound. Blood had appeared on the hip of his jeans. Wendy pulled them back and breathed a sigh of relief.

'It didn't go in, Benson. Just through the top of your hip.'

'It hurts.'

Wendy glanced up at the Judge. 'Do you have any towels?'

The Judge checked with Letitia. She nodded, and Ignatius opened a drawer to his left and pulled out a drying cloth and brought it to Wendy who applied pressure on Benson's hip.

'Back to where you were,' Letitia said tremulously.

Ignatius dropped his head slightly and retreated to the bench beside his coffee mug. 'Please, Letitia, put the gun down now. Someone will have reported the gunshot and the police will be here within minutes.'

She shook her head fiercely. 'Not until I hear from him.' She aimed the gun back at Dave.

Later, much later when I saw the judge, he told me about his emotions at *that* moment, the thoughts and regrets after Letitia said that. He said his eyes had wandered to the fridge behind her, and his thoughts to the photos on the walls, the bookshelves and coffee table. Dave was the son Ignatius never had – and it was love that placed him in his life. Dave had been with him from adolescence to the adoptive relationship. After Edward Soto's death and through the swirling stream of discontented, casual relationships. Ignatius spoke of Dave's fierce love of people, but his inability to get close because of what happened to his parents. That was why he kept his distance from Ignatius, Benson, Letitia, Meg, me. He was too afraid of killing us unintentionally by his curse. Deep down Dave believed that others' lives were the cost of living his.

At that moment in the kitchen, Ignatius wished he would have hugged Dave and held him back. They had never before truly embraced other than awkward side hugs and a few back slaps. Dave's protective nature wouldn't have allowed the closeness, but it was also the Judge's professional distance that kept them separated.

Surely, Dave knew love, right? He and Letitia were going to get married. He would have embraced her, kissed her, grown close, but even now, I can't remember ever seeing him outwardly showing his affection. Did he think that love was transactional rather than sacrificial? Did he ever act in order to receive, or was everything a gift to keep the deep darkness away? I have a sneaky suspicion, it was the latter – sickly indulgences as a price paid for purgatory.

As Benson moaned on the floor, I remember hearing the grandfather clock in the living room, that stately timepiece positioned next to the television, tick tocking into the future, the pendulum endlessly swinging and slicing time like a horrible guillotine. *Tick tock, tick tock,*

41 – Marty

marking the small seconds of wonder and dread. Can anyone really predict the long and arduous journey of pain and loss? Could any of us truly have understood the depth of Dave's pain that came from the death of loved ones, and the guilt that arose from surviving their departure?

On that fateful night as he retreated from the 'normal' world, his emotions were hindered by each fearful step into the future. You could see it. It was not a decision, but an unrepentant force pulling him towards the chasm.

That was how we all ended up in the judge's kitchen, three standing (while one knelt next to another prone on the ground) opposite a desperate woman fighting for the life of her child, while the man she loved remained impassive, even to the agony of his best friend on the floor to his left. Dave's hands still covered his ears from the gunshot, but his face was empty, void of anything.

'Dave,' Ignatius implored. 'Dave, you must remove your hands. Listen.'

As if awakened from a conscious nightmare, Dave slowly lowered his hands and allowed the sound back in. He turned his gaze to Letitia whose eyes were full of tears.

'Please, sweetheart, you have to talk to me. I didn't mean to shoot. It just happened. Forgive me. Can you speak to me, please?'

Dave's eyes turned to Ignatius and then fixed on the window behind his shoulder where the darkness peered through the window like a malevolent demon. All that could be seen was the ghostly, snowy limbs of an elder tree which had trespassed close enough to the house to be illuminated by the kitchen light. 'Memory is what I have instead of a view.'

Dave was imprisoned, trapped by an unenviable past, left with only a few memories of his parents and Edward Soto and Meg. There was no key.

'Are you okay?' Wendy asked Benson who winced as he allowed himself to be pulled up. Thankfully, the bullet had not done permanent damage. It had lodged in the wood panelled staircase and splintered it.

The little hole was symbolic of the entire event – a point into the dark unknown from which no one knew would come out.

'I'm all right,' Benson said as he made his way to his feet. At that point, I was separated from Dave by both Wendy and Benson.

If only I could have been closer.

'Are you okay, Dave?' Benson asked.

'See what I mean?' Letitia shouted as she took a threatening step towards us. 'Everyone is worried about Dave, not me. Not Meg. Not cancer or death or the end of love! Just Dave and his past which NOBODY WANTS TO TELL ME ABOUT!'

'I'm sorry, Letitia,' Benson said.

Letitia was about to respond. Instead, Dave spoke, his voice spooky. 'That's a popular question today. No, Bensonian. I can't say I am okay.'

'You're sad, then?'

Dave sighed. 'Perhaps.'

'What do you want to know, Letitia?' Benson asked through gritted teeth. 'We'll have to hurry.'

Already, from somewhere in the distance, sirens could be heard. It wouldn't be long before the house would have more visitors with guns.

'Be gentle, Benson,' Dave said softly.

At that moment, Dave appeared like any number of portraits of Jesus looking down on the big ol' world of badness with something resembling resigned love. His brown eyes were soft and luminous as they alit on Benson, then Wendy. As he caught my eye, the right side of his mouth twitched – a small smile, maybe, or hope? – and then to Ignatius who was biting his lower lip. Finally, he turned to Letitia and took one step towards her.

'May I?'

'May you what?' she responded, taking a step away from him.

'I want to be near you as the story comes out. I may need to hold on to you.'

'No, Dave. You cannot. That time is past. Stay where you are.'

41 – Marty

He stopped. His body partially blocked our view of her, but enough to still see the gun trained on him.

Benson leaned around Dave. 'We know almost everything, Letitia. About his parents, his upbringing. The Mannings, the Sotos, Ignatius…'

Wendy gripped his arm. 'And *The Silence of the Lambs*.'

At this, Dave turned his head toward us revealing the left side of his face. One eyebrow furrowed. 'What do you mean?'

'Can we ask you a few questions, Dave?'

'I don't have time for this, Benson,' Letitia said as she stepped to her right revealing herself entirely to us.

'I know. I'm sorry. But I think if we ask the right questions, everything will work out just fine.'

Dave slowly turned his head back to Letitia while providing another quote: 'Problem solving is hunting, Benson. It is a savage pleasure, and we are born to it.'

'Wendy and I think we know why you do it. Why you quote from the movie all the time.'

'Proceed,' he said and leaned on the kitchen island. He almost seemed casual, as if we were having a lovely dinner conversation.

'Every character in the movie is part of you. Clarice Starling and her once-removed-white-trashness, even though your parents were quite wealthy.' Dave's facial expression didn't change, but his head tilted to the side. 'Letitia, they owned a coal mine in Pennsylvania. Dave was adored. He was an only child. But then they got sick.'

'I know those parts, Benson. The Judge told me before you got here. It was one of the few things he revealed. You should be thankful, Dave, that your friends are always looking out for you.' Her voice was tinged with vitriol. 'And he got sent to his mother's brother, Ted Manning. And things didn't work out so well.'

'Yes, but did the Judge tell you why Dave is so averse to telling you that he is a match for stem cell donation for Meg?'

Letitia's eyes widened and her mouth trembled. 'You're… You… What…' Her face crumbled, then imploded in anger. 'You bastard! All along, you could have helped my daughter. Meg!' She staggered closer to Dave.

With each word, Dave flinched. I could tell it was all true. Every single terrible word. I was shocked. Why in the world would Dave not help Meg out? She was going to be his daughter, for God's sake. I felt myself recoil slightly from him, not physically, but mentally. If he could be so cold-hearted to a five-year-old, what about an old, alcoholic, gun-seller like me? How long before he abandoned me?

'Easy, Letitia. There's a reason. Hear us out. Please.' Benson pleaded.

'You knew about this?' Letitia turned on the Judge.

'I promised Dave I wouldn't say anything.'

Her finger tightened on the trigger as she pointed it at the Judge. 'You both deserve the pain I've been going through.'

Like father and son, they both nodded slowly. 'Yes, Letitia. You may be right. I deserve it,' Ignatius said.

'Letitia, Dave's parents got sick. Cancer.' Benson took a step closer to Dave. 'It wasn't your fault, Dave. It was nobody's fault. When people hurt, or they get sick, or they suffer tragedy, blame is useless.'

'Unless,' Letitia said, 'you're a heartless human who purposelessly refrains from helping Meg.'

These words were bullet holes in Dave's defense, and he recoiled.

'Cancer, Letitia. Cancer. They both got it at the same time. It was horrific for him.'

Dave's hands began to tremble. He moved them under his arms, but his torso began to shake.

Tick tock, the mouse ran up the grandfather clock. Time, history, doesn't ease off. Just relentlessly marches into the future.

'When Dave donated his stem cells to his parents, he hoped he could save them. The doctors torturously pulled the marrow from his hips, but it did no good. Even though he was a match, they died. Both of them. Like Clarice Starling, Dave wanted to stop the true Buffalo Bill, the true Mothman – death by cancer.'

41 – Marty

A low moan started in Dave's throat, but he stopped it. His head bowed and his shoulders hunched inwards. He was beginning to implode.

'After they died, and before Jane Manning and Edward Soto were killed in that terrible traffic accident, you believed you had become the very people you detested most in life – Buffalo Bill and Hannibal Lecter. You felt as if you were taking the lives of the beautiful people you loved, and the happiness you so coveted, so you backed into your lonesome corner pushing everyone away, because the pain of helping them, in whatever way that happened, was penance for stealing your parents' lives. Edward's life. Jane's life.'

Wendy stepped forward next to Benson. 'Until Letitia and Meg came along. Dave, you must have thought it had been long enough. You'd outlasted the curse. No one close to you had died for a while. Perhaps you believed you'd served enough time in the prison of loneliness, painted your pictures, gone crazy with grief, that you could dare live again. You escaped the dreadful two-story house you'd lived in, with that deep and dark basement holding your buried pain, where unmentionable things called out to you in the dark.'

Dave's moan began again, this time longer and eerier.

The Judge told me later he wanted to cry out, 'Objection! Objection! This is Dishonor!' but no one could speak, not even Dave. The facts fit the case. The defendant needed to hear the accusations before judgment could be delivered.

Dave clapped a hand over his mouth. Eyes frightened, emotions breached, the dam had broken. It was only a matter of time.

'Dave, dear Dave,' Wendy said, 'you are not Clarice Starling – you don't need to search for Buffalo Bill or interview Lecter anymore. You are not Buffalo Bill – you don't kill people; and you certainly are not Lecter himself. There is not an evil bone in your body. You are not Dave Soto or Dave Stackworth. You are Dave Scholl. Dave Scholl. That's all.'

That Dave's wall had been broken down was apparent. One feature at a time, his eyebrows and eyes, lips and cheeks, trembled and creased. His nostrils flared just above his clapped hand, and a sound unlike any I'd ever heard in my life issued from between his fingers and his nose. It was a thick wave of grief, torturous in depth and fury, and it crushed him.

The sound of his shriek seemed infinitely louder than the gunshot that wounded Benson, and it rang between the walls, in and out of copper pots, behind the stove, under the cabinets; it increased in size and seized the room, echoing and magnifying until we could handle it no longer.

'You have to stop!' the Judge shouted. 'Make it stop! He can't handle it.'

Letitia's eyes blazed and she rushed to Dave. 'DAVE! YOU HAVE TO DONATE YOUR CELLS TO MEG!' She grabbed his shirt with her left hand. This diminutive woman began to shake Dave like a ragdoll until mercifully, the shriek ended, and light came into his eyes.

'Letitia?'

'Did you hear me?'

'Letitia?'

'Meg's life is dependent on yours.'

If only she would have said something else, but in the demand, Dave was paralyzed. The process of losing his parents had been too much, and this request, as his love for Meg was even deeper than for his parents, overwhelmed him.

'I can't. I can't bear the thought of losing her.'

'You will lose her,' Letitia said through tears. 'If you don't do this, you will most certainly lose her. She will die because of you.'

'No... No... I can't.'

Suddenly, Letitia whirled Dave and shoved him against the back blank wall and jammed the gun into his ribs. 'Dammit, Dave. Listen to what you're saying.'

Dave was facing the rest of us. Because Letitia was so short, he could see us over her head, and we could see him. That face, that tender face, kind of beautiful, loving, sorrowful, glowed in those last moments. Though the gun was in his ribs, it was his goodbye to us. How he cared for everyone but himself!

41 – Marty

I want you to know how incredibly difficult it is for me to write this. It is the full reason I drink because of what I saw in his eyes at that moment.

'Letitia,' Dave said softly, 'the little lambs have to stop screaming.'

'What?'

Dave reached down to the gun pointed at his chest. Letitia tried to pull it away from him, but he smiled at her instead.

I couldn't see what happened, and I'm glad I didn't. I tried to get to him – to them – I really tried, but it felt as if my feet were buried in cement. The second explosion was far worse than the first. Though the report was muffled slightly by its proximity to Dave's body, the bullet entered his chest. There was a brief moment of suffering on his face before he began to topple towards Letitia.

He was far too large for Letitia to catch, but even if she could, she wouldn't have been able to because she was screaming.

'I… He… It wasn't me! I tried to pull it away but he…' The rest of her sentence was lost in the uproar.

Dave crumpled to the floor and landed on his face. There was a large hole in his back where the bullet had punched a hole. Blood oozed from the wound, and as I reached him, I flipped him over.

He was conscious, barely, but it wouldn't be long. 'Another towel!' I shouted. Benson threw me his and Wendy leapt into action. She pressed the cloth into the wound in an attempt to stem the bleeding, but his back was pooling bright red blood onto the white ceramic tiling beneath. It was vivid and awful and gory. Insulting. Life should never end on the floor, and yet gravity always won. Always.

I felt the blood streaming under my hands and beneath my feet.

Letitia dropped the gun on the island bench. Her hands had blood on them, in more ways than one. If only she hadn't bought a gun… If only I hadn't sold it to her.

Suddenly, the front door crashed open, and four police officers rushed into the kitchen between us. One of them, seeing the gun, hurried to it and pushed it off to the side. Two others controlled the situation, while the last one called for backup and an ambulance.

'What happened?' he asked.

What happened, indeed? I ask that question every day.

Eventually, as the paramedics wheeled Dave from the Judge's house, Ignatius by his side, I dared look up at the wall where Dave had been standing.

If I didn't know any better, the spatter looked exactly like a set of wings.

42

Meg

I'm better now.

I don't feel like getting sick anymore, but I still have to stay in the hospital for a while yet. Mommy told me that Dave saved me. I knew he would. I just knew it.

I asked Mommy if I could see him, but she didn't say anything. She started crying.

'Where is he?'

'Shh,' she said. 'Just rest.'

'I'm tired of resting. I want to do something else. I want to go home.'

'We all do, Sweetheart. We all do.'

'Is Dave going to come home with us?'

Mommy didn't respond.

A little while later, Pastor Jonathan knocked on the door. 'Can I come in?'

'Yes,' Mommy said quietly.

He was dressed in black and carrying a black Bible with gold pages. I thought it was pretty. It must have cost a lot of money.

Pastor Jonathan laid his coat over a chair and then stood on the opposite side of the bed from Mommy. He smiled down at me. 'Hi Jon Nathan,' I said, remembering how Dave called him.

'Hello, Megamix.'

Mommy started to cry when he said it. I didn't want to hear her crying anymore, so I said, 'I'm going to sleep.'

I wasn't really going to sleep because I still wanted to hear what they were going to say. Adults never talk in front of me, but hopefully they would now.

Mommy tousled my hair. She's letting me grow it out again after the treatments. She is too. I guess she wants to be different than she was.

'How is she?' Jonathan asked softly.

'Getting better.'

'Stem cells?'

Mommy was quiet. I wanted to open my eyes, but I wanted them to keep talking even more.

'Would you rather not talk about it?'

'It's okay. Just give me a second.' Mommy blew her nose loudly, then began speaking in a whisper. 'He didn't make it.'

'I heard that. How horrible.'

'It's my fault. All my fault.'

'You can't blame yourself,' Pastor said.

'I can and I will.'

It was quiet for a little bit until Mommy talked again. 'They kept him alive until we reached the hospital. Ignatius was with him. His last words to Ignatius were, 'What does it feel like to be so beautiful?''

'That's another quote, isn't it?'

'I looked it up. It's the last words Buffalo Bill says to Clarice Starling before he dies.'

'Why do you think he did it?'

Mommy blew her nose again. 'He couldn't do it. There was too much agony in the past. He had to… not live in order for Meg to live.'

'He's a hero.'

'Yes.'

'Meg is alive because of him.'

'Yes.'

'Did they…'

Quiet, then Mommy spoke again. 'They harvested just before he… passed. He didn't feel a thing.'

'What are you going to do?' Pastor Jonathan asked.

'The funeral. Will you do the funeral?'

'I would be honored.'

'You know it will be strange.'

'I would expect nothing less.'

42 – Meg

Mommy reached out to touch my hand. 'Can you reach out to Benson for me, please? He… won't want to talk to me.'

'Why is that?'

'I don't think anyone will want to see each other for a while after that night.'

I think Pastor Jonathan wanted to ask more questions, but he didn't.

He stayed for a little while longer and they talked about me, and church, and Dave, and Christmas. Mommy said that she didn't think Christmas would ever feel the same, but Pastor Jonathan said that was okay. I think I did fall asleep after that, because when I opened my eyes again, he was gone.

'How are you feeling?' Mommy asked.

'Splendiferous.' I couldn't wait to tell Dave I was using his word.

43

Benson

It's been just over a year since my best friend Dave died.

I can say it now. It took me a long time.

Died.

Dave was full of life and peculiarity. You know, you were there. And now at the end, it's almost Christmas one year later, and I'm about to get married.

The wedding is in Davenport. Wendy and I have decided on a pretty little church, nothing fancy. Having it in a church was not necessarily my first choice, but I listened to my bride-to-be, or more importantly, my future mother-in-law who was absolutely insistent on a church wedding for her only daughter.

Whatever, it's just a place. If Dave would have been here, he would have it done outside, in the snow, probably by a casually ordained celebrant dressed in a Santa costume. That would not have gone over well with my future mother-in-law, but she did allow me to make one imposition: Judge Stackworth was going to officiate.

Ignatius took Dave's death the hardest of any of us, I think. He had lost his wife and then Dave, the nearest thing he had to a son. Both died in his home. He doesn't live there anymore. Ignatius bought a home in Arkansas, somewhere near Fort Smith, and has retired in the Ozarks, far away from all this tragedy.

Months before he died, Dave asked specifically if he could be my best man. He knew. As if I had any other options. Since he is now unavailable, I asked Marty. He was surprised when I posed the question. He'd been drinking a lot, but once he said yes, he said he would go back to AA. Maybe Dave's absence would save his life also.

Neither Wendy nor I thought it appropriate to invite Letitia to the wedding, although we both thought Meg would have made a great flower girl. Meg is doing fine, by the way; now six years old, long curly black hair, taller, and somewhat different – odd, I guess. Eventually she might turn out to be 'normal,' but I hope not. The world needs more people like her and Dave.

Letitia, though, has not recovered. Though she still is employed at Drake, she has taken a year off. The stress of what happened was too overwhelming for her, and before you become outraged by saying it was her fault – well, it was Dave, supposedly, who pulled the trigger. No one saw it, but her reaction was honest, so I believe her. I was angry with her for a long time, but I can't hold it against her anymore, not even the fact that she shot me. The police investigation pondered why there were two gunshots, but in the end, we all said that the first was an accidental discharge. Dave would have been adamant about that.

I'm writing this last part of the story as I'm attempting to go to sleep the night before the wedding. It's the 23rd of December and the Mississippi has almost frozen over. I've been pondering the words Dave spoke when we took an excursion here eighteen months ago. He talked about the River and the endless stream of stories that roll from the north, in Minnesota, to the delta, in Louisiana; and once we dip our feet or our fingers into it, we become part of that story. For me, Dave will always be part of the river, and we've had a chance to dip our souls into his even for a little while. Sometimes I think he's still around, just outside the door, ringing the bell or calling people to eat together.

After Dave died, I moved from the Palms to Davenport. It was hard to say goodbye to everyone, but to be fair, the place was never the same after he was killed. No one felt like rehanging the bell, and no one called people to gather. That's not to say people don't get together anymore; it's just different. Empty, you know?

Tomorrow, at the wedding, with Marty at my side, Pastor Jonathan and Ignatius leading the ceremony, Dave will be with us at the altar. His urn, in the shape of a cowboy boot, will supervise, and when we are done, we will tip his ashes into the lock and dam before heading to the reception at Wild Bill's.

I wish I could have seen Dave ride the bull.

www.ingramcontent.com/pod-product-compliance
Lightning Source LLC
Chambersburg PA
CBHW071953290426
44109CB00018B/2011